THE

SECRET
LIFE

OF

SPECIAL
ADVISERS

THE
SECRET
LIFE
OF
SPECIAL
ADVISERS

PETER CARDWELL

Biteback Publishing

First published in Great Britain in 2020 by
Biteback Publishing Ltd, London
Copyright © Peter Cardwell 2020

ISBN 978-1-78590-631-2

10 9 8 7 6 5 4 3 2 1

A CIP catalogue record for this book is available from the British Library.

Set in Minion Pro by Adrian McLaughlin

Printed and bound in Great Britain by
CPI Group (UK) Ltd, Croydon CR0 4YY

To my parents, Ken and Sandra Cardwell; to my best friend, Michael Selby; and to James Brokenshire, all of whom have been tremendously, unfailingly supportive in the peaks and the troughs of the past four years.

CONTENTS

PREFACE

U ntil Dominic Cummings made clear he disapproved of the practice, special advisers – ministerial aides personally appointed by UK Cabinet ministers as their political sidekicks – often worked from home on the occasional Friday.

Having spent Monday to Thursday being grilled on matters of state in the gilded rooms of Whitehall and Parliament, their Secretary of State generally will work in their constituency on Friday, spending the day in a dingy community hall at a constituency surgery, dealing with planning, drains, passports and sewerage.

This life of contrasts means ministers often deal with vastly differing matters simultaneously. I remember armed police officers guarding my main employer in government, James Brokenshire, in an airport one afternoon as we waited for a flight to Belfast, as liveried waiting staff served us tea. James leafed through official documents in his ministerial red box when his phone rang with an urgent matter. The lock on his constituency office door was broken and he needed to organise a locksmith immediately. Such is the nature of ministerial life.

As special adviser to four Cabinet ministers in four departments for three and a half years, I found my own life was full of contrasts too in the very odd, unpredictable job I did alongside about 100 other SpAds across government. Whether that involved purchasing a pair of rainbow-coloured underpants for a junior minister, explaining what a dental dam is to the Justice Secretary, or having your inside leg measured in a government office, SpAds featured in this book have done it all.

So this Friday, 22 February 2019, I took the opportunity to work from home. I spent the morning in my university hoodie and jogging bottoms, happily tapping away at my laptop and working on my two phones. I often got a lot more done at home than when I was in the office, as I avoided constant interruption by civil servants. Two groups of people always work on two phones, by the way: SpAds and drug dealers.

That morning, I got a call from a senior *Times* journalist, Oliver Wright. Had I heard, he asked, that the controversial housing giant Persimmon was rumoured to be about to post profits of £1 billion? I had not. As I was special adviser to the then Housing Secretary, James Brokenshire, Wright was asking me for comment. I did a little bit of digging before coming up with a short comment from 'a source close to James Brokenshire', as media special advisers are frequently described in the press. I pinged the lines through to Wright and thought little more of it. It was quite strongly worded; the company had not always acted entirely properly in regard to the government Help to Buy scheme, which allows first-time buyers to get a foot on the property ladder.

I checked Twitter that night for the front pages of the next day's papers, which are put online about 10.30 p.m. *The Times* screamed:

'Help to Buy house giant faces loss of contract', with the first paragraph of a story by Wright and two other journalists reading:

> Britain's most profitable housebuilder faces being stripped of its right to sell Help to Buy homes after allegations of poor standards and hidden punitive charges. James Brokenshire, the housing secretary, is reviewing Persimmon's participation in the government scheme, which accounted for half of the homes it built last year, *The Times* has learnt.

A few paragraphs later, Wright quoted the source (me):

> 'James has become increasingly concerned by the behaviour of Persimmon in the last 12 months,' the source said. 'Leasehold, build quality, their leadership seemingly not getting [that] they're accountable to their customers are all points that have been raised by the secretary of state privately.
>
> 'Given that contracts for the 2021 extension to Help to Buy are being reviewed shortly it would be surprising if Persimmon's approach wasn't a point of discussion.'
>
> They added: 'James is clear any new government funding scheme will not support the unjustified use of leasehold for new homes, including Help to Buy.'

All of this was absolutely fine, and *The Times* acted entirely honourably in publishing it. A few other journalists from other outlets asked me for similar thoughts over the weekend, but aside from the *Times* front page it didn't strike me as a huge story.

Then came the following Monday morning, when the markets opened.

The story – which was largely the result of my text to Wright as James's spokesman – resulted in a 4.9 per cent drop in the value of Persimmon by market capitalisation. In layman's terms, the company's worth fell by £387 million in one day.

My phone was red-hot the whole day, with journalists asking for further detail about the story and whether other, similar companies could be affected. A very wise civil servant urged caution in my words to journalists, as the markets were moving rapidly and other housing companies were watching their share price too.

The drama of that day rammed home the importance of being very careful about what we said to the media. It wasn't just during my previous posting with James at the Northern Ireland Office – in a part of the UK where in my experience people often literally go out of their way to be offended – that every word mattered.

But sitting in your jogging bottoms in your bedroom on a Friday morning, it's hard to anticipate that sending a text message could create a series of events which end up with nearly £400 million wiped off the value of an enormous company.

~

People who did the job I did, special adviser (the contraction 'SpAd' is a more recent innovation), have been a major part of political life in this country since the 1960s. Some contemporary SpAds are well known to anyone who follows politics: Alastair Campbell, Damian McBride, Fiona Hill and Nick Timothy, for example. And one person, a 2020 survey by the pollsters YouGov suggests, is actually known to 40 per cent of the UK public, with a further 23 per cent at least recognising his name. He is, of course, the aforementioned Dominic Cummings, the most senior aide in Boris Johnson's Downing Street – the man I worked alongside for six months.

That is, before he sacked me.

But despite acres of newsprint devoted to Dominic, many volumes of diaries by Alastair Campbell, various insider accounts by Jonathan Powell and others, and an explosive, jaw-droppingly indiscreet tome by Damian McBride – which is the best book I have ever read about Westminster politics – what special advisers actually do from day to day is still a mystery to many.

The past decade has been a defining one for the United Kingdom, its politics and especially for the Conservative Party – moving out of opposition, into coalition government and then stand-alone Conservative governments, via four elections and two referendums. It has been a defining period, too, in terms of what it actually means to be a special adviser at the heart of Whitehall. The dynamic nature of politics has necessitated huge changes in the ways SpAds operate and the level of influence they wield. As I outline in Chapter 1, SpAds did not properly exist until 1964; now, six decades later, no government can function without them. With that in mind, amongst the questions this book asks are: how did this almost completely unaccountable group become so powerful, and is that a desirable thing?

One of my bosses in government, the former Home Secretary Amber Rudd, once asked me which wing of the Conservative Party I am on. 'Amber,' I answered, 'I'm on the sunshine, lollipops and rainbows wing of the party.' So this does not aim to be a partisan book; rather, one readers of all political persuasions can enjoy. I will attempt to lift the lid on who SpAds are and what they do, how Cabinet ministers use and interact with them and how much influence they actually have in relations with the civil service and No. 10.

It is quite a personal story, in part about the triumphs and disasters of being an adviser; sometimes a sort of media-savvy Jeeves character, armed only with a mobile phone, the government's 'lines to take' email for that day and a Snickers bar (the latter in case your minister has a meltdown and needs a sugar hit).

Loyalty and friendship are qualities I came to value very strongly in the sometimes shark-infested waters of politics and, while at times indiscreet, I don't believe anything I reveal in this book will substantively damage anyone. It's certainly not designed to. I retain the greatest admiration for anyone, from any party, who becomes an adviser, mostly putting their life on hold for a few years in the service of what they believe to be a greater good.

I hope anyone interested in politics will find some nuggets of helpful advice, fun anecdotes and sometimes almost unbelievable stories about what actually happens in a SpAd's life.

And it's a job that doesn't last for ever. A TV interviewer asked me in the days following my sacking, 'What was it like to, well, to, erm, er—' I interrupted him: 'To be dumped the day before Valentine's Day from a three-and-a-half-year relationship? Not great to be honest, but I am very much an adherent of Dr Seuss, who said, "Don't cry because it's over; smile because it happened."'

And there were plenty of smiles along the way. I travelled in the Home Secretary's car with armed police officers, discussing what we would say to Prince Harry and Meghan Markle at a Foreign Office reception as the police opened a road for us. I sat by James's side as we met the President of Colombia in Belfast, who was over on a state visit. I advised the Prime Minister what to say in interviews about Brexit and the Irish border, and discussed the issue with the EU's chief negotiator, Michel Barnier, at the famous glass table in his office in Brussels. I flew in an RAF plane used by members of the royal family with a Cabinet minister to get to international peace talks. I had meetings – sometimes several times a week – in 10 Downing Street, occasionally with the Prime Minister present.

I lived an amazing, crazy, draining, fascinating life doing the best job in the world, which I had been lucky enough to be asked to do – quite literally, helping to run the country.

As you might imagine, there were myriad stories along the way. Some will never be told, because they cannot be. But the ones I can tell you within the law and without breaking the Official Secrets Act will hopefully make this book a little like my time as a SpAd: sometimes mad, sometimes exasperating, but never, ever, dull.

Peter Cardwell
Richhill, County Armagh
June 2020

1

From the Time of SpAdam:
A History of Special Advisers

Perhaps it was not just the expertly hit croquet ball that scuppered David Lipsey's potential job at Roy Jenkins's side, but it probably didn't help.

David, now Lord Lipsey, had been interviewed by a panel including the then shadow Chancellor for a position as his adviser. The interview had gone well, and Jenkins had invited the young Lipsey to his country home the next day.

'We had a most agreeable lunch,' remembers Lipsey.

> I can't say that this was conclusive, but after lunch Roy proposed a game of croquet. He wasn't to know that I was actually pretty adept at croquet, having played it at school. Anyway, everything had been going well until I roqueted [hit] Roy's ball into a nearby flowerbed and a deep froideur fell over proceedings.

The job with Jenkins disappeared. Instead, Lipsey was made adviser to Jenkins's great friend and rival Tony Crosland, joining him at the Department of the Environment as his special adviser after Labour regained power in 1974. Lipsey soon became a close confidant to Crosland, later following him to the Foreign Office, where he served him loyally for a further nine months until Crosland's sudden death from a cerebral haemorrhage in 1977.

Lipsey had been what was known as a 'chocolate soldier'. In the early 1970s, these advisers to shadow ministers were funded by the Rowntree Trust, hence the name. Previously, opposition parties hadn't received any special funding for advisers. The 1974–76 Wilson government introduced Short Money, a fund which pays for opposition parties' advisers, amongst other costs. This move was inspired by anxieties within the 1964–70 Labour government that ministers were being dominated by the civil service, as outlined in some detail by the Cabinet diaries of Richard Crossman, Barbara Castle and Tony Benn. Wilson's logic was that the public purse should pay for the opposition to have advisers as well as the ruling party, in order to best prepare for government. There was also a feeling that the Treasury just didn't appreciate or understand the left-wing economics Wilson wanted to pursue. It was in this atmosphere – and after a long period of Conservative government – that these figures suggested several ministers should have one or two political allies at their side in ministerial offices.

These efforts to formalise the role of special adviser were only the latest in a long history. Until the Northcote–Trevelyan Report of 1854 and subsequent reforms, civil servants could be appointed by ministers and were not required to be politically impartial. Prime Ministers often brought in friends or even relatives to assist – Gladstone, for example, employed his son. Disraeli's adviser, Montagu Corry, was accused of being 'the real Prime Minister', as he was so influential. A sort of Dominic Cummings of his day, some would argue.

After the reform of the civil service, and up until the 1920s, a number of personal and political appointees were brought into No. 10 in the Prime Minister's private office, which is the name for both the physical office and the group of people who interact with the Prime Minister day-to-day, running his or her professional life.

As the twentieth century unfolded, many titles were given to political aides: irregular; outsider; policy adviser; special assistant; research assistant; economic adviser; political assistant; consultant adviser; and special adviser, with its contraction 'SpAd' only used widely more recently.

During the Second World War, there were people from various professional backgrounds in Downing Street whose daily tasks probably didn't differ hugely from today's SpAds. Frederick Lindemann, Lord Cherwell, for example, was a scientist and logistics expert who had more access to his friend Winston Churchill than any other civilian adviser during that time. A eugenics enthusiast, at one stage he even tried to block the development of radar. Cherwell was later made a Cabinet minister.

Most Prime Ministers of the twentieth century also had a political secretary, a role which still exists today. (It is held, at the time of writing in 2020, by Ben Gascoigne, a Hull University graduate and political lifer who worked for Boris Johnson both at London's City Hall and, later, at the Foreign Office.) Later, Thatcher created the powerful role of chief of staff to the Prime Minister, which was at one stage held by Michael Dobbs, later Lord Dobbs, the creator of the political thriller and TV dramas *House of Cards*. While political secretaries I worked with stuck to party management and associated non-governmental affairs, the chiefs of staff have generally been the key advisers to the Prime Minister as well as de facto leaders of all special advisers across government more generally.

Aside from No. 10, of all Whitehall departments, the Foreign Office has the longest and most consistent tradition of ministers appointing 'outsiders'. In 1925, the Labour Party's international advisory committee insisted that any Foreign Secretary from its party must have a politically appointed private secretary who was a party member.

As late as the 1964 Labour government, a number of economists were recruited as 'irregulars' but were not specifically political advisers, and indeed some went on to serve Conservative governments.

John Wyndham was Harold Macmillan's private secretary from 1957 and, in total, worked for him for over twenty years. The aristocratic Wyndham, son of the 5th Baron Leconfield, sidestepped the question of how he would be paid by going unpaid. In his memoir, he described his role simply as that of 'a classic example of a court jester who lightened the tone of the place', but this is to vastly underplay his influence as Macmillan's right-hand man, advising Supermac on fundamental issues daily.

At around the same time, and on the other side of the aisle, Harold Wilson was appointing Marcia Williams as his personal and political secretary. Williams, later Baroness Falkender, was thought to have more influence over Wilson than anyone else, making her the most powerful woman in politics at the time. Their close working relationship came under the spotlight when it was alleged that Williams was responsible for the Prime Minister's controversial resignation honours list, dubbed 'the lavender list', which awarded peerages and gongs to a number of wealthy businessmen of dubious reputations. Critics claimed that the fact that the list was written on lavender-coloured notepaper proved the names were chosen by Williams; others pointed out that it is not unusual for a secretary to take down a dictated list. It has been suggested that Williams and Wilson had an affair in the 1950s, with press secretary Joe Haines claiming in his memoirs that years later Williams told Wilson's wife, 'I have only one thing to say to you. I went to bed with your husband six times in 1956, and it wasn't satisfactory.' At the very least, those closest to the Prime Minister were astounded and dismayed at how much influence she appeared to have on Wilson. Yet, intriguingly, he did not mention her once in his memoirs.

So it was in this atmosphere that David Lipsey became one of the early, Wilson-era SpAds. In government, he had access to an army of civil servants. Unlike some colleagues, he saw them as allies, rather than the enemy. 'Many special advisers will tell you they had a war with the civil service, or the civil service tried to block them out, but I didn't find that at all,' Lipsey explains.

> As a special adviser, I could do all sorts of tasks that civil servants rightly thought weren't appropriate for them. If Tony was going off to give a political speech, I could write it for him, whereas the civil service was inhibited, and anyway they hadn't got a clue how to write a political speech.

In the 1970s, under Wilson and then James Callaghan, the most powerful political appointee on the policy side was Bernard Donoughue, an academic from the London School of Economics, who set up the No. 10 Policy Unit. This small band of advisers works directly for the Prime Minister, fleshing out what the government will do on the big issues of the day. In 2005, Donoughue described the Policy Unit as 'the most important Whitehall institutional innovation in the last forty years ... both an integral part of Whitehall and yet independent of the machine and which, against the odds and under five different Prime Ministers, different political parties and various directors, [has] survived'.

Donoughue's creation still survives. At the time of writing, it is headed by Dr Munira Mirza, another former City Hall adviser to Boris Johnson, who has been on quite a political journey from her membership of the Revolutionary Communist Party some years ago to running policy for the Conservative Prime Minister. But the Policy Unit's roots can be traced back even further, to Lloyd George's Prime Minister's Secretariat, otherwise known as the Garden Suburb, a group of six advisers who were based in huts behind Downing Street during the First World War. The group was to be Lloyd George's eyes and ears, a close band of Whitehall troubleshooters. Historians differ as to how effective they actually were, but they were certainly controversial, with *The Nation* labelling them 'a little group of Illuminati'. A similar team of eighteen advisers, known as the Statistical Section, served Churchill during the Second World War.

By the time Donoughue established Wilson's more formal Policy Unit, its work was generally limited to the No. 10/Cabinet Office/ Treasury circle. It was not until much later that other departments were fully involved. Callaghan himself noted in his memoirs that neither he nor Wilson really trusted the Treasury. Both saw the Policy Unit as a mechanism by which they could be armed with the intellectual tools to go into battle with their Chancellor's officials.

More generally, by 1974 Wilson was clear that outside advisers were necessary because, as he put it, the privileged background of many civil servants meant they could 'become isolated to changes to the mood and structure of society'. He described the special advisers of those days, such as David Lipsey, as 'an extra pair of hands, ears and eyes, and a mind more committed and politically aware than would be available to a minister from the political neutrals in the established civil service'.

In his thoughts to the Commonwealth Heads of Government Meeting in Jamaica in 1975, outlined in a paper titled 'The Political Advisers' Experiment', Wilson also noted that his SpAds worked very closely with his No. 10 civil servants, as well as the network of special advisers serving other ministers across government. The paper formed, and indeed still forms, the basis for the special advisers' code of conduct and model contract.

Numerous economists and industrial advisers were appointed to assist Wilson's Cabinet too. The Conservatives of the day had been critical of the proliferation of advisers around this time, but in reality, Labour in the 1960s was expanding and formalising a scheme that governments of all stripes had been undertaking for some years. Labour advisers of this era tended to be journalists, academics or lawyers. Under Thatcher, advisers were often business figures or former party workers in, for example, the Conservative Party's Research Department, based at party headquarters.

The author Jon Davis notes that civil servants' power had grown hugely throughout the twentieth century. The 'pendulum politics' of the many governments of the 1960s and 1970s was an unsettled time for those elected – to say nothing of the country – with the swings back and forth between the differing ideologies of the two parties of power, as well as the lack of continuity, allowing civil servants to fill policy gaps. Heath's Conservative government also sought to assert its authority, embracing the use of special advisers to try to counteract the civil service in much the same way, albeit in a different direction of the pendulum.

By the 1970s, special advisers were subject to restrictions which seem odd today. Attending party conference was prohibited during the Heath administration, a notion which seems absurd to today's SpAds, whose task is to be glued to their minister and to do everything from sourcing cough sweets to writing the conference speech (see Chapter 6). One special adviser in the 1970s, Brendon Sewill, was even prevented from crossing the threshold of Conservative Central Office, despite the fact he had previously been a long-serving director of the Conservative Research Department. SpAds didn't always follow these rules, of course.

The number of SpAds rose significantly under the New Labour governments of 1997–2010 and was sustained under the coalition and then Conservative governments after 2015. But in the 1960s and 1970s, things were quite different. Even after a slight increase in 1972–73, there were still only seven special advisers in No. 10, a huge contrast to the forty or so today. Most of these continued to be paid by the Conservative Party, rather than from the public purse, as is the case nowadays.

Barbara Castle served as Employment Secretary in the first Wilson administration and would later go on to be Health and Social Services Secretary from 1974 to 1976. In opposition, she gave a speech on special advisers at Sunningdale, the civil service college, outlining her belief that the advisers of the 1960s were not as fully integrated as they should have been. She advocated a greater and more powerful role for special advisers in future Labour administrations.

Castle was soon to get her wish. The February 1974 election of the Labour government saw many, but not all, Cabinet ministers in Wilson's second period of prime ministerial office appoint political advisers. Wilson himself claimed in 1976 that the system had, by 1974, been 'regularised'. He had a point – SpAds by this stage were treated as discrete, politically appointed advisers to ministers, with almost forty in post by 1975, and almost all of them were appointed as temporary civil servants. Ten of these special advisers made up the Prime Minister's Policy Unit under Donoughue. However, the number dropped to twenty-four by the middle of 1976 as Callaghan reacted to criticism on numbers by both his Conservative opponents and Labour's backbenchers. This number remained broadly consistent until Thatcher became Prime Minister in 1979.

Costs were criticised too. In 1975, the total bill for SpAds was £196,000, prompting the Conservative MP Ian Gow to flatter his fellow MPs by telling them:

> I sometimes think that it would be better if ministers were to accept rather more advice from my right honourable and honourable friends, which they would get free, gratis and for nothing, rather than that they should pay out £196,000 a year to get advice that is leading the country to economic disaster.

Another Conservative backbencher, Iain Sproat, told Parliament in March 1976 that it was 'totally repugnant that special advisers on political matters should be paid out of taxpayers' money'.

David Cowling worked for the Labour politician Peter Shore in the Department of the Environment from September 1977 until the Thatcher government took power in 1979. At the Greater London Council, Cowling had spent much time working on housing, then one of the key areas covered by the Environment Department. This made him a prime candidate for Shore.

'It was the strangest interview in my life,' Cowling remembers.

> Obviously, it was in 1977 when Labour had lost its majority and I was being interviewed by Peter and going through the normal stuff when suddenly one of his private office staff burst in and announced, 'I'm terribly sorry, Secretary of State, there's a division [vote in Parliament].' So the rest of the interview was conducted in the lift going down and in the back of his car. I'm sure that his driver mounted the pavement at least once to get through because I suspect he knew he would have more chance of escaping execution if he mowed down several pedestrians than if he lost the government its majority by virtue of not getting his Secretary of State to Parliament in time. Peter came back after the vote and the interview was completed in a more orthodox fashion.

The job, says Cowling, gave him

> an immensely privileged view of the upper echelons of the civil service. I got access to a Secretary of State that many of the brightest people in the country, ten times brighter than me – which doesn't take much – would have spent a lifetime virtually, or much of their career, trying to get to that degree of seniority,

that kind of access, that I, swanning through the door, got almost immediately.

Cowling recalls that his relationship with the private office was key, with the diary secretary a vital contact. 'I didn't understand at first what gold dust time with the Secretary of State was. Many people from outside would totally blow the opportunity to spend time with him, spending half the time introducing themselves.'

During that era, there were arguments in Whitehall about Cabinet ministers' relationships with Permanent Secretaries, the civil service heads of government departments. Cowling says Shore took the view that

> if a minister did not know what he or she wanted, if they dithered, they just didn't have it, then of course the departmental officers would take over. Not take over in the form of a military coup, but they wouldn't allow a vacuum. If they didn't act decisively, they would get comprehensively stuffed by other competing departments.

Cowling believed that being very clear with civil servants – engaging them in intelligent debate – was the way to get things done. To him, they were allies rather than a group to be resisted. In contrast, at Tony Benn's Department of Energy, there was, in Cowling's words, 'open warfare between Benn and his private secretary, who must have been in a state of nervous collapse. A special adviser in that situation can do nothing but be a frontline stormtrooper for their Secretary of State.'

In the May 1979 election, Cowling stuck by Shore's side throughout the campaign. The day after the election, the change was dramatic. Shore was no longer a Cabinet minister with thousands of civil servants awaiting his instructions. Rather, he drove his own car with just Cowling and his constituency officer for company. The change was 'brutal', says Cowling, 'but also vital'.

Initially, the incoming Thatcher administration had only a dozen or so SpAds, such as Oliver Letwin, David Willetts and David Young – all of whom later became government ministers. But the early total increased steadily, with around double that number by 1987. The Prime Minister's Policy Unit got back to its mid-1970s strength, but some of its number were seconded impartial civil servants rather than political appointees. It was not always the case that Prime Ministers acted on the advice of their Policy Unit, strong and powerful though it was. For example, Thatcher rejected a suggestion by her Policy Unit to introduce school vouchers. Later, Major and Blair were largely disposed to accepting their Policy Unit's suggestions, but there was occasional resistance both from them and from others. In 1998, one of Blair's Cabinet ministers, Trade and Industry Secretary Margaret Beckett, refused to accept Policy Unit amendments to a government proposal called Fairness At Work unless they were written in Blair's handwriting.

The political scientist Simon James argues that the main problem with the Policy Unit, certainly under later Prime Ministers, including John Major, is that its proximity to the PM means it is often used for day-to-day firefighting rather than long-term thinking. This was the case for Sarah Hogg, now Viscountess Hailsham, a former journalist who ran John Major's Policy Unit. Due to the tiny Conservative

majority, the number of rebel backbenchers and Major's pre ___
hold on both power and his own party's leadership, Hogg said she
felt her job after the 1992 election was to 'keep on hammering in the
tent pegs round Whitehall while the storm tried to take the tent off
the grass'.

Thatcher decreed in the 1980s that ministers were to have just one
SpAd per department, although the Treasury got three. In the mid-
1980s, she believed there remained different categories of advisers,
referring in a parliamentary written answer in 1984 to a distinction
between special advisers who were civil servants and political advisers
who were 'not civil servants and ... not paid from public funds'.
Thatcher even appeared to believe the use of SpAds was 'a sign of
weakness' – a phrase she wrote, somewhat ironically, to Nigel Lawson,
who was then Energy Secretary and petitioning Thatcher for a SpAd
himself. Lawson would later resign over Thatcher's own refusal to part
with her economic adviser, Sir Alan Walters.

Even by this stage, who was classified as a special adviser was not
as tightly defined as today, with the title being given both to senior
advisers such as Policy Unit SpAds and to three people who worked
in what was essentially a secretarial capacity to the Chief Whip. When,
under Thatcher, departments were eventually given an additional
SpAd, the idea – in theory, anyway – was that the second was to
support junior ministers, rather than the Secretary of State.

In 1983, Northern Ireland Secretary Jim Prior appointed Edward
Bickham as his SpAd. Bickham had been president of the Oxford University Conservative Association. After a brief stint in publishing, he
joined the Conservative Research Department in the party's central
office. An attempt to recruit him to work for Chancellor Nigel Lawson

as SpAd was vetoed by Ian Gow, then at No. 10, as Bickham was not deemed Thatcherite enough. He was in good company – Thatcher also vetoed the 21-year-old William Hague from a Treasury SpAd role, writing that his appointment would be 'a gimmick'. Bickham eventually ended up at Prior's side at the Northern Ireland Office during one of the most dangerous times of the Troubles.

Indeed, the day before he joined Prior, thirty-eight IRA terrorists escaped from the high-security Maze Prison, although nineteen of them were immediately recaptured. 'It was always said by my so-called friends that my first piece of advice to him was to resign,' Bickham remembers, 'whereas, in fact, I instead assembled a dossier showing why that was not in line with constitutional precedent.'

Without consulting his special adviser, in the spring of 1984 Prior announced to his local BBC radio station that he intended to leave government at Thatcher's next reshuffle. Bickham found out that his time working with Prior would be ending sooner than expected when he was telephoned about the BBC Radio Norfolk interview by a Westminster journalist. Special advisers' employment then, as now, was directly linked to the tenure of the minister for whom they worked.

'Jim had quite a relaxed style of operating, and it was always possible that it slipped out on the radio,' says Bickham. Either way, Prior hadn't told Bickham, and they didn't have a plan. By the time the news reached Bickham, Prior was in a car somewhere between Norfolk and London. Mobile phones were uncommon, and Prior didn't have one. Bickham, still in the dark, was deluged with enquiries.

Sympathy came from an unexpected quarter. 'I got a call from a guy called John Lyttle, who had been special adviser to [then Labour

MP] Shirley Williams under the previous regime,' Bickham recalls. 'He said: "I can only imagine what you are feeling like because that's how we had to deal with Shirley the whole time. She never thought about what she was going to do." It was an unusual political friendship that came out of that.'

Luckily for Bickham, he knew the next Northern Ireland Secretary, Douglas Hurd, well, having worked on the Europe desk at the Conservative Research Department when Hurd was Europe Minister. The working relationship was clearly successful: Hurd not only hired his predecessor's SpAd but took Bickham with him to the Home Office in his next move, less than a year later, and would eventually recruit him to the Foreign Office. 'Douglas was a class act in both the Home Office and the Foreign Office,' Bickham says. 'There was rarely a day that ended without me thinking I'd learned something from watching him and how he handled decisions.'

Bickham puts the success and longevity of his relationship with Hurd – six years across three departments – down to the fact the two men were in tune personally and politically.

> It is very helpful to be able to be a sounding board for officials when they ask the question of what the Secretary of State is likely to think about such and such. If you're a raging ideologue, not necessarily in tune with your Secretary of State, or you have just got prejudices in different directions, that makes you a much less effective special adviser. Having worked with him for a longish time, once we got used to each other's foibles, I was much better able to predict how his mind worked and what his underlying agenda was.

Bickham left the Home Office for a job in the private sector but was tempted back about two years later when Hurd, having moved to the Foreign Office, rang Bickham to ask him to come back to help with the 1990 Gulf War. 'When I was eight years old, I remember being asked what I wanted to do,' recalls Bickham. 'I had said I wanted to be Foreign Secretary. And lo, here was a chance to work in my dream department. The world was being remade in a much more optimistic vein than has happened since, and I couldn't resist the opportunity.'

It was a hugely eventful time. Bickham advised Hurd not only during the Gulf War but also at the end of the Soviet Union, the Balkans War and negotiations with the Chinese about Hong Kong. And that was to say nothing of the Conservative Party's own internal struggles over Europe. One particular memory of Bickham's was accompanying Hurd on a visit to South Africa shortly after Nelson Mandela was released from prison.

'Whilst there, we needed someone to go and meet Thabo Mbeki,' Bickham says of the man who would later succeed Nelson Mandela as President of South Africa. 'I was sent off to his house and he wasn't in! I found myself sitting on his doorstep. When he eventually returned, we spent an hour or two getting to know each other.' Bickham later met the last National Party President of South Africa, F. W. de Klerk, and Mandela too. He felt he was experiencing history as it happened.

> That was a great privilege. But because you were in that bubble, it all did seem quite normal. You didn't think you were living history, but you were – and gosh it was fascinating. It's a bit like life in a gilded cage. You have extraordinary access to exciting developments, debates, discussions and fascinating people – such as having

> dinner with Shimon Peres [then Prime Minister of Israel, later President]. It's intense but great.

Gilded cage perhaps, but Bickham and his colleagues certainly had more freedom to spread their political wings than SpAds previously. Thatcher decreed there were to be exceptions to the civil service regulations regarding political activity for special advisers, and their terms of employment were changed. Subject to the approval of their minister, SpAds were now allowed to attend party functions and conferences (though only as observers) and to participate in party policy reviews. This was designed to ensure that anyone undertaking an analysis of any policy was completely informed about the government's view and the relevant minister's thinking on the issue.

In Bickham's time as a SpAd under Margaret Thatcher, special advisers would be collectively summoned twice a year to account for themselves to the Prime Minister. It was also an opportunity for Thatcher to find out what her ministers' bright new ideas were. On one occasion, the subject turned to the perennial problem of controlling public spending. Bickham, then an adviser at the Home Office, suggested a Green Paper setting out the long-term problem. Thatcher imperiously swept the suggestion aside and the discussion ran on. Then at one point in the discussion, suddenly, to Bickham's amazement, the Prime Minister wheeled round and declared, 'You know, Edward is right!' Some months later the Green Paper duly appeared.

Since the rules were codified in 1974, most advisers have been engaged as temporary civil servants and paid out of public funds. Salary scales, the location of offices and even the quality of office furniture made available to SpAds began to be linked to their status.

Jack Straw, the future Labour Cabinet minister, was SpAd to Barbara Castle in the 1970s, and she insisted that he be put on the same salary scale as civil servants who held the fairly senior job title of assistant secretary. Straw was only twenty-seven at the time, and he later described this move as 'a signal to the department that I was to be taken seriously'.

Press interest has increased hugely as the role has taken on greater importance. In 1981, there were just three articles in the national press about SpAds; that total rose to over 1,000 per year by 2015. A Blair-era SpAd, Andrew Adonis, now Lord Adonis, who was head of the Policy Unit between 2001 and 2003, thinks people such as Straw and later SpAds such as Ed Balls and Ed Miliband crossing over to elected office is no bad thing. In 2015, around 80 per cent of former SpAds in Parliament were ministers or shadow ministers.

'However maligned the office of SpAd may be,' Adonis wrote in 2011,

> it is an excellent preparation – in many ways an apprenticeship –
> for ministerial office … Far from decrying the reign of ex-SpAds
> – David Cameron, George Osborne, Ed Miliband, Ed Balls et al. –
> we should welcome the fact that at least some ministers come to
> office with an apprenticeship worth the name, beyond service in
> the House of Commons.

With the Conservatives back in power from 1979, a rule was introduced that a special adviser's salary could not be more than 5 per cent greater than that of the role they had just left. Given the paltry salaries for desk officers at the Conservative Research Department then – as now – this decision was deeply unpopular, leading to numerous and large differences in rates of pay, particularly by comparison with new special advisers who had come from better-remunerated jobs in the private sector.

SpAds at that stage had a number of privileges and responsibilities which endure, for instance examining papers going to the Cabinet minister and commenting and amending some of them; managing personal access to the Cabinet minister; writing speeches; preparing reports; keeping in touch with backbenchers, other departments and No. 10; and attending meetings alongside their minister.

The two main classifications of special adviser now – policy SpAds and media SpAds – were in evidence in the 1970s too, though perhaps more as a division between academic 'specialist' types and political 'operators'. As Straw later recalled, Barbara Castle once drew a distinction between him and his fellow SpAd Brian Abel-Smith, an academic economist and an expert on health and social welfare, saying, 'I've hired Brian for his brains and Jack for guile and low cunning.'

In more recent years, the number of academics turned special advisers has declined markedly, with Dr Munira Mirza and Professor John Bew in Downing Street and Dr David Shiels at the Northern Ireland Office three of the very few PhD holders in the SpAd world at the time of writing.

While Lipsey, Cowling and Bickham had fairly straightforward routes into SpAdding, one environmental activist who ended up with a key role as adviser to a very influential Cabinet minister under Thatcher and then Major was anything but conventional. Tom Burke was a maverick appointment by a maverick Conservative Cabinet minister, Michael Heseltine. In fact, Burke has been a member of three political parties – Labour, the SDP and the Lib Dems – but never a Conservative, despite advising three Tory Cabinet members.

After Heseltine stormed out of Thatcher's Cabinet so dramatically over the Westland affair – a dispute over the future of a British helicopter company – in 1986, he took time to tour Conservative grassroots organisations, picking up on anxiety about the environment. The issue was then newly in vogue, with Thatcher speaking at the UN about it. Heseltine was keen to capitalise on the growing sentiment, especially after the Chernobyl nuclear disaster in 1986. Introduced by a mutual contact, Burke started writing speeches for Heseltine, simultaneously attempting to encourage competition amongst politicians to, as he put it, 'capture the green flag'. An environmental expert, Burke was running the Green Alliance charity and independent think tank in the late 1980s and early 1990s, so he made for an invaluable ally. In 1991, Heseltine, back in Cabinet for a second time at Environment, appointed Burke as one of his SpAds. Burke would go on to serve two further Environment Secretaries – Michael Howard and John Gummer – right up until the Conservatives' defeat in the 1997 election. So why did Heseltine choose an environmental campaigner – who was certainly not a Conservative – as his special adviser?

As Burke explains, Heseltine liked the idea of 'putting a barbarian inside the gates. It seemed like too good an opportunity to pass up.' For Burke, it offered a chance 'to see what government was like and see it from a rather interesting and privileged position'.

Like many SpAds, it took Burke several months to decode how everything worked in the department, adjusting as time went on.

'Heseltine ran a regular sort of round-up every week and it took me at least three or four weeks before I realised I ought to be saying something,' Burke remembers. 'I was just so enthralled by knowing what was going on and realising, as you do when you get inside government, just how connected to lots of other things the things you're interested in are.'

Heseltine's intention was that Burke would add a non-partisan political insight into the policy process, something quite different from the roles of many other SpAds in government. Because of his environmental expertise, Burke was able to offer huge detail in that analysis. He worked alongside more partisan political SpAds too, including a young Gavin Barwell, now Lord Barwell, later to become an MP and minister and latterly chief of staff to Theresa May in the final two years of her administration.

Civil servants frequently sought Burke's view, but he didn't think that he was there to be his master's voice, as other SpAds did. 'I didn't try to pretend I was speaking for Michael and in a sense I think that's part of the piece,' Burke explains.

> You've got a bunch of bright people in the civil service who know what they're talking about a lot of the time and if you add a judgement to it, they pay attention because it's a good judgement. I don't think I ever said 'what Michael thinks' or 'Michael won't like that' because that's kind of bullying in a way unless it's very tailored, unless there's a specific context where that's an appropriate thing to say, but mostly I said what I thought.
>
> I remember once having written a speech for Michael on business and the environment, which he hadn't looked at. We were

driving and he was just glancing at it as we drove down to the venue. He just read it straight out. It was slightly terrifying, really, so it was a trusting relationship. I didn't abuse his trust or try to get things done because I knew him. He trusted me and that's central to that relationship.

In 1997, in the dying days of the John Major administration, Burke didn't head off to work on the election campaign, as most other, more party political, SpAds did. Rather, he stayed in his department, watching the officials as they planned for what they considered the very likely scenario of a Labour government. 'The assumption that somehow the civil service gets captured politically is damaging and increasingly held. What I saw was that there was far more focus on, and professional interest in, preparing for the new government even than in taking forward the existing programmes,' explains Burke. 'I was very privileged, in a way that most people aren't, to see the reality of the civil service close up for six years,' he continues. 'I don't mean to say it's remotely fault-free, but I do feel a bit about them as I think lots of people now feel about the NHS.'

Another SpAd around this time was Jeremy Mayhew, whose career straddled the administrations of Margaret Thatcher and John Major. He worked with the same Cabinet minister, Peter Lilley, in two departments: from 1990 to 1992 in the Department for Trade and Industry; and between 1992 and 1993 in the Department for Social Security.

Lilley made it clear that he wanted someone who had more 'world experience' than a party researcher, and Mayhew's CV, which included both a Harvard MBA and stints as a current affairs producer at the BBC and Channel 4, was of interest. Mayhew, for his part, saw one aspect of his role as increasing the space within which Lilley could operate – for example, reminding civil servants at the DSS that the Conservative Party's manifesto had committed the government to reducing public spending as a proportion of national income. Mayhew felt it was essential that the largest-spending department kept this firmly in mind as it inevitably faced pressures for an even greater outlay. 'I sufficiently understood where Peter came from intellectually and ideologically – and, over time, my understanding improved,' explains Mayhew.

> In addition, I would often have a better understanding of Peter's strategic priorities, instincts – and the questions he would frequently ask – in a way that few officials would have the opportunity to acquire. I wasn't bothered if he didn't accept my advice, but he always gave the impression of listening to me in front of the officials and that was important.

Mayhew says it is vital for any SpAd to establish very quickly that they have the right to walk into the Secretary of State's office without anyone's permission.

> You need to be the only person, other than the private secretaries, who can just go in. That says to officials that they cannot control the relationship.
>
> As you get to know somebody, you can sometimes efficiently, reliably, usefully do things that you believe your minister would like done – for example, when talking to a range of interested parties and communicating political messages to journalists and

other opinion-formers. You have to know someone quite well to do that with confidence and you have to be quite skilled in dealing with journalists.

Any SpAd's links to No. 10 are also crucial. By that stage, the No. 10 Policy Unit employed an 'opposite number' for each departmental special adviser – in Mayhew's case, before the 1992 election, Howell Harris Hughes.

> Howell, in particular, became one of my closest colleagues for a period of time. It was probably relatively unusual that the person in No. 10 had such a very high level of trust in the Secretary of State. It meant that there could be complete openness, as far as I was concerned, with No. 10, and Peter never encouraged anything different.

Following the Labour landslide in 1997, Tony Blair appointed twenty-eight SpAds in No. 10 and a further thirty-nine in departments – such a marked expansion, notes Jon Davis, that the SpAds now 'formed a significant new third tribe of government, a development that occasioned a short-lived furore'. As is often the case with changes of governing party, the new Labour administration distrusted the civil service and decided to bring in as many special advisers as it could reasonably get away with. Blair himself acknowledged that 'it was considered by some to be a bit of a constitutional outrage', but nevertheless asked, 'Why shouldn't you, if you are the elected government, have people who support what you are doing?' It was a sentiment Blair would come to regret, though he later defended the increase in

SpAds under his watch, pointing out in 2002, at a parliamentary committee, that in the American system there were '3,500 or even 4,000 political appointments. We have eighty special advisers for the whole of government.'

Special advisers in the Blair era, under communications director Alastair Campbell, also had a vastly differing and more engaged role in attempting to manage the media than their predecessors. While Wilson and Thatcher's press secretaries, Joe Haines and Bernard Ingham, were immensely influential in the development of press management, or 'spin', it was clear from the outset that Blair's SpAds were to redefine the relationship between the government and the media. SpAds had always briefed the press to some degree, but under New Labour this practice accelerated hugely. As political journalist Matthew d'Ancona wrote in the *Sunday Telegraph* in October 1997:

> What distinguishes this government from its predecessors is the belief that presentation is not a secondary activity to be delegated to officials, but the first and most pressing task of every minister. New Labour does not regard news management as an ancillary function of government, but as its very essence.

Arguably the most significant shift in the development of special advisers' power over the past six decades, though, was another move by the Blair administration in 1997: it allowed a small number of SpAds the power to convey ministerial instructions to civil servants. Blair's chief of staff, Jonathan Powell, and Campbell were given this power under a type of legislation called an Order in Council, which made the two men the most powerful unelected figures in the country. Some have questioned the significance of this move, however: Sir Richard Wilson, for instance, Cabinet Secretary from 1998 to 2002, said he didn't think that the Order in Council made much difference, and Jonathan Powell has written that he agreed with that assessment – it was perhaps formalising a practice that was already widespread. The Order in Council was ended by Gordon Brown on assuming office in 2007 – somewhat ironically, given the degree of power Brown's own SpAds enjoyed in the Treasury. The special advisers' code was updated in 2015 to allow SpAds to pass on ministerial instructions once again.

In 1997, the updated Ministerial Code decreed that all major interviews and media appearances be cleared with Downing Street, perhaps a reaction to the sheer number of government ministers who went rogue during the Major administration, which was less known for policies such as the Citizens' Charter and more for some of its ministers being involved in sleaze, such as numerous cash-for-questions scandals involving ministers such as Neil Hamilton. In theory, media appearances were supposed to be cleared with No. 10 previously, but this did not always happen. A coordinating unit of media SpAds, known as the strategic communications unit, and a further rapid rebuttal unit were also established in No. 10 in the late 1990s.

It was during the Blair administration that some of the greatest scandals involving special advisers occurred. Jo Moore, who was SpAd to the Cabinet minister Stephen Byers at the Transport Department, sent an email on 11 September 2001 suggesting that given the blanket global news coverage of the attacks on the Twin Towers of the World Trade Center in New York, 'it is now a very good day to get out anything we want to bury'.

As the scandal raged for about a month after 9/11, Moore appeared on camera to apologise, an extremely rare occurrence of a SpAd being front and centre in a news broadcast. The following year, an email exchange was leaked that appeared to show the department's civil service director of communications, the former BBC journalist Martin Sixsmith, instructing Moore not to use the burial of Princess Margaret as an opportunity to release unhelpful statistics. It later emerged that the email had been doctored, but both Moore and Sixsmith were left with little choice but to resign.

The Permanent Secretary of Moore and Sixsmith's department, Sir Richard Mottram, had a sterling career in the civil service. He led three Whitehall departments, became an international security and counter-terrorism expert and was appointed a knight of the realm. But he will be remembered for posterity simply for a remark he made during that chaotic time: 'We're all fucked. I'm fucked. You're fucked. The whole department is fucked. It's the biggest cock-up ever and we're all completely fucked.'

Before Moore, SpAds had seldom been the story. Then, in 2003, Alastair Campbell's role in the decision to declare war on Iraq came under scrutiny after the BBC's Andrew Gilligan alleged that he had 'sexed up' a dossier making the case for military action – something Campbell hotly denied in an extraordinary live interview in the *Channel 4 News* studio.

Policy SpAds who fall on their sword due to public controversy are rarer. Nigel Lawson resigned as Chancellor in 1989 after demanding that Thatcher choose between him and her personal economic adviser Sir Alan Walters, who also quit the same day. And in 2012, then Culture Secretary Jeremy Hunt's SpAd Adam Smith resigned after providing information to a senior executive at News Corp about internal thinking over the company's proposed takeover of BSkyB. In 2020, Boris Johnson's most senior adviser Dominic Cummings faced intense questioning over a number of journeys made during the coronavirus lockdown. The media maelstrom resulted in Cummings giving a press conference in the Downing Street garden. Unlike many others caught in the media headlights, though, Cummings did not resign.

Behind the scenes, internecine battles between SpAds from different departments are not unknown. During the final years of Tony Blair's premiership, such campaigns became increasingly vicious. Gordon Brown believed he had been promised that Blair would step down many years before he did, leaving the way clear for Brown to become Prime Minister, and as their relationship disintegrated, Treasury SpAds took numerous opportunities to advance their master's interests against those of Blair. Later, under Cameron, Theresa May's Home Office SpAds Nick Timothy and Stephen Parkinson were removed from Conservative candidate lists in 2014 on the grounds that they had not campaigned in an important by-election. They protested that, as SpAds, they were not allowed to campaign. The local Conservative association was even told by party headquarters that Timothy had withdrawn from the selection process when he had not. For many commentators, the incident pointed to tensions between No. 10 and the Home Office.

Stewart Wood, now Lord Wood, worked alongside Campbell, Powell and McBride, first at the Treasury under Gordon Brown and later at No. 10. As a Labour-supporting politics don teaching at Magdalen College, Oxford, Wood wrote to Tony Blair, the newly elected Leader of the Opposition, in the mid-1990s, and was surprised when Blair asked to meet him personally.

'Everyone knew he was going to win in 1997 and everyone wanted him to do well, but he didn't really have any policies at the time,' Wood explains. 'We had this idea of essentially trying to start a network of academics with policy ideas to feed them into Blair's team. So in a very vain gesture I wrote Blair a letter in 1996 saying we've got lots of academics on board, and policy ideas to help out.' Blair's aide David Miliband then rang Wood, inviting him for a cup of tea with the Labour leader. With minimal delay, Wood was informally advising the next Prime Minister.

Early on, Wood remembers, he felt cowed.

> There was already that mystique about the professionalism of advisers around Blair. I felt slightly intimidated by the Campbells and David Miliband. They weren't intimidating individually. They just seemed to know what they were doing. At the time there was a feeling that professional politicians had arrived in some way.

At the end of 2000, Ed Miliband, who worked for then Chancellor Gordon Brown as a SpAd, suggested Wood go and work at the Treasury full-time. Wood said he was not sure Magdalen would give him leave to do so, but fate was about to intervene.

A comprehensive school-educated girl called Laura Spence had applied to Wood's college, Magdalen, and been rejected, despite having exceptional academic credentials. Brown mentioned Spence's rejection and state school status in a speech in May 2000, making her a cause célèbre. The story about access to one of the UK's top universities dominated the press for days. Magdalen, in Wood's view, handled the affair badly at the time, but the upshot was that the college wanted to repair relations with the government. Part of this plan was to allow Wood five years' leave to work for Brown at the Treasury.

I went for an interview with Gordon and sat in the Treasury waiting room on three occasions for about an hour. Eventually, the secretary came and said, 'Sorry, the Chancellor's busy. Can you come back another day?'

And then the fourth time I walked in and he was sitting there reading. He basically started talking at me for an hour and a half. He didn't ask me a single question. He talked about Britishness, he talked about the paradox of Madison and constitutional design, and it was nothing to do with being Chancellor. It felt a bit weird. At one stage, Ed Miliband came into the room. I turned round and saw Ed putting two thumbs up and raising an eyebrow. And then I went home and Ed rang and said, 'Would you mind coming in a fifth time?' and Gordon talked at me again. He asked me a couple of questions about Europe. He leaned across his desk and burrowed through his papers, started scrawling on some of them and said, 'Can you get me something back tomorrow?'

And I left, and Ed said, 'That's great, he has given you a piece of work – you've started.' It was classic Gordon.

Wood says that, despite the tensions between Prime Minister Blair and Chancellor Brown, their advisers generally got on well during that period. 'We were drinking together. There were even a couple of people going out with each other in that group.' And the Milibands, of course, are brothers. They got on well in those days before David became the first politician to leave politics to spend *less* time with his family.

And the true business of the week was done not in the Treasury but in a café nearby on a Tuesday morning. Ed Balls, then Brown's principal SpAd, would hold the meeting with his co-SpAd Ed Miliband. Also in attendance were the high-flying civil servant Jeremy Heywood, who was Brown's principal private secretary at the Treasury, his right-hand man, along with SpAds from No. 10, such as David Miliband and Matthew Taylor. 'That Tuesday morning meeting was a functional meeting of the government when everything got cleared. That was the point when No. 10/No. 11 functionality happened,' remembers Wood.

He has fond memories of the Treasury. 'It was intellectually the most stimulating place I have ever worked, and I am very lucky – I worked at Oxford University. It was the perfect peak of a combination of factors. Gordon was supreme. The Treasury was self-confident, and Gordon was reshaping it.'

Wood says the influence of Ed Balls as SpAd between 1997 and 2003 cannot be overestimated.

> Ed Balls ran the Treasury. If you were a junior official, the peak of your work cycle, the clearing moment for a decision, was a meeting with Ed Balls. Gordon was basically shielded from day-to-day running of the Treasury by Ed Balls and Ed Miliband, so that he could focus on thinking about wider subjects – including multiple pieces about constitutional reform, changing the governance of the world economy, looking ahead to when he was Prime Minister, as well as producing high-level speeches and proposals on economic

policy. After Ed Balls left, Gordon's team never really worked as well again.

In 2006, Magdalen told Wood he would have to come back to teach or he would lose his position. A compromise was reached for the following four years until Brown left No. 10. 'I used to go to Oxford on Friday afternoons – I would get on the bus or train and teach on Friday night and Saturday morning,' says Wood.

> The students loved it. When I was at No. 10, sometimes I was in Gordon's office at 1.45 p.m., thinking, 'My first tutorial is at 4 p.m.! How am I going to get to Oxford?' And I would just say, 'I am going to the loo, I'll be back in a minute' – and I would never come back that day. I basically relied on the fact that life in No. 10 was so chaotic.

Wood remembers that Brown had a unique style as Prime Minister. 'On his first day in No. 10, Gordon went down to the small café in the basement of the building. They gave him a gammon steak with oven chips – it was pretty horrible, but he loved it. The next day, he went down again. They hadn't seen a PM down there for about fifteen years.'

Wood not only gave policy advice but became a close and trusted friend of Brown. As his closest confidant, Wood was even thought by many to be the person who would manage the Prime Minister emotionally. 'So I became a personal aide – I was originally a policy person and then I ended up doing media as well in the last few years.'

Brown announced early in his premiership that he wanted a 'spin-free era', in reaction to the characterisation of the Blair years as spin-heavy. But while the number of SpAds initially decreased, it slowly crept up again. Further change came with the Brown government's Constitutional Reform and Governance Act in 2010, codifying special advisers as per their code of conduct and position as temporary civil servants.

As the Brown years came to an end and the Conservatives and Liberal Democrats embarked on a coalition government in 2010, the role of SpAds remained a thorny political issue. Cameron had pledged to keep the number of SpAds low after the scandal over MPs' expenses, but the realities of the coalition pushed the figure up to over a hundred, later reduced to eighty-seven when the coalition ended and the Conservatives won a majority in 2015.

Meetings of SpAds at No. 10 or elsewhere in Whitehall have happened weekly, sporadically or not at all during various administrations. During the first such meeting when David Cameron was Prime Minister, he asked SpAds to introduce themselves and say for whom they worked. After they did, Cameron thanked them but told them they were all incorrect: 'None of you work for the person you just said you work for. You all work for me, No. 10, and for this government.'

One of the key SpAds for the majority of the coalition was Jo Foster, Nick Clegg's deputy chief of staff from 2011 to 2014. Foster had been chief executive of the Welsh Liberal Democrats and was in daily contact with grassroots members. Consistent contact with them meant she could accurately gauge the immediate reaction within the wider party to the Lib Dems' position as junior partners in the coalition. 'It was a massive learning curve to work together as a party with this new arrangement,' remembers Foster. 'The London guys had gone into government, and then we had a Welsh party and a Scottish party who were up for election in the first year. People said we had massively disorientated a lot of Lib Dem voters. It felt catastrophic, actually, despite being the right thing to do.'

The Welsh campaign Foster ran within months of the coalition being formed in Westminster was very different from the one her Scottish colleagues ran for the Edinburgh Parliament. Tavish Scott, then leader of the Scottish Liberal Democrats, distanced his offering to voters as much as possible from London, refusing to shake the hand of Vince Cable, the Liberal Democrat Cabinet minister, during the contest.

'In Wales, we realised people actually did want to talk about the coalition on the doorsteps. They wanted to talk about things like pensions, tuition fees. You can't hide from issues. Scotland got annihilated and we held our own,' says Foster.

Following her success in running the Welsh Assembly election for her party, then Deputy Prime Minister and leader of the Lib Dems Nick Clegg invited Foster to become his deputy chief of staff in Westminster.

In that role, Foster says:

> You run their entire life and political programme. Whatever their strategic goals are, you're involved in setting them. You are the one that has to come out of the meeting and think about how to get them done. I spent an awful lot of time saying 'no' to people on Nick's behalf, even when he'd go behind my back and say 'yes' anyway. So it was effectively a gatekeeper role. On a strategic level, it was about making sure he was delivering what he was meant to be delivering.

Relations between Foster's Liberal Democrat SpAd colleagues and those of the senior partner in the coalition, the Conservatives, were not always good.

> For one of the meetings about reforming political party funding [Cabinet Office minister] Francis Maude just didn't turn up or wasn't going to turn up. I spoke to [No. 10 chief of staff] Ed Llewellyn and he said, 'You're just going to have to cancel that, Jo.' He didn't give a shit about the things that were important to us, and sort of spoke to me in this imperious kind of way and I thought, 'Gosh.' I didn't say anything because I was too shocked in the moment. I thought, 'Good Lord, is that how we speak to each other here? Is this what we do?'

The substantial size of Clegg's team of SpAds wasn't to Foster's taste either.

> This sort of royal court drove me mad, because I was the one who had to keep things moving and get things done. I thought the world of Nick and really enjoyed working for him, but towards the end I didn't feel like I was learning anything or that I was making a meaningful contribution. It just felt like we were going round and round on the same issues and not really doing anything differently. We weren't quite there for each other in the same ways the Tories were, either.
>
> At the start, you jump out of bed in the morning and you do it and you live it. And I just stopped feeling like that. I had run elections, I had been delivering leaflets in the rain in Bridgend in

my early twenties. I just didn't have the sort of swagger or approach that others did. I just didn't feel like I fitted in, in the end.

However, Foster still has many fond memories of her time in coalition government.

> When Justine Greening was Transport Secretary, there was a question about a matter in Nick Clegg's constituency involving transport. Nick had this call with Justine. I'm listening in with one or two other advisers.
>
> Justine says, 'Hi Nick, really nice to hear from you, how are you doing? I'm out drinking with Pete Waterman.' So she's the Transport Secretary and she's out with Pete Waterman, the train enthusiast but also the guy who made Kylie Minogue a pop star.
>
> Nick starts to talk very seriously about the issue, and Justine says, '*Especially for you*, Nick, I'm going to get that done.'
>
> The Transport Secretary was quoting a Kylie Minogue song title, but the Deputy Prime Minister didn't get it, replying, 'Oh, well, great, that's great, Justine. Thank you.'
>
> And she says, '*I put my hand on my heart and tell you* it's definitely going to get done.' Then she worked in 'Ten Good Reasons'. I think she also said 'Sealed with a Kiss', and Nick was like, 'Excuse me, Justine, what?'

Listening with her phone muted on the conference call, Foster monitored the exchange outside The Clarence pub on Whitehall, a favourite watering hole for SpAds.

'I had my drink in my hand,' remembers Foster, 'and I was just roaring with laughter.'

For over a century and a half of the impartial civil service, politicians have brought partisan aides of some description into government to help them. It is clear that Wilson was the instigator of the key role SpAds have today, as well as the codification of their position. But, as this chapter illustrates and others make yet clearer, the influence of SpAds is currently at its zenith, a culmination of six decades of the accumulation of power. The political aides of 1964 may well recognise a number of the tasks today's SpAds undertake – some have perhaps not changed drastically – but they may find it difficult to conceive of the level of power and influence some of their successors now wield. They may also find it intriguingly ironic that in 2020 it was announced that the Sunningdale civil service training college where Barbara Castle gave her speech advocating a greater role for SpAds is to be redeveloped … into a retirement home.

2

Welcome to the SpAd
House: Recruitment

Sending the email with my CV attached to the Downing Street chief of staff who I wasn't sure really remembered my name, I looked at the screen and muttered the following sentence to myself: 'I will never hear another word about this.'

I was on the dreaded reporter's night shift at *Good Morning Britain* at ITV's headquarters in central London. We weren't quite down the mines, but the occasional twelve-hour overnight marathons we had to do were starting to take their toll after two fascinating years, during which I had learned a lot from a great team.

But it was time to move on, and I'd been interested for some time in going from covering politics to perhaps actually taking part in it. The email I sent that night was to Fiona Hill, who had been Theresa May's most loyal aide for years, alongside her co-chief of staff, Nick Timothy. Fiona and I had known each other for about six years, dating back to the days when she was a special adviser to May at the Home Office.

A 'morning round' is a series of media interviews undertaken by a government minister, where they go to studios at 4 Millbank in Westminster and do anything up to around a dozen interviews on the same topic over the course of the early morning. SpAds accompany these ministers, with sometimes a press officer in tow. All three will have been up late at night preparing the minister, getting up again very early in the morning to get into Millbank. The minister will then be grilled in quick succession, sometimes literally running between interviews (especially after Piers Morgan overruns yet again), shuttling between the floors of 4 Millbank to the various studios of broadcasters such as the BBC, ITV, Sky News, LBC and Talk Radio. As well as the main announcement of the day, they can be asked any question whatsoever on any aspect of government policy, or indeed any other topic. 'Secretary of State, exactly how many NHS intensive care beds have been scrapped in the past five years?' Or perhaps: 'Were *Love Island* bosses right to eject the controversial contestant last night?' With James Brokenshire at the Northern Ireland Office, occasionally the London, Belfast and Dublin morning programmes would all want to question him. I think our record in one morning was fourteen interviews in two and a half hours.

But back in the early 2010s, when I worked on *Newsnight*'s political production team, I was on the other side of the equation: my job was to convince SpAds such as Fiona that they should do yet another interview that night. Yes, you've been awake since the early hours of the morning and are just back in the office with a cup of tea and a full day ahead, despite feeling as if you've just done one. But this was not enough.

No, Fiona. What you really, really want to do now is to forgo that glass of wine you were going to have at 7 p.m. followed by a nice hot bath and an early night. Instead, what you really want to do – though you might not know it – is to go to west London with the Home Secretary at 10.30 p.m. for a longer, more detailed evisceration on exactly the same policy by Jeremy Paxman, with all the associated, potentially career-ending consequences. The 8.10 a.m. *Today* programme interview with John Humphrys wasn't enough. The 5 Live grilling by Nicky Campbell hasn't sated the BBC beast. Your minister must do *Newsnight*, too.

Unsurprisingly, this was often a big ask of both SpAds and their ministers, and they increasingly said no. At the time of writing in 2020, *Newsnight* is one of a number of programmes that now only very seldom have a government minister on air, so this is clearly a problem with which its producers continue to grapple.

The basic logistical point that an already extremely long day would be made even longer by staying up to do the *Newsnight* interview was compounded by the fact that the newly announced policy would already have been picked apart by the media, the opposition, interest groups and other commentators over the course of the day. During the early morning interviews, much of the detail of the new policy may not yet have been digested by those opposing it. It was often a very different story by 10.30 p.m. The story might have dominated the news cycle, but it also might have gone horribly wrong. Why risk Paxo? Why indeed, many asked.

Another factor was that Andy Coulson, then director of communications at No. 10, had basically decreed there was no need to do *Newsnight* any more as the programme was, in his view, past its best. I disagreed, of course, arguing robustly that Paxman was the best interviewer in the country and that the way to demonstrate to the public that the policy was a good one worthy of their support was to show that it could stand up to the very toughest scrutiny. We were in-depth, intelligent and asked the questions no one else would. Plus, we would make the SpAd a nice cup of tea and sort out a taxi home after the interview.

Nonetheless, the guest-booking producer's task was, you'll have gathered, a tad tricky. It would frequently get to 7 p.m. without an answer, leaving an empty seat in the *Newsnight* studio that had to be filled at short notice.

Hello? Is that the backbencher famous only in his own household who's on the relevant select committee and has been biting my hand off to get on *Newsnight* for the past three months? Philip Hammond's SpAd says his boss has a late-night Pilates class, so you're on in two hours, mate – pour that glass of wine down the drain, hoist your suit back on and be prepared to waffle for Britain. Thus the media careers of the Andrew Bridgens of this world are born.

Most SpAds were fine to deal with when I put in the requests for their ministers. Most said no most of the time, and that was entirely their prerogative. There were ways to try to persuade them, of course – as one of my *Newsnight* superiors, Robert Morgan, told me on my first day in that particular job, 'The great Cardwell schmooze-a-thon begins today.' Indeed, much drinking and dining was done in the bars and restaurants of Westminster so that SpAds would at least take my call in a crisis. But the SpAds were in control, and it was extremely rare for any minister to do an interview they did not want to do.

Occasionally, SpAds would spend the day negotiating with me, No. 10 and/or their minister, sometimes putting ridiculously strange conditions on the format of the interview. Only a junior minister would do it, they sometimes said, but the junior minister wouldn't sit on a panel. Or Paxman could interview the minister at the start of the interview, the panel in the middle of the interview, and then return to the minister at the end – but panel members couldn't address questions to the minister. This largely pointless negotiation often took up the whole day, eating into valuable time needed to work on the briefing and suggested questions, much to the chagrin of the presenters and my editorial superiors. Indeed, Paxman once mentioned live on air the conditions on which we had been granted the interview: namely that the minister wouldn't engage with the rest of the panel during the programme. It was a reasonable thing for Paxman to point out on air, but it earned me a hairdryer session from the department involved. They also complained that Paxman was 'very withering' in his questions. I asked the person on the other end of the phone if they had ever before seen Britain's most famous interviewer on television. Besides, their conditions were ridiculous; I avoided imposing these when I later became a SpAd.

One person who was very helpful at that time was Michael Salter, then head of broadcasting at Downing Street, who was part of the press SpAds team there. He met me regularly at No. 10 for catch-ups, always took my calls and was unfailingly helpful with coming up with some solution, or at least being realistic if we weren't going to get a minister. It was during this working relationship that I got my first taste of what SpAds did, and Michael, who is hugely impressive and completely unflappable, was a major part of my early inspiration to get into SpAdding. But the amount of faffing from a small number of media SpAds at that time was enough to drive you to drink.

Fiona was different from most SpAds. You could ring her at 11 a.m. and ask whether Mrs May would do *Newsnight*. Yes, she would say. Or, no. Or, a junior minister will do it. There was no mucking about, no dilly-dallying, no keeping you hanging on until 7.30 p.m. only to be told no one was available, or that an under-briefed junior minister was being sent out to be thrown under a bus. Chloe Smith discovered the perils of this latter practice in a notorious interview, conducted by Paxman in 2012, about a fuel tax U-turn by the Treasury. Chloe was then a Treasury minister and was sent out on an impossible mission. Paxman repeatedly asked Chloe when she had been told of a certain decision and grilled her about the ins and outs of a change in policy in which she, as a junior minister, would have had no say. Paxman's final question was: 'Do you ever think you are incompetent?' The failure of that interview, now I have seen both sides of the equation as producer and SpAd, was entirely the fault of whoever put her forward for it, and not Chloe herself, who did the best she could under almost impossible circumstances – though those more senior ministers who should have done the interview themselves can share some of the dubious credit.

Being a pretty direct person, I got on with Fiona Hill, who would call me 'chuck' and send me kind texts. I found her reasonable and she took my calls; many SpAds were much more difficult to pin down and much less friendly. Fiona's reputation throughout Whitehall, however, was somewhat less positive, with civil servants cowering as she and Nick Timothy, her co-SpAd at the Home Office and later her co-chief of staff at Downing Street, took a rather more muscular approach than some. I remember starting at the Home Office as a special adviser in April 2018 and being asked by a member of private office how I became a SpAd. 'It was Fiona Hill who got me in,' I said, 'and I will always be grateful to her.' 'Congratulations,' they shot back, 'you're one of the 1 per cent.' 'The 1 per cent?' I queried. 'The 1 per cent of people who have anything nice to say about Fiona Hill.'

Fiona was eventually sacked by David Cameron's No. 10 over a row Theresa May had had with Michael Gove, who was then Education Secretary, about extremism. Many people dropped Fiona like a stone, as often happens when SpAds are sacked and their usefulness is deemed to have passed. It can be brutal. But I stayed in touch and wished her well.

Quietly occupied in other jobs for a few years, she re-emerged as one of the key people helping to run May's campaign for leader in 2016. A couple of weeks after May became Prime Minister, and having been one of probably hundreds of people who contacted her to congratulate Fiona on becoming chief of staff at Downing Street, I thought I would take a punt and email her about a SpAd job. I had absolutely nothing to lose – except those dreaded, draining night shifts.

I don't come from a political or journalistic family, and growing up I had barely any connection to either field. What I had, though, was curiosity, determination and – perhaps the most crucial quality – shamelessness.

I leapt at the chance to do politics at A-level, under an inspiring teacher at Portadown College in County Armagh, Sean Dunlop. (Later, as SpAd at the Ministry of Justice, I had a group of Sean's students into the Lord Chancellor's office and I'm afraid I breached protocol by allowing my former teacher to try on the Lord Chancellor's wig. His students' phones were quickly snapping away, though I forbade them from putting it on social media.) I'd watched the news almost from infancy, and indeed remember aged five writing to – and receiving a reply from – the local news presenter on Ulster Television, Paul Clark. So I always knew I wanted to be a journalist.

Ten years into my career, having known, met and sometimes become friends with SpAds, I had done most of what I wanted to do in journalism. I had written suggested questions for Paxman on *Newsnight* as my first job, worked for the BBC in Washington, New York, Belfast and London, been senior producer on *Question Time* aged twenty-seven and been a reporter for five years too, on both radio and telly, reporting from Downing Street and the White House. Having interviewed everyone from Cate Blanchett to Timmy Mallett, I fancied a change. Reporting especially is a ruthless game – your face either fits or it does not. Sometimes in my career it did, sometimes it did not, and that could change with the wind. I remember asking a senior editor in a national newsroom what I needed to do to get on screen more. 'You could start by losing two stone,' he countered, in a totally matter-of-fact tone, without looking up from his computer. And he was right (and sadly still is).

The night after I sent the email to Fiona, I was at the National Theatre to see Sean O'Casey's *The Plough and the Stars* alongside an Irish journalist friend, Ruth Dudley Edwards. I checked my phone in the bar before the play and found that less than twenty-four hours after my email to Fiona she had replied: 'Would you consider NI SpAd?'

I replied four minutes after her email reached me: 'Yes. Would love it.' She replied within one minute: 'James Brokenshire is about to call you.'

James had been appointed Northern Ireland Secretary about ten days previously as one of May's Cabinet appointments. My heart was in my mouth. This was actually happening. Now, what on earth was I going to say to James Brokenshire? I knew very little about him, except that he had been a Home Office minister for the entirety of the Cameron administration and was seen as one of Theresa May's most loyal supporters. Incidentally, I have a terrible, terrible confession to make. Fiona once offered me James as the guest for *Newsnight* as a replacement for Theresa May, then Home Secretary. I rejected the offer because I had never heard of him.

So I didn't know him from Adam, and he, similarly, couldn't have picked me out of a police line-up. Mildly panicking that I was about to be rung by a Cabinet minister, we actually missed each other's calls due to the play starting and the fact James was on a train. We eventually spoke in the interval for a few minutes, arranging to meet on the following Saturday.

Mutual friends and contacts can be an invaluable source of advice on any minister with whom a potential SpAd may be working. I consulted former Sky News deputy political editor Joey Jones, who as spokesman for Theresa May at the Home Office had worked alongside James. Joey was very complimentary about James and advised me to go for it. One thing he did mention, however, was James's loquaciousness – James is the opposite of taciturn, as I came to learn. Saying that, James was far from the worst offender. I recently learned that some of the Downing Street SpAds who sat behind the rows of ministers during Cabinet meetings used to have a sweepstake on how long Greg Clark, then Business Secretary, would speak continuously in Cabinet meetings. Clark's record? Twenty-six minutes without a pause. In a ninety-minute meeting.

Two days after my initial discussion with James, we met in the plush surroundings of the five-star Corinthia Hotel just off Whitehall, over a gin and tonic. (Aside from the Carlton Club, I doubt there is a more Tory setting – or indeed beverage – for an interview.) During our hour-long conversation, I attempted to convince James that I was the person for him. I had rather stupidly considered wearing jeans and a jacket and was only persuaded otherwise by my housemate, *Newsnight* producer Sam McAlister, who convinced me to at least wear a suit, if not a tie. I later learned James had removed his tie before the interview when he spotted me, realising he was more formally dressed than me. I was to discover that this was a typically thoughtful gesture.

Our initial conversation at the Corinthia ranged from my motivation to move into politics from journalism, my media experience, the perception of the Northern Ireland Office (NIO) both in Belfast and in London, and what I thought I could do for him as special adviser. James had never had SpAds before, as he had been promoted to the Cabinet only a matter of days earlier, having previously served as the Minister of State for Security and Immigration at the Home Office. With his big promotion to the Cabinet, he suddenly had two SpAd roles to fill.

As I was to learn, SpAds play a weird daily role to their ministers, somewhere between friend, gatekeeper, adviser and general dogsbody. As his media SpAd, I was to advise James both on what to say in the crucial 8.10 a.m. interview on the *Today* programme as well as reminding him to have a pee beforehand. From a Cabinet minister's point of view, it must be a tremendously difficult task to choose one of your key aides, with whom you will be working extremely closely, based on little more than a chat. Not every SpAd likes their minister by the end of it, and indeed some are barely on speaking terms. I know one former Cabinet minister whose wife can hardly speak the name of his former SpAd. But as my erstwhile co-SpAd Liam Booth-Smith said of James, 'Usually, you admire a politician from afar, then you get to know them and see them up close and see all their foibles, warts and all. With James, it's the opposite. I have more respect for that man every single day I work for him.'

I now feel exactly the same about James, whom I am proud to call a close friend. But back then, we were sizing each other up and seeing if it was going to work in a semi-formal, interview-style setting, accompanied by our gins and tonic and James's untied tie in his pocket. Having seen just how much time SpAds spent with their minister even in my limited experience, at one stage of our conversation I was pretty direct. 'What you essentially need to decide, Mr Brokenshire,' I said, 'is whether you can spend twenty-four hours in an airport with me.'

James said he would ring me the next day, as he wanted twenty-four hours to think about it. Whatever the result of the interview, I told him, I wished him well for his time in Northern Ireland.

But he didn't take twenty-four hours, much to my surprise and relief. About two hours later, he rang me at home, telling me he wanted to employ me. I was ecstatic and could hardly believe the extent to which my working life was about to change. James said the Permanent Secretary of the NIO, Sir Jonathan Stephens, would be in touch the following day to arrange the next steps, and that I should come into the offices on Monday for a preliminary chat with Sir Jonathan. The job was mine, bar the paperwork.

On the Monday morning, barely five days since I had sent the original email to Fiona Hill, I was in the Northern Ireland Secretary's cavernous office in the Treasury in Whitehall – a huge building that houses a number of bits of government – sitting with Sir Jonathan and his private secretary.

We spoke for about an hour, outlining the processes that came next and the role of a SpAd, and Sir Jonathan made it very clear that I was not to be unreasonable to civil servants, otherwise he would come down on me harshly and not hesitate to report it to the Secretary of State. Sir Jonathan pointed out that he did not know me or how I operated, and that he would have said the same to anyone because any new SpAd needed to hear it. Had I been one of his civil servants, I would have been very impressed that the Permanent Secretary was standing up for his juniors even in advance of the new SpAd's first day.

Next came salary negotiation, this time via a phone call with the redoubtable Cabinet Office director general, Sue Gray. Many SpAds felt the process for arriving at their pay could charitably be called opaque, but my first experience of negotiating my salary with Sue was actually quite an interesting one for me.

She offered me £60,000, which was more than I had ever earned as a journalist, but I argued for £64,000, as I knew a couple of SpAds around my age with the same level of experience were on that amount. The chiefs of staff at Downing Street were both on £140,000, the SpAd salary ceiling then as now. What helped in my negotiations was that just before Christmas each year, the Cabinet Office published the salaries (now salary ranges) of all SpAds. It's all on the Cabinet Office website, if you're bored – and nosy.

Sue is an intriguing character. She actually had a rather curious career break in which she ran a pub in deepest, darkest, south Armagh in Northern Ireland, sometimes known as 'Bandit Country' due to the number of IRA terrorists who lived there during the Troubles. Northern Ireland's police service, then called the Royal Ulster Constabulary, could not safely patrol the area for many years without an Army escort. I've often wondered what the locals made of the Englishwoman running the local boozer, the Cove Bar.

I was curious as to why Sue had left such a high-powered job in Whitehall to run a pub, and later found out that her husband is a Northern Irish country music singer called Bill Conlon.

'I tell you what, Sue,' I said, after a fairly long negotiation. 'We'll compromise on £62,000 and I'll take you for a gin and tonic and you can tell me all about living in south Armagh running that pub.' The drink never happened, but I got the cash.

Sue actually later returned to Northern Ireland and is now Permanent Secretary at the NI Department of Finance, whose minister, at the time of writing, is Conor Murphy MLA. Like many Sinn Féin politicians, he is a former IRA terrorist. In the 1980s, he went to prison for possession of explosives. And guess what? He's from south Armagh – the staunchly Irish Republican village of Camlough, just a few miles from where Sue ran the pub. Small world.

Of course, moaning about how your £62,000 salary – nearly three times the national average wage – isn't fair or equitable when you've been given a fascinating, rewarding job that many would kill for is probably not going to win you many fans; I write this safe in the knowledge that the world's tiniest violin has struck up an aria already. However, I should point out that there is now a very different process for the setting of SpAd salaries, which is both better and worse than what I experienced in 2016. It's done by a committee these days, rather than by negotiation, but there are still of course grumbles about some disparities. When you have a group of people whose job it is to have an opinion on stuff for a living, you're going to get a few comments when the list of salaries comes out each year.

SpAds need two sets of approval to be appointed: the relevant Secretary of State and the Prime Minister both need to sign them off. As there are dozens of SpAds appointed very quickly when a new Prime Minister takes office, in practice the PM's final say will be granted after recommendations from their senior team. In my case, the No. 10 approval was a formality, as Fiona Hill was one of the chiefs of staff, and her verbal reference is largely what got me the job in the first place, but nevertheless I waited for the formal offer letter before I resigned from *Good Morning Britain*. Days later, the letter came through on government-headed paper from Sir Jonathan, officially offering me the job as special adviser. One for the memory box.

Other SpAds have not been lucky enough to have such seamless approval. In 2010, one of Michael Gove's senior advisers in opposition actually accompanied him in person up Downing Street following the coalition negotiations, waiting inside No. 10 as Gove had his meeting with newly appointed Prime Minister David Cameron. Gove was duly appointed Education Secretary, and discussion soon turned to those he wanted to appoint as his SpAds. But it was quickly made clear that Andy Coulson, who wielded so much power over the appointment of SpAds at that time, was going to block Gove's choice. The name of the person patiently waiting in Downing Street for Gove, expecting to be swiftly confirmed as special adviser to the

Education Secretary? Dominic Cummings – whom Cameron would later dub 'a career psychopath'.

Luckily for Cummings, Coulson resigned from government just months later, before he was sent to jail as a result of the phone-hacking trial. Cummings was swiftly appointed Education SpAd.

Such is the serendipitous nature of the trade. Fiona Hill, too, fell afoul of No. 10, in her case over the extremism row with Michael Gove during her time as a SpAd at the Home Office. No. 10 withdrew their approval, so even though May was happy for her loyal lieutenant to continue at the Home Office, Fiona's time was up. And then suddenly, just a few years later, she was back at the very top of the tree. That, though, lasted only a year, before the 2017 election led to her resignation.

It's a tumultuous world, and a dog-eat-dog one. I knew what I was getting into, and hopefully I played the game to some extent. Well, until I got sacked, obviously.

My new employment secured merely a week after I had sent the speculative email to Fiona, I worked out my notice at *Good Morning Britain*. My bosses wished me well and I left on good terms. I didn't so much have a leaving do as a night out to celebrate my new life. I said a fond farewell to a decade in journalism by going to perhaps an odd choice of gig – Chesney Hawkes's twenty-fifth anniversary concert in Putney, south-west London. With my *Good Morning Britain* colleague Anne Alexander, *ITV News* anchorwoman Charlene White and my friend Becky Pedder in tow, we drank, danced and belted out 'I Am the One and Only', Chesney's one and only hit record. We even met the singer's family at the concert – his mother, Carol, was very charming.

Although I had loved being a journalist, and the team at *Good*

Morning Britain were – with only a few exceptions – the friendliest with whom I had ever worked, I felt liberated, and truly excited about what would come next. Walking from Westminster Tube to the Treasury building for my first day as special adviser to the Northern Ireland Secretary in late August 2016, barely a month after that email exchange that changed my life, I played Chesney's anthem on my phone through my headphones. Like Chesney, there was nobody I'd rather be.

Mine was a very swift and very straightforward way into SpAdding – there were perhaps not an abundant number of people who knew both the Northern Ireland and the London media and were willing to put their life on hold to jet between Belfast and London several times a week. It would have been a tricky job to do had I had children to care for, or even just a relationship. I had neither.

On this, Dominic Cummings is absolutely right. In 2019, when he advertised on his blog for a personal assistant, he wrote: 'You will not have weekday date nights, you will sacrifice many weekends – frankly it will be hard having a boy/girlfriend at all' – and this is a sentiment with which all SpAds can concur. It is also a weakness of SpAd life, in that there is a lack of diversity – caring for very young children alongside the job or working part-time as a SpAd has proven particularly difficult for some.

The frequency of travel between Belfast and London was one of the things that struck me the most when I first started, but it is entirely necessary for the Northern Ireland Secretary to do the job. As special adviser, I tended to operate a 'where James goes I go' rule, and we were usually accompanied by his principal private secretary, the Permanent Secretary and my co-SpAd, Lord (Jonathan) Caine. I dubbed it The Brokenshire Travelling Circus. In 2017, the only full year I worked at the NIO, I kept a record of how many flights I took – mostly between Belfast and London, but we went to Dublin and Brussels too, occasionally. (There were also several trips to Washington DC and New York, but Jonathan Caine pulled rank on every one, leaving me in London.) My flight total was eighty-five in 2017; not the best carbon footprint, but the upsides were that the very nice flight attendants on Aer Lingus knew how I liked my tea (with four sachets of milk and a KitKat) and I can still recite the Aer Lingus and British Airways safety instruction presentation. One Aer Lingus flight attendant, Louise Annon, even became my Facebook friend. In one memorable week, I actually had four flights in four days between London and Belfast. It was unavoidable on that and every other occasion: if it's not justified, it doesn't get approved, and the civil servants at the Northern Ireland Office are very careful with taxpayers' cash.

Another route into SpAdding is to gain relevant policy experience. Many SpAds, at least in the past ten years, have come from think tanks. One of the best examples is Arminka Helić, who advised William Hague at the Foreign Office. A Bosniak foreign policy expert who fled the Yugoslav conflict in the 1990s, Arminka advised a number of Conservatives in opposition, while her work on the Global Sexual Violence Initiative saw her strike up a partnership with the Hollywood actress Angelina Jolie. David Cameron was so impressed with her efforts that he later made her Baroness Helić.

In early 2020, the Johnson administration introduced a website, SpAdJobs.uk, which has a four-stage process involving a CV; a phone interview; a face-to-face interview with former special advisers, strategists, recruiters and experts in the relevant field; and an interview with Lee Cain, Downing Street director of communications, who signed off all SpAd appointments at that time. It strikes me as a fairer and more straightforward process, based less on who you know and more on the candidate's skills and expertise. A key figure in this selection arrangement is Paul Stephenson, a former SpAd to Philip Hammond who is well respected throughout the political world. A true believer in Brexit, he was a key member of the Vote Leave campaign team and turned down the job of Downing Street director of communications to run Hanbury Strategy, which he set up with several former special advisers.

Hanbury is the number one consultancy that has the ear of Dominic Cummings, Lee Cain and other senior Downing Street figures, and Paul was a frequent visitor to No. 10 during the latter stages of my time in politics. Indeed, on Brexit night, 31 January 2020, he was pictured on a sofa in the White Room – one of the main staterooms – with bearded Antipodean Svengali Isaac Levido, who ran the hugely successful Conservative 2019 election campaign, and Dominic Cummings. It is a photograph of three of the most powerful people in Westminster politics at the time of writing.

The move to bring Hanbury Strategy into the selection process followed the blog written by Dominic Cummings in the final days of 2019, in which he called for a greater diversity of SpAds into government. His blog mentioned that people with very specific and sometimes strange skills were needed, adding that SpAdding should be a haven for 'misfits and weirdos'. I am not aware whether this blog ever actually resulted in any SpAds being appointed from those who emailed Dominic's team through it. I can certainly say that my SpAd experience had its fair share of people matching that famous description. Indeed, it probably describes me.

For my money, any good SpAd needs to understand that it is not all about them. It's about their minister, it's about what No. 10 wants, and it's about reacting nimbly and with diligence when there is a crisis. The best SpAds I saw in action were always 'on it', and you would trust them in any organisation. The worst were those who didn't realise that you are the servant and not the master, and that you are utterly dispensable.

Unless you're No. 10 SpAd Sheridan Westlake, of course, whom three Prime Ministers have found totally indispensable. Leaving aside his somewhat recherché name (Ross Reid, a former No. 10 SpAd, has suggested it sounds more like an upmarket home furnishings shop: 'Where did you get those lovely curtains?' 'Oh, they're from Sheridan Westlake.'), when it comes to political 'lifers' in the SpAd world, Sheridan is unparalleled. Super SpAd, Dean of SpAds, whatever you want to call him, if Sheridan didn't exist, you would have to make him up. He is whatever the Conservative Party equivalent of a shop steward is, knowing every single line of the SpAd contract and code of conduct by heart, and he has absolutely no fear in representing SpAds against Whitehall officials in regard to their pay and conditions.

I remember only a few days into one of my SpAd roles when a senior official told me I was 'not allowed' to have a meeting in my own office with a party colleague without a private secretary present. I knew the senior official was wrong and I was right, but I didn't know why. Enter Sheridan. The Westlake Hotline was dialled, the breezy greeting 'Sheridan speaking' uttered as usual, and within ninety seconds the relevant paragraph of the SpAds' code of conduct was in my inbox. I called the senior official back into my office, emailed her the paragraph and told her that if she had any further questions she could take it up with Sheridan Westlake, uttering the magic words that brought terror to the eyes of many a civil servant across Whitehall. Off she went, nothing more was said about it and my meeting with a researcher from Conservative Party headquarters went ahead unhindered by her attempted roadblock.

Once a week, Sheridan holds court at SpAd drinks, held at a rotating selection of Westminster pubs. He sends out an email to SpAds, always with a link to the online weather report and a suggestion of whether or not it would make sense to stand outside for, as he always terms it, a 'cheeky' pint of Foster's, his chosen tipple. These drinks evenings were my finishing school: I learned far more from Sheridan and Amy Fisher, another long-serving SpAd, from their collective institutional knowledge imparted down the boozer than from anyone else. I owe them both a huge debt of gratitude for the many times they have assisted me with patience, wisdom and, above all, humour. Conservative headquarters newbies and seasoned SpAds alike sit at the feet of the master as Sheridan dispenses his hard-won wisdom on how to deal with recalcitrant officials, Treasury obfuscation and personnel matters such as pay and conditions. Sheridan's treasure trove of stories, accumulated over two decades in politics, is imparted to the eager gathering, which laps up every word of the Westlake wisdom. On your way up, down, in or out, Sheridan will always help, and his war stories of the bad old days of the early 2000s when the Conservative Party was in the wilderness abound, as well as more recent triumphs.

Unlike Sheridan, for example, who was fairly clearly going to have a role following the 2010 election if the Conservatives won, many Liberal Democrats appointed as SpAds in the coalition were some-what shocked by the fact they were actually going to be entering Whitehall departments and taking important decisions. Some appeared overwhelmed by the transition to government – indeed, one had a particularly badly timed trip to the 2010 World Cup in South Africa planned as a post-election treat, bought and paid for. Instead of enjoying his time in Cape Town, the SpAd in question spent the trip on email and phone to his new department, dealing with the many queries as the vuvuzelas blared.

Occasionally, a SpAd might be recruited from their minister's parliamentary office, but this is less common, and it doesn't always work out. Parliamentary aides mostly do a brilliant job, but SpAdding is a very different life with a different skill set needed, and too often I have seen SpAds recruited this way sink rather than swim, though there are exceptions.

Some SpAds have even been elected representatives themselves, for example Gavin Barwell, now Lord Barwell, who became May's chief of staff after losing his parliamentary seat in the 2017 election. As outlined in Chapter 1, he had been a departmental SpAd in the 1990s before becoming an MP. May also made a number of defeated MPs SpAds following the 2017 election, including Kris Hopkins, Stewart Jackson and Jane Ellison. Sir John Randall at No. 10, now Lord Randall, and my own co-SpAd at the Ministry of Housing, Communities and Local Government, Lee Scott, were likewise ex-MPs.

Lee represented Ilford North for ten years from 2005 to 2015. I once mentioned the boy band Blue in the office, to which Lee piped up, 'Blue? I used to be their MP!' before promptly launching into an impromptu rendition of the band's hit 'One Love'. It's not every 62-year-old former Member of Parliament who could remember the lyrics to the entire song, with the actions.

Lee also represented many of the good people of the ITV2 series *The*

Only Way Is Essex, frequently regaling the young wide-eyed private secretaries with stories about how he had had lunch that weekend in a pub and seen, for example, the show's star Gemma Collins. As MP, Lee once joined La Collins to cut the ribbon for a fish and chip shop in Gants Hill, Essex.

Lee revels in his wheeler-dealer, wide-boy image, complete with sheepskin coat; I used to call him 'The Del Boy of Westminster'. He is full of stories, usually ending with his filthy laugh. A particular favourite recalls the time a list compiled by Desmond Swayne revealing his frank views on his fellow MPs made it into the public domain. Spotting Swayne in one of the Palace of Westminster's tea rooms a few days later, Lee told Swayne he had a complaint about how he was described on the list. Apprehensively, Swayne asked Lee what the problem was. 'You spell "tosser" with two "s"s,' Lee replied, before nonchalantly walking off.

On one memorable occasion, Lee told a few of the men who worked on our floor that he was getting a mate of his, a very talented tailor called Keith Ashby, into the office to fit us for bespoke suits. Lee, who I'm not convinced has ever paid the full retail price for anything in his life, had, of course, negotiated us a discount. Keith has been making suits and uniforms for those around Parliament and indeed in Buckingham Palace for decades. He's a fascinating character whose own book would be an interesting one – but I doubt he will ever write it.

Enter Keith with his measuring tape. It was a slightly curious experience deciding whether you wanted a single- or double-vented jacket in offices which had, at that point, seen everything from major matters of state being decided to my inside leg measurement being taken, but Keith was extremely professional. I think he got about eight suits out of it, and very well made they were too.

I remember sitting in the SpAds' office later that afternoon with the always-tactile Lee, saying to him, 'Lee, I honestly don't know anyone who would bring in a tailor to take over a government office so we could get our inside legs measured for suits. You are a complete one-off, mate.' Not missing a beat, Lee walked the few steps to my desk, put his arm on my shoulder and replied, 'I know a guy who does shoes.'

Sadly, Lee did not continue in his post under the Johnson administration. However, he was absolutely delighted some months later to be made a member of the Board of Deputies of British Jews. He is a man whose Jewishness is at the very core of his being, and I was absolutely honoured one day when he told me that to him I was 'an honorary Jew' – about as nice a thing as he could possibly say.

So I do worry that the more mainstream the process of SpAd recruitment becomes, the less the eccentrics, characters and, yes, perhaps even the misfits and weirdos will make it through.

3

The Devil's SpAdvocate: Policy SpAds

Barely across the threshold at the Ministry of Housing, Communities and Local Government (MHCLG) after the reshuffle that made James Brokenshire Housing Secretary, I had a ministerial submission thrust in front of me by my private secretary. 'They need a decision on that in the next thirty minutes,' she explained. Until hours before, the department had had three SpAds – two policy and one covering media – dealing with everything. For the moment at least, it was just me.

The heat was on to read through the various bits of information put together by officials, which recommended spending £28 million on an innovative programme called Housing First, designed to help people sleeping rough long-term.

I read the submission carefully, crossing out just a few words before it went to James. It was odd to be asked my opinion on a policy area I hadn't considered much until a few moments previously, but that is the life of a SpAd starting in a new department. Everyone has an opinion on homelessness, and I was clear we should do what we could for such vulnerable people, but was this the right scheme in which to put so much taxpayers' money? I hadn't long to 'clear' the submission before it went into James's ministerial red box for his immediate decision.

Suddenly it struck me. Just five weeks before, I had been in the Northern Ireland Office, whose budget for *the entire department* was £21 million, significantly less than this single proposal. And now I had less than half an hour to recommend to James whether to go ahead with the policy, as well as a planned visit to Birmingham – one of the pilot areas for the scheme – later that week.

I was on the third page of the ten-page ministerial submission when Cathy Brokenshire, James's wife, rang about an interview he was doing with the *Daily Mail* later in the week. Was it OK to wear jeans for their photo in the paper? No, I quickly said, it is better to go slightly smarter for the photo if that's all right, as the *Mail*'s readership would expect something a little dressier. We chatted a bit about how busy the week had been and how, already, the work was mounting up, and said our goodbyes. Cathy has always been the backbone of 'Team Brokey' – we couldn't have done nearly as much either in Northern Ireland or at MHCLG without her constant support. The eventual interview with the *Mail*'s Jack Doyle about James's return to the front line of politics, having recovered from the lung cancer diagnosis which necessitated his resignation from Cabinet, was one of James's best to date. The headline was 'From cancer to Cabinet in four months', accompanied by a lovely picture of Cathy and James.

Cathy was endlessly patient when a planned family weekend was wrecked for the umpteenth time with preparation for one of the

Sunday morning political programmes, such as the *Andrew Marr Show* or *Sophy Ridge on Sunday*. The work would take up much of the Saturday, to say nothing of most of the Sunday morning for any last-minute briefing, travel and visit to the studio. And she was good enough to ask my fashion advice.

We went ahead with the Housing First programme and when the two other SpAds were eventually appointed at MHCLG, James gave me responsibility for advising on the entire policy of homelessness in the department, as well as my other, cross-cutting, media duties.

Tall, raffish and with a filthy habit of nipping out for a fag, Liam Booth-Smith became our main SpAd on policy matters. I didn't quite know what to make of Liam when I first met him. Very shortly after he was appointed, I had a few days off and flew to Northern Ireland to see my family. When I returned less than a week after Liam had started his job, he was already running rings around No. 10 and the Treasury to get policies through. Even though I have never smoked, I soon started taking a short break from the grindstone to chat policies through with Liam as he lit up outside the departmental building, usually indulging my own bad habit of downing a can of Diet Coke. We were a great team, and he soon gauged the level of detail I needed to know about policies in order to explain them to the press. Liam quickly came to the notice of No. 10, the Treasury and others, and in 2019 the Treasury poacher became the gamekeeper with a job at No. 10 under Boris Johnson.

Policy SpAds aren't necessarily experts in every single area of the fields they cover, though Liam is a housing expert, having run the think tank Localis. Many policy SpAds learn the details of their department as they go along and must quickly establish what is politically useful for the Secretary of State to push through. As one former Ministry of Defence SpAd once told me, 'My job is politics, not tanks.'

Policy SpAds work just as closely with their minister as media SpAds. They usually attend more meetings than media SpAds, feeding in the important political policy points and driving through the detail of the politically important initiatives. They hold their own meetings with officials too, making clear to each department what is a priority for the Secretary of State and what is not, which is sometimes half the battle. Policy SpAds engage with many MPs, including key people such as the chair of the relevant select committee. It's important, too, that they have a close relationship with their counterpart in the No. 10 Policy Unit.

Regarding homelessness, James made a clear decision from the outset that we had to reduce the numbers of rough sleepers. They had been rising for eight years, and that was a major failing for which the government was at least partly responsible. My view is that the austerity policies of the Cameron administration were certainly a contributory factor to that trend, but there are many factors at play.

The government definition of a rough sleeper is someone who is sleeping in the open air, such as on the streets, or in doorways, parks or bus shelters. Rough sleepers might also be in buildings or other places not designed for habitation, such as barns, sheds, car parks, cars, derelict buildings, boats, railway or bus stations. There is a subtle but important difference between someone who is homeless but not rough sleeping and a rough sleeper who is homeless. It may appear abstruse, but it's actually fundamental to the issue.

A £100 million Rough Sleeping Strategy had been established by James's predecessor as Housing Secretary, Sajid Javid. Thanks to some excellent work by civil servants, with input from the charitable sector and local government, we managed a small reduction – 2 per cent – in the number of people rough sleeping in England, that first year, 2018. The 2019 figures showed a 9 per cent fall. This was not nearly enough, of course, but it was a start. James and I had brokered a £30 million fund with the Department of Health targeted at the mental health of rough sleepers. I was delighted when the 2019 Conservative manifesto committed to eradicating rough sleeping entirely by 2024.

Ironically, there are enough shelter beds in London to go round, but people choose not to sleep in these shelters for a variety of reasons. I only began to understand these as time went on. The person who taught me most about this deceptively simple area was an outstanding civil servant called Jeremy Swain. Jeremy is a former chief executive of Thames Reach, a major homelessness charity, and his no-nonsense attitude and reforming zeal shone through from the moment we met. He's about the least 'civil service' civil servant I have ever come across – Jeremy has no hesitation in calling a spade a shovel, which was probably a big part of the reason we got on. He was brought in to MHCLG to challenge official thinking, and for thirty years he has been obsessive about his work. You could ask Jeremy what his favourite colour is and he would still somehow bring the conversation round to reducing the rough sleeping numbers. Jeremy arranged for me to visit a number of shelters, both with and without James. Late at night on a number of occasions, I shadowed the workers from St Mungo's homelessness charity as they offered to arrange beds for people sleeping rough around Victoria in London and, on another very moving occasion, at the terminals of Heathrow Airport. On these shifts, I was astonished at just how many people refused a bed for the night, for often complicated reasons such as mental health, an aversion to being inside, personal safety and addiction. Some charities and religious organisations think they are helping by giving people tents. In reality, knives, drugs, unsanitary conditions and incidences of coercive control are all too frequent in these primitive forms of shelter.

I remember asking Jeremy whether people should give money to people begging on the street. What he told me was exactly the same view he has held for decades. 'Firstly,' he said, 'how do you know they are homeless?' I explained that if someone was sitting on a tent in the street and had a cup or hat with money in it, it was reasonable to assume they were.

No, said Jeremy, many people begging have access to benefits, temporary accommodation or in some cases own their own homes – a thesis backed up by research by police in Nottingham in 2019, which investigated and indeed followed people begging in the streets. In 2015, a Freedom of Information request showed that fewer than one in five people arrested for begging in England and Wales was actually homeless, and some were making £45,000 a year. Obviously, people beg for all sorts of mental health and circumstantial reasons and should be helped out of this life, but it is also clear that many people begging do have somewhere to stay.

So should we give money to people who are genuinely homeless, I asked Jeremy. The answer from the man who had run one of Britain's biggest homelessness charities was blunt, and consistent with what he had been telling people for years: 'If you give someone rough sleeping money, you may as well just cut out the middle man and give it directly to a drug dealer. Anything you do – even giving someone a sandwich – sustains their life on the street.' He argued that access to medical attention, social workers and getting people a proper, sustainable plan to get a roof over their head as quickly as possible is what is needed to solve the problem, not a few coins with no proper purpose. He also cautioned against giving money to people who said they needed cash for a hostel, pointing out that most hostels are free at the point of access.

On the nights I went out with Jeremy, he questioned rough sleepers constantly about what they were going to do, how they were going to work with the outreach workers, how they saw a path out of this way of living. It might sound harsh, but it was quite the opposite – Jeremy was very clear that people had to make a choice for themselves for their life to be better, so they would stick with the difficult path of getting back on their feet. 'If it was a member of your family, God forbid,' he would say, 'you wouldn't give them a tent. You'd do everything possible to help them out of their predicament.' It may seem harsh, but Jeremy's brand of 'tough love' has helped thousands of people over the years. 'Real compassion is when you give people a life chance, not a few pence in a hat,' Jeremy told me.

> When I left Thames Reach, seventy-eight of the staff were former rough sleepers, including the manager of our team that worked with rough sleepers on the London Underground. And who are the outreach workers who are the most direct and unrelenting towards rough sleepers? The ones who used to sleep rough themselves. They can't be doing with prevarication – staying on the street equals an early death.

In 2018, James did a Christmas Eve shift with outreach workers. He didn't want the media there; rather, he simply approached people in great need and asked their view about how government policy could most help them. Some experts from homelessness charities were also on the shift, and they told James how they would ensure the rough sleepers they met would eventually get a roof over their head, as well as a hot meal on Christmas Day. James definitely used these first-hand experiences to inform his actions as Secretary of State.

At the Northern Ireland Office, one of the areas of policy I took a lot of interest in was same-sex marriage, which is now, finally and belatedly, legal in Northern Ireland, as it is in the rest of the British Isles. I had the odd experience at university of feeling left-wing when at home in the socially conservative surroundings of Northern Ireland, and, despite holding exactly the same views, feeling right-wing when I was in more liberal England for my studies. The rest of the UK legalised same-sex marriage in 2014, and attitudes on the island of Ireland have shifted since. The Republic of Ireland showed how far it had come since being a state beholden to the Catholic Church when a whopping 62 per cent voted in favour of same-sex marriage in a 2015 referendum. But Northern Ireland still lagged behind, although it had allowed same-sex civil partnerships since 2005.

One of our junior ministers at the NIO, Kris Hopkins is a blunt Yorkshireman who was in the Army for many years. To the naked eye, Kris probably doesn't come across as a social liberal, but he is one of the most left-wing Conservatives I have ever met. His strong advocacy of the extension of equal marriage to Northern Ireland was one of the many surprising aspects of Kris's political philosophy – he was a book I had judged by its cover, and that was both wrong and unfair. We clubbed together to see how we could advance the cause of equal marriage in Northern Ireland, having one particularly fun meeting with Ruth Hunt, then head of Stonewall, who got on with Kris famously. In a memorable meeting with ministers in the Northern Ireland Office, Kris remarked in his Yorkshire drawl, 'It's probably about bloody time I got on my big rainbow underpants and told the DUP what's what on equal marriage.' The Democratic Unionist Party, headed by Arlene Foster, spearheaded the resistance to any reform, although the might of social conservatives in her party is arguably on the wane since the retirement and subsequent death of the Reverend Ian Paisley.

As Kris left the NIO to fight the 2017 election, my leaving present to him was a bottle of wine, nestling in a gift bag alongside a large pair of rainbow underpants I had purchased on eBay for £2.99. I have no idea whether Kris ever tried them on, but he laughed heartily on receiving them, holding them up to display them to the private secretaries.

Kris sadly lost the 2017 election, in part due to a row over a local incinerator in his constituency. I rang him at 5 a.m. on election night to commiserate and he told me, 'I'm all right, dude. I've had a bottle of red wine and a packet of Frazzles.' And eventually, after a drawn-out public battle, same-sex marriage became legal in Northern Ireland in 2020 thanks to the Westminster Parliament – rather than the suspended Northern Ireland Assembly – passing it into law.

The other area of policy in which I was most involved at the Northern Ireland Office was the legacy of the Troubles. My co-SpAd Jonathan Caine was the key person on all political policy at the NIO, but I generally fed in when there were media elements to discuss.

The Belfast Agreement – otherwise known as the Good Friday Agreement – was signed in 1998 and there is a reason 'Legacy', as the issue is termed in government, has taken so long to resolve. In truth, it is perhaps an unsolvable element of the peace process, as so many people want so many different outcomes. Indeed, as a student journalist, I remember interviewing Paul Murphy, then the Northern Ireland Secretary under New Labour, in 2005. He told me that an announcement he was about to make concerned 'the process of dealing with the past in Northern Ireland'. Fifteen years later, despite much progress, it is clear to anyone who deals with Legacy that it is a tremendously difficult area, still without any clear answers.

Speaking to dozens, if not hundreds, of victims during my journalistic and political career, it became abundantly clear that one of the main problems with tackling the past is that almost every victim wants a slightly different outcome. Some want the full truth, some want justice in the courts, and some – from whom we hear less, by the very nature of their thoughts on the matter – want to put the entire nightmare behind them and move on with their lives without legal redress.

With Legacy, sections of the media and very vocal campaigners are clear – there should be no prosecutions of soldiers at all. The notion that 'our boys' are the subject of a 'witch-hunt' for their actions in Northern Ireland decades before is a narrative with which I profoundly disagree. It is just not backed up by hard evidence. Examples of elderly veterans being 'dragged from their beds' and arrested make for very strong stories in some newspapers, but often these veterans are accused of some very serious crimes, and arrests are rare. Those who perpetuate this 'witch-hunt' narrative usually do not agree that *anyone* who served in uniform in the Troubles should be prosecuted for anything they did. I would also like to ask these people if they do not believe that those accused of crimes will receive a fair trial, and whether that means they do not believe in our justice system?

Having spent time as a journalist in Northern Ireland, it is all too clear that the effects of the Troubles are a daily reality for people who have lost family members or friends. It is a physical reality for the thousands of people who sustained injuries from that period, and I too would want justice, even for something that happened decades ago. A total of about 270,000 people served in uniform throughout the Troubles – the vast majority with great bravery and distinction. But the suggestion that not one of them did anything wrong permeates this debate. It became increasingly difficult to make clear to the media that, while we owe an enormous debt of gratitude to the armed forces in Northern Ireland, without whom the peace process would not have been possible, there were nonetheless those who fell short of the standards most upheld.

If I were a veteran who had followed the rules – as the vast majority did – I would want proper justice meted out to those who had not. There is also a perceived inequality in that veterans have been pursued, yet many former terrorists who many believe should be subject to the full force of the law – including some Sinn Féin politicians who were involved in violence – have not been. At the time of writing, the issue continues to be a very difficult one for the Northern Ireland Office, the Ministry of Defence, the Ministry of Justice and the Attorney General. It is a complex and nuanced policy area and my role in explaining it to journalists was a key element of my time at the Northern Ireland Office.

On a brighter note, Julian Smith, who was Northern Ireland Secretary for just over six months, from July 2019 to February 2020, finally got a piece of legislation passed which would give a pension to civilians who sustained injuries in the Troubles through no fault of their own. This group comprises some of the most dignified people I have ever met. One of my great regrets from my time at the NIO is that we didn't make more progress with these pensions – the political will was just not there, and it was always going to be part of a wider deal. Julian and his team did an excellent job getting it over the line.

One of these injured people is a man called Alex Bunting, who received an MBE for his bravery and campaigning. I was the first journalist ever to interview Alex, in 2009, for BBC Radio Ulster. In that interview, he spoke for the first time publicly about having his leg blown off when a booby-trapped bomb under his taxi exploded. He also lost a finger and was made deaf in one ear, and his other leg was damaged. During our interview, Alex even took off his prosthetic leg to show me the stump that was left. The IRA, the terrorists who carried out the attack, insisted it was a case of mistaken identity.

Alex hadn't done anything wrong whatsoever. He had been about to go to work in his taxi when his entire life changed for ever, and he could no longer do his job. Surely people like him – totally and completely blameless, and living with horrific, life-changing injuries – should be afforded a pension? Thankfully, that is now the case, and I take great satisfaction in this. It is a constructive example of politicians in Northern Ireland – from all sides – making a tangible difference.

I had told James Brokenshire and Karen Bradley the same thing at the start of their respective periods as Northern Ireland Secretary: there was no way they could ever be as popular as Mo Mowlam, the

Secretary of State at the time of the Belfast Agreement, who had the common touch. When I had a cup of tea with Julian Smith in his office in Whitehall in early 2020, I told him he had become so popular in Northern Ireland due to his successes with pensions for those injured and getting compensation for victims of historical institutional abuse – to say nothing of getting Stormont up and running again – that my new nickname for him was 'Mo 2.0'. He laughed and was very gracious about how much preparatory work had been done by James and Karen. Just days later, we both lost our jobs in the February 2020 reshuffle: me as SpAd at Justice; Julian as Northern Ireland Secretary.

Julian's sacking was a brutal reminder, as if one were needed, that policy success, popularity and even an award as Minister of the Year from *The Spectator* were not enough to save his Cabinet career. Reshuffles – and political careers in general – are rarely about merit. They are more often about patronage; rewarding or punishing perceived or actual loyalty or disloyalty (Julian, I am told, was seen to be disloyal over Brexit); balancing wings of the party; gender; and sometimes simply the recommendation of fellow politicians, for example the Chief Whip, who has a key role in the promotion into the more junior ranks. In a reshuffle, literally dozens of people – Cabinet ministers, more junior ministers and SpAds – can change jobs over the course of a very short period and for reasons which are not always clear.

I played an absolutely tiny role in advancing the causes of both equal marriage and the injured victims in Northern Ireland, but I am proud of both. Having grown up in a country ravaged by terrorism, I have very strong views about how it should be dealt with. At the Ministry of Justice some time later, I was privileged to be involved in discussions in regard to the government response to the Streatham terror attack on 2 February 2020. Two people had been stabbed in east London by a terrorist who had just been released from prison. The next morning, I found myself at a meeting with the Prime Minister, Home Secretary Priti Patel, Justice Secretary Robert Buckland (my then boss), the Metropolitan Police and various senior advisers including Dominic Cummings. The whole question of terrorists being released from prison was a live issue, and it was clear that action needed to be taken quickly. There was praise for the immediate response of the counter-terrorism officers in killing the terrorist in Streatham, as well as discussion of the 'next-day' issues of the release of terrorist offenders, or non-terrorist offenders who had been radicalised in prison. The Prime Minister was clear we were to take tough action, and he spoke with huge determination.

Dominic Cummings is often criticised, but his absolute commitment to progress and getting the law changed as soon as possible gave complete clarity to everyone in that and subsequent meetings in which I took part. Keeping the country safe is the first duty of any government, and I never imagined I would ever have a role – however small – in helping with that task. When signing up to be a SpAd, I just didn't imagine it would ever be part of my day, but here I was, discussing the response to a horrendous attack and what the best options were to keep people safe. As I sipped water from the crystal glasses on the Cabinet table embossed with the 'ER' insignia, I was both nervous and keen to help as much as possible when the safety of my fellow citizens was discussed. I believe that through his decisive action and clear instructions to us as more junior SpAds, Dominic Cummings – acting with the full authority of the Prime Minister –

showed great leadership that day. The subsequent legislation that came out of that meeting showed how effective SpAds could be in dealing with a horrendous tragedy, acting in the interests of both their political masters and the public more generally. The result, just weeks later, was emergency legislation ensuring that terrorist offenders would spend longer behind bars in future. One of our junior ministers at Justice, Chris Philp, ably guided the bill through the House of Commons.

Many people criticise Dominic for his bullishness and bluntness, but while he may not be everyone's cup of tea, there is absolutely no doubt in my mind he is a strategic genius. Even in August 2019, when things looked very bleak on all fronts for the new Conservative government – bereft of a majority and having come through all the problems of the May administration – Dominic was adamant that Brexit would happen, that an election would be called and that it would be successful for us. That looked entirely impossible to many of us, especially the veterans of the May administration, left exhausted and dejected by months of political stalemate.

Fast forward four and a half months to our final SpAds' meeting at Downing Street before we broke up for Christmas and the Brexit withdrawal agreement had passed its second reading in the Commons, and the December election had produced a majority of eighty for the Conservatives. I stood at the back of the room and raised my hand during the questions section, saying, 'Dominic, in August, you said we would get Brexit done, we would have an election and we'd win a majority. I thought that was actually pretty counterintuitive. I was 100 per cent wrong. You were 100 per cent right. Thank you very much, and Merry Christmas.'

As we've seen, policy SpAds get into the weeds of what the government is doing, and it is their job to make sure that it is politically desirable. Wiser – and more academic – heads than mine advised my ministers on most of the substance of what we did, though I loved homelessness policy and I do feel we made a difference to the lives of some of the most vulnerable people in our society. But knowing the media as I do, it was clear that my talent lay in handling that particular beast, and that was always the main part of my job. Public perception in politics is so important – frustrating as that may be sometimes – and if what you do in Westminster is not relevant to people's lives then, rightly or wrongly, it is seen as of little importance. James's and my two mantras by the end of the three years we worked together were 'Perception is reality' – if enough people think it then it's accepted as fact, no matter what the facts actually are – and 'You can't put the toothpaste back in the tube.' Being a media SpAd, as I outline in the following chapter, has a lot to do with cleaning up that metaphorical toothpaste – and occasionally going through the looking glass to deal with the perceived realities in which we found ourselves.

4

Calling a SpAd a SpAd: Media SpAds

Although I'd done some policy SpAdding at the Ministry of Housing, Communities and Local Government, the recruitment of Cambridge DPhil legal eagle Rajiv Shah as my co-SpAd at my next department, the Ministry of Justice, meant there was little merit in my advising Robert Buckland on anything other than media. Like his fellow policy SpAds Jonathan Caine at the NIO and Liam Booth-Smith at MHCLG, Rajiv was a walking encyclopaedia on his area of expertise; with Robert and Rajiv together, a great partnership of legal knowledge, experience of criminal justice and insatiable gossip about the legal profession was born. For me, too, there was plenty to be getting on with: daily enquiries about celebrity prisoners such as Rose West, Julian Assange and Charles Bronson; the thorny issue of terrorists in prison and associated sentencing policy; insatiable home affairs desks on Fleet Street; and the occasional judge or prison governor popping up to say something controversial to keep us on our toes.

My role as media SpAd, whether at the Northern Ireland Office, MHCLG or Justice, was, mostly, to decode the complex policy in bite-size chunks so journalists could write or broadcast about them, working closely with the press office of each department and frequently asking each of my three very knowledgeable co-SpAds how best to explain things.

Liam later moved to an exalted role in No. 10. Initially a senior adviser to Boris Johnson and a key member of his inner circle, Liam still retains that role, but at the early 2020 reshuffle he was appointed to head the joint No. 10/No. 11/Treasury advisory unit. One of the first requests of the new Chancellor of the Exchequer, Rishi Sunak, was that Liam be his right-hand-man. Rishi, Liam and I worked together very closely at MHCLG when Rishi was Local Government Minister. It was clear even then my two colleagues were destined for great things. Liam combines a ferocious intellect with being an extremely down-to-earth, loyal friend; he is the son of a single mother living on a council estate in Stoke and has risen to one of the most important jobs in the country. He would make an excellent chief of staff to Rishi when – and I am convinced it is a when rather than an if – Rishi becomes Prime Minister.

When we worked together at MHCLG, Liam helped explain policy to me so I could brief the media. He learned quickly that I only needed the headlines to satisfy some journalists' fruit fly-like attention spans. Saying that, one of the longest briefings on any topic I have ever given to a hack in Westminster resulted in a 350-word article containing no fewer than seven factual errors in a prominent position in one of the biggest newspapers in Britain. Some of the journalist's copy was in direct contradiction to factual information I had told him on the phone the previous afternoon during our 45-minute conversation.

Keeping the departmental press office – staffed by dozens of impartial civil servants in large departments – on side is a key part of any media SpAd's role, and it's important to remember the long hours any press officer can be called upon to work, with weekend and evening duties very much part of the job. Likewise, a SpAd is always on call, and I've had phone calls at 1.45 a.m. and again at 5.30 a.m. too many times to remember. Just about every possible family or social event has been ruined by some crisis or another, and I think I ended up cancelling at least one holiday every year that I was a SpAd. But that's the game, and you know that when you sign up.

One way I recognised excellent work at the MHCLG press office was by creating a little award called the Brokey Cokeys. A press officer going beyond the call of duty gained themselves the coveted Brokey Cokey award, consisting of a can of Diet Coke from my mini-fridge in the SpAd Pad, which James had christened Fridgey McFridgeface. The winner also received a specially designed certificate, which a particularly artistic colleague knocked together in a few minutes.

I was having a drink in one of the House of Commons bars one evening shortly after I launched the Brokey Cokeys when I got talking to Caroline Nokes, then Immigration Minister. She told me her civil servants had heard of the scheme and were demanding she implement her own awards: the Nokey Cokeys. News of the copycat scheme somehow made its way into one of the gossip columns of the *Daily Mail*, with James getting full credit for the idea and me not mentioned. On the morning the *Mail* published the item, James was looking through that day's newspaper clippings and was baffled to see the article giving him credit for something he knew nothing about. Incredulously, he enquired where on earth it came from.

'Put it this way, James,' I said to the morning meeting where we daily discussed departmental issues, including press coverage. 'You're getting praise for something you didn't strictly do yourself. A fellow minister is implementing your policy across Whitehall and there is an article in a national newspaper pointing out that you are a nice guy to hard-working civil servants. Breakfast is barely over, but let's face it: my work today is already done.'

This illustrates another key part of the media SpAd's role: to promote the minister, keeping their profile up and feeding the media with sympathetic stories. This can be done through formal means such as agreed stories on the government 'grid' – literally written in a grid in a spreadsheet so that one big announcement doesn't clash with another – or informally through briefings about announcements as they come up. On my first day in the Northern Ireland Office, Jonathan Caine, who I am fairly sure is the longest-serving SpAd in the same position since the establishment of the role in the 1960s, gave me some good advice: 'I don't leak and I don't brief against people, and that is why I have survived in politics for thirty years. It's up to you how you operate, but I would recommend that.'

Much to journalists' frustration, I can honestly say that in three and a half years as a SpAd I did not put a single thing into the public domain that was not beneficial to my minister, the government or, mostly, both. It also wasn't really my choice – had I acted in the way some SpAds were getting away with, especially in the latter days of the May administration when things were truly falling apart, James would have sacked me, and rightly so.

My mission was to attempt to have as much integrity as James in my dealings with people – I have only ever met one person who has more of that characteristic than James, and that is my father. I felt the same way about leaking as I did about briefing against people – pouring out poison to the press to write negative stories about them. The opposition? Yes, fill your boots – attack them as often as possible and promote your boss and the government. But blue-on-blue action was not for me. Most SpAds most of the time were generally fine in both regards – I remember one senior journalist telling me that in the May administration there were just four SpAds (out of about a hundred) who properly and consistently leaked, and I could make a fair guess as to who they were. Cabinet ministers weren't much better – towards the end of the May administration, statements were being made in the supposedly confidential Cabinet meetings which were actually designed to make good copy for journalists. Others felt they could not say what they truly thought, because it would simply appear in the media within hours. At one stage, James even darkly suggested that it would be simpler just to put Cabinet on Sky News as that would mean at least an accurate version of what was said would be on record.

Following the confidence vote in Theresa May just before Christmas 2018, there was the hope that the Yuletide break might focus minds. But the New Year did not involve much of a change of mood; rather, it signified an almost tangible moment when it became clear that the May government was in office but not in power. Brexit had simply meant Theresa May's authority had drained away, and for Mayites such as James and me, it was bleak. Perhaps the best piece of political analysis at that time came from my best friend, Michael Selby. 'The problem is', he said, 'you just can't have a Prime Minister who people feel sorry for.' I remember texting the *Mail on Sunday* columnist Dan Hodges: 'If this really were the last days of Rome, at least we would be getting some more sex.' Similarly, when Andrea Leadsom resigned in May 2019 in protest at Theresa May's Brexit strategy, I WhatsApped one of the few journalists I actually trusted, making a reference to Leadsom's membership of the so-called Pizza Club of pro-Brexit Cabinet ministers, who met weekly: 'Let's hope the first resignation of a member of Pizza Club doesn't lead to a Domino's effect.' Humour was my coping mechanism, and if you didn't laugh you would cry. If people asked how I was during the final, dark months of the May administration, I would reply, 'Oh, strong and stable.'

But as Dominic Cummings told us in one of our first SpAds' meetings as part of the Johnson administration, 'There are leaks and there are leaks.' A letter James Brokenshire wrote to the Mayor of London, Sadiq Khan, about what we believed was Khan's appalling record on social housing miraculously made it onto the front page of the *Evening Standard* – obviously I gave that to the political team of the *Standard* in a coordinated briefing which suited their deadline and was timed to make life as difficult as possible for the mayor. My course of action was technically a leak, but it's helpful to the government and to your minister, so it's an authorised one and therefore acceptable – indeed, encouraged.

What sent me completely crackers were the totally unauthorised briefings criticising people in our own party, or just making life difficult for them – for instance, when details were leaked from what is called a write-round. Towards the very end of the policymaking process, a letter is sent to every member of the Cabinet, asking if they have any objections to proposed legislation. By that stage, perhaps months of work will have gone into a policy and there is a torturously choreographed process of speaking to interested and affected parties, warming up the national press and the trade press and coordinating the launch. It will have been 'gridded' by No. 10, and often there are 'trails' – part of the announcement briefed out – in the Sunday papers, with maybe an article by your minister explaining some elements. For instance, if the policy involves changes to housing legislation on eviction, the article might outline how the policy will help renters and note that extended tenancies will ensure children will have to move school less. The article is usually ghost-written by the press office, the media SpAd or both. And if your announcement is 'top of the grid', your minister will generally do the morning media round of interviews to announce the policy.

But all that work by officials, the private office, the press office, No. 10, departmental SpAds and politicians can be undone in one stroke if someone leaks it from the write-round, which happened to us a few times. It puts the policy in the public domain at a time that can be difficult for the government, is often angled towards one aspect rather than showing the full picture, and allows interest groups to pile in with their opinion (and, sometimes, opposition) to a policy that might not be entirely ready. It's a nightmare in government and hugely frustrating to all involved. Added in for good measure was occasionally a quote slagging James off, sometimes for reasons that were far from clear. We could generally easily trace who the leaker was, or at least take an educated guess, and it never seemed to be out of any animosity to James, rather that the leaker wanted to show journalists he – and it was always a he – was Jimmy Big Balls with all this secret information. I found this testosterone-filled

THE SECRET LIFE OF SPECIAL ADVISERS

one-upmanship tiresome. Even as a journalist, when someone in government leaked to me, I rarely respected their motives, which were seldom honourable.

Journalists thrive on the practice, of course, and love the access. They claim transparency is the objective, and good luck to them. But from the perspective of anyone in government it is totally mad, counter-productive and extremely annoying, and I vowed never to do it.

Of course, I'm not saying I was Mother Teresa: when talking to journalists, I certainly omitted facts or kept silent or worked with my policy colleagues to ensure that I was genuinely ignorant of the more sensitive facts about a story so I could honestly say 'I don't know the detail of that' or 'I'm just not getting into that'. I promoted my bosses in every way I could – but I'm pretty sure I never intentionally lied to a journalist. The truth can hurt you, but the lie will kill you.

I certainly wasn't above employing a few elements of the dark arts to promote my boss, though. One way to do this was to 'create' a story out of a 'Dear Colleague' letter. These are quite literally when a senior minister writes to his or her colleagues to tell them about a policy or give some further explanation about something that is happening. The Dear Colleague letters often go to all 650 MPs, so they are generally considered to be in the public domain. To 'create' a story, I would pick a journalist – usually one who wasn't familiar with the Dear Colleague process – making clear that they were the only one who was receiving my briefing about the letter. 'I've a wee exclusive for you…' I would tell them, and that was technically factually accurate – I wasn't giving it to anyone else, after all. The journalist would write up the 'story' – usually 'revealing' absolutely nothing that we didn't want in the public domain anyway – as 'a leaked letter to MPs, exclusively obtained by X news outlet', which then led to many other journalists following up the story as if it were something big. And so good publicity was created for my boss. I did this a number of times to take the heat off during periods of the Northern Ireland peace talks. It was a simple and effective process.

In times of crisis, a chat with a journalist reminding them of the virtues of your minister never goes amiss, either. When Gavin Williamson was sacked as Defence Secretary in May 2019 after a leak from the National Security Council about the Huawei technology company's involvement with the UK's 5G network – a leak he continues to deny responsibility for – SpAds were on heightened alert. There was a period of about twenty-five minutes between the news of Gavin's astonishing defenestration and news of his replacement, a time when SpAds oscillated between shock and frenetic speculation.

The obvious question for all SpAds was: who was going to be the new Defence Secretary? And could we be on the move? I remember the exact moment my co-SpAd Liam walked into the MHCLG SpAd Pad about ten minutes after Williamson's dismissal. He remarked, 'I suppose if you were really Machiavellian you would be getting friendly journalists to talk up Brokey on Twitter as the new Defence Secretary.'

I looked up from tapping away at my phone and said, 'Liam, I am literally in the middle of doing exactly that.'

'Senior government source tips James Brokenshire as next Defence Secretary' was my draft tweet. But sadly it was not to be, and Penny Mordaunt was given the post.

About two weeks later, I bumped into the reporter who got the Huawei leak, Steven Swinford of *The Times*, one of the best-informed political journalists in Britain. He would frustrate SpAds continually with the quality and frequency of the confidential stories he obtained from inside government. But he was always courteous and good humoured when asking us to react. Steve had been given a couple of weeks off in the immediate aftermath of the Huawei leak story, taking his family to the sunshine of Tenerife to escape the heat of Westminster.

'How was your holiday, Steve?' I asked him when I saw him buying his breakfast in Parliament. 'Did you have a nice time when you were Huawei?'

He had the good grace to laugh.

Steve was also the journalist who rang me for our reaction when a 'government source' told *The Times* that Home Secretary Priti Patel and Justice Secretary Robert Buckland, my then boss, were 'split' over tougher sentences for assaulting police officers. The source told the paper, 'The Ministry of Justice seem more focused on making the life of criminals easier than protecting our police officers. Robert Buckland needs to understand the public's priorities.'

So this source was alleging that the Lord Chancellor and Justice Secretary, a man who had been a criminal barrister for twenty-five years and a part-time judge who had locked up more criminals than the source had had hot dinners, cared more about the welfare of criminals than that of police officers. And this demonstrably inaccurate sentiment had just been shared with arguably the most important broadsheet newspaper in Britain.

Just about keeping my calm on the phone, I asked Steve to give me an hour to respond, which I eventually did with a very anodyne statement agreed with No. 10. But I knew exactly who the government source was, and I absolutely hit the roof the moment the phone was set down. I immediately rang the person who I am convinced to this day leaked it and confronted him. He denied it outright. What the source should have done is had the argument about the policy with us in private, rather than mouthing off to *The Times*. These sorts of incidents of inter-departmental rivalry are always part of government, but leaking to the papers about currently active government policy makes my blood boil.

One event that stopped a lot of leaking was the clarity of Dominic Cummings's thoughts on the matter in an early meeting, just days after Boris Johnson became Prime Minister. A mandatory gathering of all SpAds was scheduled in Downing Street for the odd time of 7.55 a.m. I am not a morning person, so to be summoned to a 7.55 a.m. meeting, even at 10 Downing Street, was not a development I was thrilled about. Dominic stood at the front and told us, 'If you leak, you will be marched from your desk by the head of security at your department, your pass will be taken off you and you will be sacked. You have no rights.' Duly, these sentiments appeared in *The Times* the next day in an article by – you guessed it – Steve Swinford.

I was personally very glad to hear about this new zero-tolerance approach, having grown increasingly frustrated with the behaviour of some of the SpAds in the dying days of the May administration who didn't seem able to keep their mouths shut. Some of the Cabinet ministers weren't much better. I remember a SpAd WhatsApping me to complain that the usual chapter-and-verse Cabinet run-down by *Spectator* political editor James Forsyth hadn't been published online. Forsyth's version of events was usually on the website within an hour of the meeting at Downing Street finishing. Both my friend's minister and mine were amongst the very last of the May administration to observe Cabinet confidentiality, so we of course were glued to

Forsyth's coverage waiting to find out what had happened at the Downing Street meetings. 'Ah,' I noted, as a certain Cabinet minister popped up on the House of Commons TV feed in front of me. 'She's got departmental oral questions today, so she won't have had a chance to ring Forsyth and spill the beans.' It then made sense why Forsyth was later than usual with his copy.

~

The thorny issue of a Cabinet minister's style, delivery and appearance is also the bailiwick of the media SpAd, even down to very personal details such as the minister's weight. Robert and I had a number of conversations about this, mainly how on the 2019 campaign trail he was losing some and his trousers were looser.

One particular bone of contention I had with James – and there were not many in nearly three years of working together – was his preference for rimless glasses, which I have always thought do not suit his face. I'd been on at him almost since Day 1 at the Northern Ireland Office to change them to a light frame, perhaps black or brown, with a slightly softer shape, but there was no movement on that front.

Then one day, when we were at MHCLG, he rang me and told me he had just been at the optician's. 'Aha,' I exclaimed, 'at last we have an opportunity to get you some new glasses!'

'Erm, no, I don't think so, Peter,' he replied, gingerly. 'Cathy has told me I'm getting an identical pair with my new prescription. But if you want to take Cathy on and talk to her about it...'

We both laughed. There was zero chance of that happening, so I shut up and he got the replica pair.

At a wedding a few months later, I found myself sitting beside two high-end opticians who make glasses for the legal fraternity on Fleet Street in London. I showed them a picture of James I had brought up from Google, and they spent a good ten minutes over the dessert course giving me some tips about frames that would suit his face. Sadly, the advice I passed on has so far come to naught. I live in hope of a spectacular shift on the Brokenshires' long-standing resistance to my optical advice.

Indeed, it was such an ongoing issue that I teased James slightly when he recommended I watch the Netflix series *Designated Survivor*. In the series, the fictional US Housing Secretary played by Kiefer Sutherland becomes President when the US Capitol is blown up. At the White House as the new President, his staff tell him he will look more statesmanlike if he gets rid of his geeky eyewear. About a week after his recommendation, James asked me how I was getting on with the series, which he had found compelling despite the acting, which he accurately described as 'pure Oak Furnitureland'.

'Oh, I'm enjoying it very much, thanks James, I'm four episodes in,' I said. 'Now, tell me, what is it about the housing guy with the controversial glasses becoming leader of the free world that so appeals to you about the series?'

My teasing of James on that occasion was gentle, but it didn't take long in my SpAd career to realise that to rise to the highest levels of elected politics as he had, you have to have the hide of a rhino. The press can be merciless, with one particularly poisonous description of James when he was Northern Ireland Secretary suggesting he had 'the personality of a motorway service station car park'. Ouch.

The *Daily Mail*'s sketch-writer Quentin Letts was especially horrible about James. I will not repeat some of the nasty things he wrote in the *Mail*, but he tweeted in early 2017, 'Secretary of State James Brokenshire in Northern Ireland today: not so much a statesman as an ink monitor' and 'James Brokenshire, the robot who is a Cabinet minister'.

Similarly, a columnist in Northern Ireland wrote during Conservative Party conference in October 2017, 'James Brokenshire … reminds me of one of those novelty dogs that used to sit in the back of cars. All nodding; but no balls.'

This churlishness is just part of frontline politics, and the irony was that I was much more annoyed about it than James, who either ignored it or just let it wash over him. I grew a thicker skin as a result of working as a SpAd, but at the start I was very prickly about such personal remarks concerning my boss. I have very little regard for those who are needlessly nasty. Similarly, despite some very successful images shift engineered by enterprising advisers – who, for example, managed to make people think that David Miliband was in any way cool? – I am glad James has never changed his fundamental characteristics. He is truly authentic and is exactly the same in public and in private.

Personal remarks are also sometimes made about SpAds in the rough-and-tumble of Westminster – a friend of mine worked for Boris when he was campaigning to be Mayor of London and was referred to in the press as 'Boris's careworn press officer', something which very much upset her mother.

With me, it was my weight. After my original appointment as a SpAd in 2016, my former colleague Jon Craig wrote a column for *Total Politics* magazine about the new SpAds of the May administration he had worked with at Sky News. Their number included Theresa

May's chief of staff Fiona Hill, a former news editor at Sky. (Many years previously, I had mistakenly mentioned to a boss at *Newsnight* in La Hill's presence that Fiona had been a senior producer at Sky News. Fiona corrected me: 'News editor, not producer. Input, not output.' 'What's the difference?' I asked, as *Newsnight* didn't have those distinctions. Fiona replied, 'Input people's job is to say: "Look at this, it's a great story" and output people's job is to say: "Oooh, look at the sparkly graphics."') Another former colleague of Jon's is Poppy Trowbridge, a Sky News business correspondent who went on to be the lead media SpAd for Philip Hammond at the Treasury. Jon wrote nice things about both Poppy and Fiona but wrote of me:

> The other ex-Sky News spad is Peter Cardwell, a surprise appointment (to many of us) as aide to the new Northern Ireland Secretary James Brokenshire. Peter was a political producer with us at Westminster before joining ITV's *Good Morning Britain*. He's a farmer's son from Northern Ireland and has an appetite to match his beefy physique. No one who works with Peter will ever go hungry. On a Saturday evening shift in Sky's Millbank office Peter would always order takeaway pizza, curry, Chinese or Thai and then tell everyone what we'd eaten in his handover at the end of the weekend. Come to think of it, tiny James Brokenshire looks like he could do with putting a bit of weight on!

Casting aside the facts that my father is not a farmer and I was a news editor rather than a producer (input, not output), there's also the reference to my 'beefy physique'. The good news is that Jon Craig is a loveable rogue of Westminster and I completely forgive him.

Saying that, I reserve the right to poke his own not-so-svelte stomach every time I see him to remind him of his outlandish transgression.

One person who has absolutely no love for political journalists is the aforementioned Dominic Cummings. Towards the end of my time as SpAd, he infamously banned us from receiving even so much as a cup of tea from a journalist, making clear we had to pay for it ourselves. One senior columnist on a very important newspaper for the Conservatives was then hugely annoyed when I said I couldn't go to the expensive restaurant at which we had arranged to have lunch. Would it be OK, I asked, to go somewhere cheaper, as I had to pay for it myself? 'I'm not playing that maniac's game,' the columnist texted me. 'Nothing personal, mate, but the lunch is cancelled.'

I was never really in the habit of freezing out journalists, as some SpAds do, but one hack in particular faced my wrath for writing a nasty and completely pointless story about the payoff James received when he left Cabinet. Since the 1980s, the law has decreed that if you leave Cabinet for any reason – whether it's becoming pregnant, resigning because of a dodgy passport scandal or having an affair with a goat – you receive three months' salary as a payoff. James obviously received the standard payoff when he resigned to fight cancer. When he was reappointed to Cabinet four months later, having recovered from his illness, the reporter asked whether he would be paying his cash back? Obviously not, was my answer. And, by the way, you do know he had cancer? Are you honestly writing this story? Does anyone care about a few thousand quid he is legally entitled to, as is every minister who leaves Cabinet?

Heartlessly, the paper printed the story, which was technically factually accurate, but the 'fury' referred to in its headline was nowhere to be found in the article, as the paper could not find a single person to go on the record to criticise James. I lost my cool when it was printed, and I sent the reporter to Coventry for some time, though our relationship has since recovered.

~

As well as the privilege of working in Westminster, SpAds can be invited to interesting events, all of which must be declared quarterly to abide by strict Cabinet Office rules. Receptions, dinners and even cultural occasions can sometimes be technically classed as 'work'. From time to time, most SpAds will get decent invitations – for example, a swish ITV garden party I attended with James only to be quizzed on Brexit policy by the actor who plays Marlon in *Emmerdale*. But this is small fry compared to the invitations received by the person at the top of the SpAd tree on this matter. That's whoever happens to be the media SpAd to the Secretary of State for Digital, Culture, Media and Sport (DCMS). That person can generally take his or her pick of whichever cultural, theatrical or sporting occasions they want to attend, neatly passing it off as not-so-hard graft for the government department often known as the Ministry of Fun.

The trick is to make friends with whoever is in this role, and I've been lucky in that two of the incumbents when I was a SpAd have been proper mates anyway. They have both remarked how they suddenly find themselves extremely popular on appointment, with friends they didn't even know they had asking them whether they require a companion for, say, the FA Cup Final.

A man called Jamie Njoku-Goodwin was Matt Hancock's SpAd when he was Culture Secretary, and once very kindly took me as his guest to a play by an Irish playwright, Brian Friel, of whom I am a big fan. After a particularly busy week at DCMS, Jamie managed to fall asleep, starting to snore – albeit quietly – through most of the second half.

A huge chess enthusiast and gifted musician, Jamie is one of the characters of Westminster. Late at night after a particularly heavy week, he can sometimes be found tinkling the ivories in Players bar in Villiers Street in Charing Cross. On other occasions, he has conducted choirs and taken part in boxing matches. Once, Jamie was heading on holiday to Spain. He amused staff at Luton Airport when his chess set – an essential item for a three-night sunshine break in Cartagena, I'm sure you will agree – set off the security scanner.

Another DCMS SpAd during my time in government was Lucy Noakes, who in 2019 very kindly managed to wangle me three tickets to Centre Court at Wimbledon. Over the course of the day we managed to watch Roger Federer, Rafael Nadal and Johanna Konta. Coincidentally, I met Britain's best female tennis player at a Downing Street reception the following week. As Theresa May entered the side room, her SpAd Liz Sanderson, a friend, gently ushered me into the room, where we chatted for a few minutes about the match I had seen the week before. It was a special moment, and another No. 10 SpAd, Nero Ughwujabo, took an excellent photo of Johanna Konta and me.

Even more impressive on the invitations front are those who are no longer even in government, including one former DCMS SpAd who somehow seems to still be on all sorts of lists for corporate hospitality at major sporting events despite having left politics several years ago. He is known as the king of junkets. A different friend who used to be a SpAd still gets an invitation to the Brit Awards. They WhatsApped me the morning after the 2020 ceremony concerning the antics of one of her companions, Thérèse Coffey MP, the Work and Pensions Secretary. 'The image from the Brits that will be burned into the pinholes of my eyes – perhaps for ever', they wrote, 'is that of Thérèse Coffey attempting to twerk to Stormzy.'

I'm afraid I may have repeated that story to a few friends, one of whom nicknamed poor Thérèse the 'Twerk and Pensions Secretary'.

I've never been to the Brits, but I have been a last-minute replacement for both Cathy Brokenshire and Sian Buckland at a number of events. Most memorably, Cathy once had to drop out as James's plus one for a concert at the Royal Albert Hall for the centenary of the Armistice, a very moving and special occasion. I even met broadcasting legend John Suchet of Classic FM.

Sian couldn't make the State Opening of Parliament days after the 2019 election, so very generously donated her ticket to me. It was the second State Opening of 2019, due to the election. On the first occasion, I had sat in the Royal Gallery, which is just outside the House of Lords, and had a wonderful view of everyone walking past, including Her Majesty. But for the second State Opening, I was in the Strangers' Gallery in the House of Lords. Seating there is usually limited to the spouses of those taking part in the ceremony, and the gallery is directly above the House of Lords chamber itself. The first occasion was fantastic enough, but in the second I got a brilliant view of the Queen as she read her speech, which was ceremoniously handed to her by Robert as Lord Chancellor. It was such a special day, full of pageantry and constitutional history.

During the hour or so before the second State Opening started, I was sitting beside the wife of a long-serving Conservative backbencher. We compared notes on the election campaign just fought. Wearing pearls and a twinset, deploying cut-glass vowels and essentially fulfilling almost every stereotype of a Tory wife imaginable, my companion sympathised as I told her how I had worried at times about the closeness of the competition. 'Robert's majority was only 2,464 in 2017, so it could have been tight if things hadn't gone so well,' I said. 'Oh, I know all about it,' she replied. 'I really did worry my husband's majority would go below 20,000 at one point.'

When I mentioned how generous the Bucklands had been to have me stay at their home, my companion continued, 'Oh we were exactly the same! We must have had sixteen or seventeen at one point.' I wondered, silently, whether she and her husband had been forced to open another wing of their no-doubt enormous country pile.

I related this story to a Conservative friend, lamenting to her that my State Opening gallery companion's outlook and background were very much the Tory cliché people associated with our party.

'Yes, Peter,' she remarked. 'And that is why people hate us.'

5

You Don't Have to Be SpAd to Work Here: Civil Servants

For a generation, the TV series *Yes, Minister* and *Yes, Prime Minister* shaped the public image of how the government and civil service worked – with the emphasis very much on the influence of the latter. Margaret Thatcher loved the programme so much she even appeared in a specially written sketch. In the series, SpAds were banished to an office down the hall and rarely seen, with the clear intention that they shouldn't get involved with anything the minister was doing, at least if Sir Humphrey and Bernard could get away with it. Indeed, one episode of *Yes, Prime Minister* shows Jim Hacker's SpAd Dorothy Wainwright convincing her boss to clip Sir Humphrey's wings after her office is moved as far away as possible from the Cabinet Room.

Fast forward twenty-five years, and in stark contrast, *The Thick of It* placed much of the power with the SpAds. A generation of political nerds like me grew up watching the fictional Prime Minister's chief enforcer, the shouty, sweary Scot Malcolm Tucker, reacting to, or at times creating, whatever scenario the fictional government was screwing up in that particular episode. There were certainly times in my SpAd career, especially at the Northern Ireland Office, that I did have a deep sense of worry that I might be turning into the principles-free character Ollie Reeder. And that concern was only enhanced by the fact that my co-SpAd Jonathan Caine was occasionally ever so slightly like Ollie's older, sometimes wiser, sometimes infuriatingly curmudgeonly SpAd Glen Cullen. I actually used to watch *The Thick of It* to relax after work, generally after a particularly heavy day working closely with one official who was a little bit too much like the show's incompetent but very entertaining civil servant Terri Coverley. (Even before I became a SpAd, I was such a fan that when Joanna Scanlan, who plays Coverley, came into Sky News one day, I asked her as she was about to go on air to be interviewed whether she was 'nervous? Anxious? Worried?' Scanlan looked at me oddly, and it dawned on me that I knew her character's catchphrases better than the actress did. Truly, I was an obsessed fan.)

While a SpAd, I even managed to meet two of the actors from the series: Alex Macqueen, who played the pedantic prime ministerial adviser Julius Nicholson, who was extremely charming; and Paul Higgins, who played the even nastier, even more menacing and even more Scottish version of Malcolm Tucker as my favourite *Thick of It* character, press SpAd Jamie McDonald. Apparently, if you ask Higgins nicely, he will recite one of Jamie's particularly brilliant and expletive-filled rants, which is a favourite moment of mine on screen. Without being too graphic, it's about an iPod Nano and where he will stick it if his musical hero Al Jolson is criticised. I did get a selfie with both actors, which I put up in the SpAd Pad, but nonetheless felt an opportunity had been missed to be ranted at by Higgins. He was absolutely horrified when I told him that *The Thick of It* was sometimes truer to life than he could imagine.

As in *The Thick of It*, the sheer number of civil servants in most departments means that SpAds will only ever properly get to know a tiny number. There are literally tens of thousands of people working in many ministries, and only some of them actually get to interact with SpAds, and even fewer with the Secretary of State. Relationships are crucial, but there are not generally that many close working relationships between SpAds and officials outside the Secretary of State's private office, other than in key areas of policy or with the press office. The lower-ranking civil servants who actually do the work send it upwards to their bosses, who then add their wisdom/take the credit/both (delete as appropriate) and advise the Secretary of State in crowded meetings. These multiple layers are part of the reason accountability in the civil service is so blurred – occasionally, trying to find out which civil servant had actually made a decision with whose consequences I had to deal was particularly difficult.

James Brokenshire, in particular, often wondered aloud why there was a 'cast of thousands' at various gatherings, and generally wanted to keep the numbers small. I kept out of as many meetings as I could, as generally the line-by-line stage of formulating policy was left to others. When policy is in development there are not the same presentational issues that every media SpAd worries about, and my time could be better spent speaking to journalists or interested parties – or, as the civil service would have it, 'stakeholders'.

Theresa Villiers, James's predecessor as Northern Ireland Secretary, once referred to the fact that she believed the NIO was 'a four-person department', as she relied heavily on her special adviser Jonathan

Caine, her principal private secretary and her Permanent Secretary above all others. It is entirely the prerogative of Secretaries of State to decide whom they listen to or consult; however, opting for a small, powerful group rather than taking a more consensual approach, involving many civil servants giving their opinion, can cause resentment within a department, with those civil servants 'inside the tent' perhaps wielding too much power. The trick for SpAds is to find the person who *really* knows what they are talking about. As a natural extrovert, it took me time to realise that the wisest civil servant in one department in which I worked was actually a tremendously quiet, reserved gent who, when you got to know him, would tell you how things really were. I christened him The Guru and he resembled the wise, blunt, but kind character of Nigel (played by Stanley Tucci) in the 2006 film *The Devil Wears Prada* to such an extent that I, as very much the clueless Andrea Sachs (Anne Hathaway) character in the scenario, presented him with the DVD over lunch when I left that department.

In contrast to the tiny NIO, my next department, the Home Office, had some 32,000 staff, with a vast array of confusing and sometimes – to me, anyway – meaningless titles. I did wonder what some civil servants did all day throughout my SpAd career other than sit in meetings, but they may well have wondered the same about my frequent swanning off for lunches with journalists.

Departments are headed by a Permanent Secretary, usually a knight or dame, and directly beneath them they have directors general, directors, deputy directors and so on. I never fully understood the grading system of departments, but often they were different in different parts of government. All I knew was that it appeared most people around my age and level of experience were generally paid more than I was. Most civil servants were university-educated, some at top universities, and there was a very good mix of races, religions and sexualities represented in the ministries in which I worked. It is, like many institutions of the United Kingdom establishment, far too middle class, but there is good work going on to address this imbalance.

Ascending to the exalted position of Permanent Secretary in Whitehall is quite a feat: the pole is both greasy and filled with elephant traps, to mix metaphors. A Permanent Secretary in charge of the civil service side of one of the major parts of government can be the ultimate line manager for tens of thousands of people. They are also the chief accounting officers for departments, most of which have multi-billion-pound budgets. Unsurprisingly, those who inhabit these roles are generally tough as nails, often accumulating many enemies over the course of what is usually a lifetime in the civil service. Certainly, everyone in the senior level of the civil service has an opinion of the 'Perm Sec', and, unsurprisingly, it is not always favourable. Self-confidence and self-belief are needed to lead such a large organisation, traits possessed by all Permanent Secretaries with whom I worked, sometimes to a fault. At times this can manifest itself in odd ways. For reasons best known to one Whitehall Permanent Secretary, they once scheduled a one-hour meeting involving all the top brass of the press office, entitled 'Developing the Permanent Secretary's personal brand'. That particular Permanent Secretary's nickname in the department's SpAds' office was 'Personal Brand' for some time afterwards.

A Permanent Secretary will generally see the Secretary of State at least once a week, usually at the start of the week, for a one-on-one catch-up. The Perm Sec will also attend a few other, larger meetings, for instance the weekly meeting with all the ministers – sometimes called 'prayers' – and a meeting to discuss the grid of media stories. They will usually take a very keen interest in Budget and spending round negotiations as chief accounting officer for the department, as well as particularly controversial elements of government policy, or emerging issues that dominate the news cycle. However, different Permanent Secretaries interact with their political master or mistress in very different ways. Of the four I worked with, Sir Jonathan Stephens was the most hands-on, attending almost every meeting at which the Secretary of State was present. Sir Jonathan was highly skilled in negotiations and had years of experience in the craziness of Northern Ireland politics and the UK–Ireland relationship.

In contrast, Dame Melanie Dawes at MHCLG and Sir Richard Heaton at Justice were more hands-off, acting in a more classical model of the Permanent Secretary as a sort of chief executive of the department. Generally, I only saw them in a few meetings a week, but we would catch up from time to time, and their door was always open. Melanie, in particular, was very kind at times, sending a lovely text on the last occasion on which I was sacked.

I didn't see much of Sir Philip Rutnam at the Home Office in the four weeks I worked there, which was even more remarkable given that it was the period during which the Windrush affair was at its height. When I started at the Home Office, I asked my private secretary to schedule a sit-down meeting with Sir Philip, but it did not appear to be a priority for him and seemed to move back and back in our diaries on a daily basis. Eventually, one day I simply marched past his private secretary and into his office and stretched out my hand, saying I was the new SpAd and it was nice to meet him, to his obvious surprise. I only worked with Sir Philip for the very briefest of periods but did not find him particularly friendly in our few meetings. He later clashed spectacularly with Priti Patel, and his subsequent resignation from the Home Office – which was accompanied by an extraordinary press conference one Saturday morning – is, at the time of writing, subject to legal action.

A good relationship between a SpAd and a Permanent Secretary is desirable, but there is always a tension between the two. There is essentially a Venn diagram between what the Permanent Secretary and senior civil servants want for the department, what the political team – Secretary of State, junior ministers and SpAds – want, and what the private office can actually achieve. Everyone navigates the cross-over space in between the Venn diagram every day; sometimes successfully, sometimes less so. It is often ill-defined, too, so any good SpAd needs to keep informed of everyone's priorities in a department and how they shift, sometimes hour by hour.

I remember being properly bollocked by Sir Jonathan only about four times, usually with justification for some stupid email I had sent or for flying off the handle with an official, but in general I got on with and respected him. I can't remember ever being properly told off by any other Permanent Secretary.

There was a less good relationship between the NIO officials and my co-SpAd, Jonathan Caine. After thirty years of being in and out of the NIO, Caine both loved and hated the place, dubbing it 'Hotel California' – he could check out, but he could never leave. He also believed it to be full of Irish Republicans, something of which I didn't see much evidence, although of course most civil servants' personal political views are completely inscrutable. Most mornings, Caine would grumpily come into our shared office, switch on his computer and open his emails with the line: 'What has the Sinn Féin Appeasement Department got for us today?' According to Caine, there was a widespread but erroneous belief in Whitehall that Northern Ireland was on a gradual slope to a united Ireland and should therefore be managed accordingly. While it was continually frustrating when Whitehall officials, usually in other departments, referred to us being responsible for 'Ireland' rather than Northern Ireland, or asked very basic questions about one of the constituent parts of the United Kingdom, I found it was fuelled not so much by malicious intent as by pure ignorance. (The same is true in journalism – the Sky News senior Ireland correspondent David Blevins remembers advising his superiors that it probably wasn't the best idea for another reporter to refer to Martin McGuinness and Gerry Adams as 'Sinn Féin's big guns' in a report, for example, and having to tell a desk editor that, yes, Dublin was in the same time zone as London. Between us, David and I created Blevins's Law, the principle that one should never underestimate how little any English person knows about Northern Ireland.) A very strong unionist, Caine would push back at even small derogations from his self-imposed set of acceptable phrases. Any civil servant daring to send a submission with reference to, for example, 'the two governments' would have it sent back with a strong comment from Caine that it should read 'the UK government and the Irish government', lest there be any suggestion that there was any shared responsibility for the sovereignty of Northern Ireland.

I was more concerned about the poor standard of written English used by many civil servants. A combination of management waffle, meaningless phrases, terrible sentence structure and sometimes shockingly bad grammar often led me to completely rewrite press releases or submissions into plain English. I was often faced with sentences along the lines of:

> Local Government Secretary of State James Brokenshire will today meet with stakeholders and relevant ALBs as the government rolls out a five-year plan to implement a road-tested, peer-reviewed planned strategy as outlined in the 2017 Spending Review by HM Treasury to reduce, reuse and recycle local authority waste management load.

… which I would translate into English: 'Changes to the way bins are collected are being launched by Communities Secretary [his favoured nomenclature] Rt Hon James Brokenshire MP today.' I'm afraid to say that of the four departments in which I worked, MHCLG proved the biggest challenge. When I left, the press office even constructed a jokey press release with every single one of my banned phrases included, mocking themselves for the inability of the 67-strong press office to correctly title James in almost any press release.

At one stage, I was so frustrated at the grammar of press officers that I stupidly sent what I thought was a funny email – it was not – to the press office at MHCLG, with words to the effect of: 'I know most of you were educated under New Labour, but please try to use some grammatically correct sentences in your press releases.' This raised a few eyebrows in the press office – with most laughing it off as a bit tone-deaf – but I didn't repeat what in retrospect was a churlish and regrettable missive.

I'm afraid I was quite harsh with officials from time to time when things went badly wrong, as is sometimes the SpAd's duty. Once, a simple mistake regarding an appointment to a public body, which should have been rectified on a Wednesday had a civil servant done their job correctly, led to a messy and tedious situation dragging on for days. The matter was eventually resolved by a long and boring conference call on a Saturday afternoon across various parts of government.

The most frustrating thing was that the ninety-minute Saturday conference call could have been avoided had the problem been nipped in the bud earlier in the week. My patience – never my best or most durable quality – was lost and I ended the call paraphrasing Josh in one of the early episodes of *The West Wing*. 'The Secretary of State is a good man,' I told the officials. 'He's got a good heart. He doesn't worry about these things ... That's what he pays *me* for,' I barked, slamming down the phone. One innocent official who was also on the call rang me afterwards to say it was 'a beautiful moment', and completely warranted by the officials who had screwed the issue up, but perhaps I should have been nicer.

When problems escalate to reach SpAds' radar, they often are quite big problems, I found, and my job was not only to fix them for my Secretaries of State but to ensure they didn't happen again. Sometimes, marking officials' cards was the best way of doing the latter. I wasn't perfect either, but protecting my boss was my priority, and any individual civil servant's screw-up on even a seemingly minor matter can occasionally lead to a minister being forced to resign, so I was extremely vigilant at all times.

I spoke to a fairly senior civil servant after I left MHCLG and asked her whether I had ever been too harsh. Even SpAds have a conscience

– sometimes. Having worked with a number of SpAds, every one of whom, in her experience, had a very different style, she said my two best qualities were that I was always extremely clear in what I wanted for the Secretary of State and that if there was a problem with an official's work it was dealt with and I moved on quickly, without holding a grudge. My two most negative qualities were my complete lack of patience and my grammar pedantry, to an almost distracting extent. Another colleague was more direct. 'The problem with you, Carders,' he said, 'is that you're 90 per cent charming smoothiechops and 10 per cent complete and utter c***.'

One SpAd I know had a notoriously bad relationship with their Permanent Secretary. The sheer pettiness on display in this story – one of my favourites from my entire time in government – exemplifies the depths to which their dealings had sunk. A Permanent Secretary usually has a huge office with a boardroom table, and this one was no exception. The SpAd in question learned that the Perm Sec had ordered a new, sizeable boardroom table and fourteen chairs for their office. Outraged, the SpAd in question instantly arranged that new furniture of an equal quality be ordered for the ministerial board-room – that SpAd's bailiwick – with *sixteen* chairs.

The most important part of the department for any minister or SpAd is the private office, which is headed by the principal private secretary (PPS) – the Bernard character in *Yes, Minister*. He or she might be in charge of twelve or fourteen private secretaries to the Secretary of State in a medium-sized department such as Justice or MHCLG.

Private secretaries don't just do typing and filing but are often some of the brightest graduates in the country, and many are destined for great things. Many Permanent Secretaries will have been PPS earlier in their career. A PPS's job is to manage deftly, swiftly and efficiently the Secretary of State's workload, papers and everything that goes into the famous red box, which ministers take home each evening to go through all the work 'sent up', on which decisions are required almost instantly.

The PPS will generally have some policy or press office experience and is usually in their thirties or early forties. The relationship between the PPS and the Secretary of State is incredibly important, and when the chemistry is right, great things can be achieved. If the chemistry is wrong, it's just not going to work, and the PPS often gets moved onto another role, or leaves voluntarily. It is rare for a PPS to do the job for more than about two years or for more than two successive Secretaries of State, such are the crazy hours, demands from their boss, SpAds, the department more widely, and the rest of government, including No. 10.

Civil servants are, of course, meant to be completely impartial, as happy working for a Conservative administration as a Labour or coalition one, and most civil servants are very good at maintaining this impartiality. There is a huge difference, though, between the civil servants in private offices who 'get' the politics and those who don't. The best are fully cognisant of the environment necessitated by the short-term political realities under which their masters operate. This was particularly important during the period between the 2017 and 2019 elections. I have absolutely no idea how any of the PPSs I worked with vote on election day, but I do know which ones 'got' the politics and which ones did not. It was not a PPS who made the following suggestion, but it illustrates the point about the differences between the impartial world civil servants operate in and the political realities that SpAds have to navigate. James was appointed Housing Secretary just days before the 2018 local government elections. The day of the results, I was sent a press line to clear for Twitter congratulating Dan Jarvis on being elected Mayor of the Sheffield City Region. We were responsible for local government. Dan Jarvis was the first elected Mayor of the Sheffield City Region and, therefore, we should be congratulating him, went the civil service thought process. I'm afraid my response on being presented with the press release just days into my job was withering.

'It may have escaped officials' attention,' I said loudly, so the whole office could hear, 'but James Brokenshire is a *Conservative* and Dan Jarvis is a member of the *Labour* Party. James and I were knocking doors last weekend persuading people to vote for *Conservative* candidates. So as the Cabinet minister responsible for local government, James is probably not going to be sending a tweet congratulating a Labour mayor.' One of the great privileges of SpAdding is that you can quote lines from *The Thick of It* and get away with it. So my conclusion was couched in a quotation from Malcolm Tucker: 'Whoever came up with this monumentally crap idea is so dense, light bends around them.'

They got the message.

Thrust into MHCLG without a paddle when James Brokenshire returned to Cabinet in May 2018, I was the only SpAd at the department for the first month James was in post. I was working crazy hours with very little guidance, as James and I got used to a totally new ministry. I didn't know the policy, who to trust, or how the department worked. I was faced with new junior ministers I didn't know, a huge amount of briefing to read, all the time doing the work previously done by three people. I called for reinforcements from No. 10 and very happily was sent both a civil servant called Jamie Cowling, then a housing policy official, and Toby Lloyd, a SpAd who had just started on the housing brief in Downing Street. Toby knew the policy but not the politics; I knew the politics but not the policy, and we worked well together for a few afternoons until I felt I had my feet under the table a little more.

Quietly, in his calm, assured, down-to-earth manner, Jamie Cowling gently explained what I needed to know and I relaxed into the task in front of me. It was a pleasure to work with Jamie when he was later appointed principal private secretary to James.

The PPS's team of private secretaries essentially shadow each department's many policy areas and are the first port of call for ministers or SpAds when these issues come up. Private secretaries arrange meetings and look at submissions to ministers, which are important documents giving advice which require a decision from the minister. These go through many iterations and have to be signed off by SpAds, who can make changes and add comments as the final set of eyes before the 'subs' go into the minister's red box. Often, there are questions or points for clarification, which the private secretaries resolve with teams across the department. The minister approves or amends the submission, perhaps adding questions for clarification, and the policy comes 'out of the box'. The private secretary then communicates that decision to the rest of the department, and action is taken. Sometimes civil servants can be resistant to what the political team want, so there is a difficult dance for private office staff to be strong but also diplomatic. Often, I reminded private offices of one of my favourite Jonathan Caine phrases: 'The department is not a democracy.'

There are, of course, various levels in the private secretary hierarchy, and most I've encountered tend to be in the mid-to-late twenties or early thirties. Saying that, the hierarchy didn't mean a great deal sometimes – I'm afraid there were a few very experienced private secretaries who were transferred out of one particular private office I worked in for not being up to the Secretary of State's standards, but there is always a churn in the 'permanent' civil service. Indeed, I remember after James gave me responsibility for advising him on homelessness, I felt, about six weeks in, that I needed a full briefing from the relevant team to double-check I was picking up the policy correctly. When the two fairly senior civil servants designated to go over all the policy again to make sure I had a handle on it finished their briefing, I asked them how long they had been working in the team. They had both started four weeks previously.

Of course, sometimes even the most inexperienced people can be outstanding, often bringing similar know-how from a different department to a fresh policy area. But the turnover of officials was frustrating. It seemed almost every week someone was off to another department or a new person was joining. I shouldn't moan about inexperience, though – one particular civil service apprentice I worked with at MHCLG, aged just nineteen, could give most of the senior civil servants in the department a run for their money, earning him the nickname 'the real PPS'. This young man organised James's diary and movements with almost military precision and generally knew what I would ask regarding the diary before I did. Quite a character, he kept a small cactus on his desk which he christened

Eric Prickles, in honour of Eric Pickles, a previous Secretary of State. Pickles sat on a departmental board and thus occasionally came into the office. One of the diary secretary's colleagues bet him a tenner he couldn't get Pickles to sign the cactus pot with a marker. Pickles was only too delighted to autograph the pot, and the cash was duly handed over.

One of the biggest perks of the job is the opportunity to visit No. 10: even for those who don't end up working in Downing Street itself, there are all sorts of receptions, dinners and drinks parties that civil servants and SpAds can sometimes pop into as the great and the good mingle in the staterooms at the most famous address in Britain. These receptions are often a chance to meet the Prime Minister and walk up the famous staircase adorned with the portraits of all of their predecessors. On one occasion, a Conservative MP brought the eccentric actress Su Pollard as his plus one to a reception with Theresa May, who endured Pollard shouting, 'Hi-de-Hi, Theresa!' at her. I'm sure, in that moment, Mrs May felt the decades at the grindstone of political life were all worth it.

As a journalist, I had been on Downing Street, and occasionally in No. 10 itself, a number of times. For understandable reasons, it is a highly secure street nowadays, fenced off from the public and guarded by armed police, but there are constant comings and goings, whether it's the Education Secretary coming in for a meeting or a bin man driving his lorry through the great black metal gates to collect Boris's empties.

What you can't tell from watching the news is that Downing Street is always freezing, caught in some sort of weird wind tunnel no matter what the weather – as the journalists who spend long hours standing outside No. 10 will testify. There are no toilets except inside the building, so as a reporter I would often have to nip up to McDonald's on Whitehall, hoping they wouldn't force me to buy a Big Mac in exchange for loo access – and that the PM wouldn't come out to resign while I was doing a pee. Gordon Brown, at the nadir of his popularity, told journalists he would have toilets built on Downing Street in a clear attempt to curry favour. It was a deft move, but it never actually happened.

The houses of Downing Street – Nos 9, 10, 11 and 12 – are mainly offices and staterooms, rather than residences, and only an extremely small number of SpAds ever get to see the Prime Minister's and Chancellor's private quarters in the flats upstairs. Jonathan Caine told me that in thirty years in politics he was invited only once to the PM's flat, and that was by the last Prime Minister he served, Theresa May.

In the winter, the huge Christmas tree dominates Downing Street, and mulled wine and gossip are the order of the evening at the numerous receptions in the beautiful staterooms. It's quite a house, and the novelty never wears off. I remember the first time I was there, which was a day after Margaret Thatcher made what was to be her final visit to No. 10 in June 2010. Michael Salter, who was then the SpAd serving as head of broadcasting at Downing Street, brought me into a wonderful stateroom called the White Room. 'This is where Mrs Thatcher and Mr Cameron met yesterday,' Michael told me, to my wide-eyed astonishment. 'The gardener has worked here since her time as Prime Minister and remembered her favourite roses and put them in that vase for yesterday's meeting,' he continued, gesturing to my left.

One of the many elite institutions within No. 10 is 'Switch', the switchboard at the heart of the building, renowned for its calm, assured operators who connect everyone from Prime Ministers to heads of state, senior officials, MPs, SpAds and even people checking whether Boris Johnson has ever been involved in an accident that wasn't his fault.

Switch's digital Rolodex has almost every number of anyone the Prime Minister – or his SpAds – could possibly want to contact, and when you are rung from Downing Street it comes up on your phone as an anonymous number. As a SpAd, there was always a slight adrenalin rush at this sight, as it could either be No. 10 about to shout at you or, roughly as often, someone trying to get you to claim back your PPI money.

Very occasionally – and it is very occasionally – even Switch operators make mistakes. Once, a No. 10 official rang Switch and asked to be put through to the then Housing Minister Gavin Barwell, the man who would later end up as Theresa May's chief of staff. Sadly, the operator misheard and put him through not to Gavin Barwell but to a recent guest at a No. 10 reception for musicians. Take That frontman Gary Barlow was slightly baffled to receive a call about housing policy from a Downing Street civil servant. Saying that, I expect the call from No. 10 is one Gary will Never Forget.

Both No. 10 and the departments also have private secretaries who deal with the immense volume of correspondence every minister receives, and every email or letter should, in theory, receive a response. Departments often like to foist difficult bits of correspondence on to others for reply. Sometimes a delay in response to a letter can take weeks – months, even – as departments try to argue it is not they who should answer it. This level of bureaucracy drove me up the wall.

One letter we received at MHCLG from a member of the public dealt with cross-cutting issues regarding the housing of immigrants, sent in extremely offensive and intemperate language. The Home Office had very kindly passed on this letter to our correspondence private secretary at MHCLG rather than answer it itself. She asked my advice on whether to try to send it back to the Home Office yet again. 'My advice', I said, 'is that we all agree that the author of the email is a nasty racist and we delete the email and say no more about it.' 'Peter,' she countered, with a sigh, 'you just don't get the civil service way of doing things, do you?' 'No,' I replied, 'and I never want to.'

SpAds usually have their own mini-private office, and I was supported by some top-class operators as my private secretaries, who dealt with absolutely everything from making sure there were enough staples to arranging and attending meetings at No. 10 with me. Some were Oxbridge graduates who had gone through the civil service's fast stream and knew when to be firm and when a quick walk in St James's Park followed by a Greggs sausage roll was the best way to bring me back to reality. My right-hand woman at the Northern Ireland Office worked almost exclusively in Belfast, but on one occasion she was over in London for some training and I managed to get her on the list for a No. 10 reception, which was a special moment for us both.

Every private office has a diary team, which is almost as important as the PPS and guards access to the most valuable commodity any Secretary of State has: time. And of course everything, from the minister's kid's violin recital to that long-sought-after invitation to dinner at Chequers from the Prime Minister, goes into the diary, which every day is juggled in some way. Keeping track, keeping a handle on all the requests for the minister's time and, crucially, keeping everyone completely informed when changes happen, is the unenviable task of the diary secretary. The private secretary who manages the diary is the real unsung hero of private office if they get the job right (which nobody notices). Getting it wrong can be fatal. The job was most difficult for the diary secretary at the Northern Ireland Office, who faced the unenviable task of juggling airlines, civil servants, police protection officers, SpAds and the Secretary of State's family's priorities, keeping us all informed of the huge and frequent changes to the diary affecting people on both sides of the Irish Sea. On one occasion during talks with James Brokenshire in Belfast, I remember my flight changed four times over the course of the day.

Usually the whole office knows what is in the diary, and it can be difficult to keep appointments private. After being interrogated by a private secretary about why I was going for a drink with a political rival one evening, I started simply writing 'personal appointment', but then the trick became to remember what the engagement actually was. One person who sat around the Cabinet table for a decent proportion of my time as a SpAd actually had her diary secretary block out an afternoon once a month so she could go to her doctor in Harley Street and get her Botox done. 'The problem', this particular minister's SpAd once WhatsApped me, 'is when she grins heavily you can see the filler accumulate above her temples.' His advice to his boss was to smile less enthusiastically for the few days after the Botox appointments.

There are three types of people you work with in any job: proper friends, work friends and mandatory working companions. Proper friends who remain close to me now are very rare, but I had many work friends, some of whom I keep up with from time to time, although as the months and years pass your commonality inevitably wanes. But in the moment in government – in the thick of it, as it were – close bonds can be forged. Getting through a major piece of legislation or a big press win can really yield rewards, from which friendlier and more relaxed working relationships can ensue. After one of these occasions, a member of private office cheekily – and not inaccurately – said to me, 'You are not the least eccentric person I have ever met.' Facing this aspersion from a man whose desk is adorned with a ludicrously camp mirror on a stand, placed there, in his words, 'so I can look at someone gorgeous every day at work' – I replied, 'Physician, heal thyself!'

But there is a line that should never be crossed. I remember asking advice from a very wise official about whether it was kosher to ask a civil servant on a date. Absolutely not, he replied. Turn away, delete that number and forget the face. Just don't go there. Some SpAds I know have perhaps – shall we say – blurred that line from time to time, but I will take their names to the grave.

That said, there are a huge number of Westminster relationships, with the Politico journalist Annabelle Dickson publishing a now annual list of who is allegedly going out with, or married to, whom.

Speaking of eccentrics, one hilarious private secretary in the Ministry of Justice, whom it would be unfair to name, had clearly missed her calling in life as a TV producer. Always up to date on her celebrity gossip – which I expect was a welcome distraction from the sometimes extremely grim policy area on which she worked – she once explained in elaborate detail two ideas for television programmes she had. One was called *From Special Adviser to Special Forces*, where after leaving the political world, pasty-faced, podgy and unfit special advisers (I had absolutely no idea to whom she might be referring) would be taken to an SAS boot camp and knocked into shape. I immediately had a vision of my Ministry of Justice co-SpAd Rajiv Shah's effete scarves and lime green trousers being burned on a campfire by Bear Grylls as the former SAS hardman forced the two of us to do 100 press-ups in singlets and shorts – which, to be fair, would make excellent telly. But we would perhaps not actually survive the experience. Her second idea, my favourite, was *The GC Versus the DC*, in which Gemma Collins from *The Only Way Is Essex* goes around Britain in a campervan alongside Dominic Cummings, stopping in towns and villages, undertaking community-based *It's A Knockout*-style challenges, combining teams of Leavers and Remainers to heal the wounds of Brexit. The private secretary in question, like most private secretaries and almost all SpAds I encountered, worked extremely hard almost all the time, but these wonderfully implausible flights of fancy would occasionally fill the air as we trudged in and out of the latest dull but important meeting on, say, the maintenance of magistrates' courts.

And it's not just civil servants and SpAds who can be eccentric – ministers can too. A former Treasury civil servant told me of a rather odd set of Post-It notes which for a time adorned the desk of the then Chief Secretary to the Treasury, Labour's Liam Byrne. It is traditional for ministers in the Treasury, when leaving their role, to leave a light-hearted note for their successors. Reginald Maudling, leaving his post as Chancellor in 1955, wrote: 'Sorry, old cock, to leave it in this shape,' to the next Chancellor, who turned out to be James Callaghan.

Byrne's own note after the 2008 banking crash and subsequent recession read: 'Dear Chief Secretary, I am afraid there is no money. Kind regards and good luck.' The note was an absolute gift to the Conservatives, who frequently cited it as evidence of Labour's poor handling of the economy during their time in office. But it wasn't just the note to his successor as Chief Secretary that civil servants noticed and upon which they remarked. It was the series of Post-It notes that Byrne, nicknamed Baldemort after the villain in *Harry Potter*, had left around his desk to motivate himself. They included 'Get Army fit', 'Buy ski chalet in France' and, my personal favourite, 'Have my own library (like Reagan)'. Alas, at the time of writing, the Liam Byrne Ministerial Library remains unbuilt, but perhaps some day his huge contribution to our island story will be properly commemorated.

Not that big egos are confined to Labour ministers. I was also once told that Sir Alan Duncan, the former Foreign Office minister, has a fireproof vault in his home, lest his ministerial papers be lost to posterity by a conflagration. This too would be a tragedy.

~

Ministers often try to shoehorn in some time for themselves during the day, not always successfully. To keep his fitness and lung capacity up post-cancer, James Brokenshire tried to take a walk every day, and his clear head after a bit of fresh air and exercise generally made him a lot more productive than he would have been without it. Another minister I worked with, Dominic Raab, was known to try to get some iron-pumping in with a daily gym visit, though the demands on any minister mean that 'me time' can be difficult to carve out from the long and intense days they (and their SpAds) work. And the poor private secretary who has to deal with the constantly shifting ministerial diary doesn't have an easy time of it either.

MHCLG was rocked in April 2018 when a diary secretary in Raab's private office was caught in an undercover sting by the *Mirror* for being on a 'sugar daddies' website, selling sex to older clients for £750. The lurid details of her side hustle and the allegations she made about Dominic Raab's alleged behaviour towards subordinates – strongly denied – were of much less interest to SpAds than the jaw-dropping revelation that he apparently ate exactly the same lunch every day from the upmarket sandwich chain Pret A Manger.

A chicken Caesar wrap, a superfruit pot and a Vitamin Volcano smoothie was apparently known as 'The Dom Raab Special' by officials, with a private secretary dispatched each lunchtime to procure the items for the then Housing Minister from the Pret across the road from his ministerial office.

Political Twitter, of course, went bonkers with the lunch revelation, with phone-in programmes asking people whether they had the same lunch every day and whether there was actually anything wrong with that per se. The *Daily Mail* memorably employed a nutritionist to analyse whether poor Dom was getting enough nutrients, and whether the Vitamin Volcano/superfruit pot combo actually contained too much sugar and if he should vary his diet.

I was at the Home Office at the time, and after reading every word of the articles in the *Mirror* I immediately went out to Pret and bought the constituent parts of The Dom Raab Special, took a picture of myself eating it and WhatsApped it to one of the SpAds at MHCLG. Little did I know that a month or so later I would be in the department myself as her successor, having a 1 p.m. meeting with Dominic about his media profile. We had a good, honest chat, where I made clear I wanted to send him out on the media quite a lot as he was an excellent broadcast performer. But, I explained, he needed to 'own' the lunch thing, otherwise he would simply be known for it.

'With no criticism of my predecessor intended,' I said, 'had I been the SpAd here when that happened, I would probably have had you doing a funny tweet. Maybe you could have gone to Pret and been "confused" as to what to choose for your lunch – just to show you can laugh at yourself. These things are important for any politician's image.'

He was fine with that suggestion and took it on board, though he did insist that the explosive lunch revelations were overblown.

At that exact moment – and this is absolute gospel – there was a knock at the door. A private secretary walked in and set down on the desk a Pret bag containing: a chicken Caesar wrap, a superfruit pot and a Vitamin Volcano smoothie.

~

Every private secretary works long hours, not only being their minister's first port of call on all sorts of issues but often travelling with their minister to events as well, and often SpAds go too. Space in the ministerial cars is limited, and whether the SpAd or the private secretary gets to travel with the Secretary of State can sometimes be a bone of contention. At MHCLG, there was a ministerial car for James Brokenshire as Secretary of State, and then another shared by the five junior ministers. The driver of the latter car, a woman called Lynn, is a Cliff Richard superfan, known personally to the superannuated crooner; for a time, she ran his official fan club. If music was played in the car, it was always Sir Cliff, and indeed there was one occasion, during which I was not present, sadly, when one of the junior ministers, Jake Berry, joined Lynn in a verse or two of 'We're All Goin' on a Summer Holiday' while travelling between the office and Parliament.

Indeed, I remember the first time I properly made Rishi Sunak laugh was when Jake Berry's second son was born. Rishi enquired as to how mother and baby were doing. I replied, 'Yes, all is well, the delivery was flawless and everyone's happy. So they've decided to call the baby "Brexit".'

Some ministers are, either all the time or some of the time, protected by police officers. These policemen (and occasionally policewomen) are members of the Metropolitan Police's Royalty and Specialist Protection Unit – known as 'Prot' for short – and know everything that goes on in their ministers' lives from dawn until dusk. Often it is a huge adjustment for newly appointed Secretaries of State and their families to realise that teams of virtual strangers now need to accompany 'the principal' (the minister) on every occasion from a Cabinet meeting to nipping out for a pint of milk, and for quite scary reasons too.

Members of the police protection teams have a tremendously important job, with every minute of their shift revolving around the principal and where he or she may be at any given time, as well as preparing for where they are going next. A number of my ministers were protected by the brave and brilliant officers of Prot – it is hardly a secret that the Northern Ireland Secretary is still, very sadly, a target for some terrorists. I hope I always respected the Prot officers, although I'm afraid there was a running (and not particularly funny) remark I made every single time one of my bosses got into the car driven by these officers. When they radioed to base, 'Principal on board,' I unfailingly countered: 'You should probably tell them the Secretary of State is in the car too.'

The officers get to know private office and SpAds well, but personal relationships such as the one in the BBC 1 drama *Bodyguard* between principal and officer are strictly prohibited. Saying that, one SpAd I know did send a cheeky Valentine's Day card to a protection officer who had worked with their principal. The card included the line: 'No need to fire your Taser to make me go weak at the knees.'

James's protection officers got on well with him and accompanied the Brokenshire family one afternoon when they went to Chessington World of Adventures for one of the children's birthdays. The following Monday, James joked that his officers were too scared to go on the rollercoasters with his family – an experience each of them had, sadly, declined. The officers often dwarfed James, who is five feet eight and a half inches tall and mockingly refers to himself as 'The Hobbit from the Broken-shire'. With this in mind, the Monday morning after the family theme park visit, I asked the assembled officers whether James had been tall enough for the rides.

It was Sian Buckland who once pointed out the similarities between her husband, Robert, and James, with the small stature of the two ministers – my two main bosses in government – a frequent point of reference. One day, Sian ribbed me about my successive bosses' similarity on this and other points. She WhatsApped me: 'You sort of have a type who you work for, don't you?'

I jokingly replied: 'Perhaps I do! Maybe next time they could write a personal ad: "Short, bespectacled, white, male, Remain-voting, relatively liberal Cabinet minister seeks political sidekick for special advice sessions."'

She immediately countered: 'You forgot "greying".'

I was lucky to have quite good relationships with most of the non-political people I worked with in four departments. Some of the younger staff asked me to mentor them and give them some tips on their careers, CVs and even, occasionally, their desire to get into politics.

And there was actually a cyclical nature to some job movements at stages. For instance, one press SpAd in No. 10 switched to the civil service side to become director of communications at MHCLG. Before No. 10, she had been media SpAd at the Ministry of Justice, a job I then did after the 2019 summer reshuffle. Also in that reshuffle, a senior MHCLG press officer went to be SpAd to Julian Smith at the Northern Ireland Office, a job I had done previously for James and Karen. You never quite know where people are going to end up, where people's loyalties lie or how they might be able to help you (or you them) in future years, so it's best to at least try to avoid making enemies, though it is inevitable to some extent.

Not everyone takes this view, of course: Michael Gove and Dominic Cummings once referred to elements of the civil service and educational establishment as 'The Blob'. They believed parts of it to be obstructive, sclerotic and resistant to ministerial direction. Occasionally, I found this to be accurate, but in other ways it is extremely wide of the mark. What the civil service is obsessed with is process. (And, to a lesser extent, hierarchy.) Sometimes progress can be slow, but when it comes, it's tangible and difficult for the next administration to reverse. This can be both a good and a bad thing. The stereotype of the civil service as full of people who were against

Brexit is probably true, but then London is a Remain-voting city. Problems chiefly arose if that mindset manifested itself institutionally, which it seldom did in my experience.

One thing that did drive me up the wall during the path to Brexit, a policy which dominated my entire time in government, is the civil service's infuriating habit of referring to Brexit as 'EU Exit' in documents, submissions, written answers to parliamentary questions, briefings and even verbally. 'Brexit means Brexit,' as Theresa May once said. This also fed into my extreme pedantry about spelling, grammar and syntax. At one stage I refused to let any parliamentary questions go out of MHCLG unless all the references to 'EU Exit' were changed to 'Brexit'. The civil service pushed back and asked me to clarify with the Department for Exiting the EU. I told them that was a total waste of time, and they could do what they liked but the parliamentary questions weren't leaving the department until every reference was changed. I quickly realised that this team's performance was measured by how quickly they arranged for these parliamentary questions to be answered. My temporary block on the answers leaving the building appeared to focus minds, and the team conceded the point.

As I discuss elsewhere in the book, Dominic Cummings's Friday meetings, as night followed day, almost always leaked. Journalists generally knew not to ring me, because I wouldn't tell them anything about these events beyond very vague generalities, or, occasionally, precisely what Dominic had specifically instructed us to brief out. On one occasion, I grew so frustrated with the frequency with which 'EU Exit' was being used that when Dominic asked at the end of one Friday meeting whether we had any questions, I raised the issue.

It appeared to take Dominic by surprise, as he had not experienced this first-hand, but he very kindly said he would raise it with the then Cabinet Secretary, Sir Mark Sedwill. Night followed day and that comment leaked out. Not, I hasten to add, anything to do with me.

The next day, a story appeared in *The Times* detailing Dominic's exchange with 'a departmental SpAd' at the meeting. A civil servant I had worked with very closely texted me and asked me if I was the one who brought it up in the meeting, knowing my pedantry on the matter.

'Are you honestly suggesting', I texted him back, 'that I would knowingly bring up the "Brexit versus EU Exit" nomenclature in a meeting with Dominic, knowing he would be as annoyed about it as I am, so that he would then enquire about it at the highest level of the civil service, in the full knowledge that the exchange would almost certainly leak, with the possible result being a cross-Whitehall instruction from the Cabinet Secretary to call it Brexit?'

'Yes,' replied my interlocutor.

I countered, 'Well, then you'd be absolutely right.'

6

SpAds on Tour: Conference

I f you're a person interested in politics, particularly a young, wide-eyed one, the annual party conferences in the UK are sort of a nerd's Disneyland. But instead of that treasured snap with Minnie Mouse to show the family, you get a selfie with Andrew Bridgen. I absolutely loved them as a journalist, attending all three major parties' conferences for a couple of years. They are usually in the Midlands or the north of England, with Manchester, Birmingham and Liverpool frequently used by the major parties, as well as Bournemouth in the south. And that enjoyment of conferences came despite the extremely long hours, hard-drinking atmosphere and pressure to deliver the highest-ranking ministers or shadow ministers for *Newsnight* or *Question Time*.

I loved the heightened sense of drama, the interaction with politicians and their SpAds, and having a little bit of time to catch up with friends and colleagues after the programmes on which I was working. It's like being in a hermetically sealed bubble of politics, where everyone is super-informed, hugely interested in what is going on, and where even minor events have major traction – within the bubble at least. I had watched the major conference speeches and coverage for many years at school and as a student, sometimes even bunking off for Tony Blair's speeches as Labour Prime Minister. Sad, I know.

For any London-based broadcast journalist, getting outside the capital for a few days is always a refreshing break, and *Newsnight* on tour was always great – Jeremy Paxman in particular was great fun to work with at the various conferences. He was also generous to young, underpaid producers, buying us food and drinks on many occasions, especially in the main conference hotel, which was usually a five-star one and therefore out of our price range. The result was that my impression of party conferences as a journalist was a very positive one, although – whisper it – I always enjoyed the Liberal Democrats' one the best, because they were the most relaxed and off-guard. I remember supping some vodka a young aide had very kindly smuggled into the conference hotel one evening in a Lucozade bottle before the Lib Dem karaoke started up. I remember the drunken lover of a senior Lib Dem MP pitching up wearing just a vest and shorts looking like some sort of relic from a Culture Club gig in 1989 and buying us all drinks. I also remember a female friend, who would have been about twenty-five at the time, imploring me to buy her a stiff whiskey as she told me about the particularly difficult experience of extracting herself from a conversation with a nationally known broadcaster at least forty years her senior whose intentions were not that they should speak about the contents of Nick Clegg's speech all evening. In contrast, I have a particularly lovely memory of Lib Dem conference in 2010, going up and round in the Liverpool Wheel, a sort of London Eye-like Ferris wheel, with a friend from the BBC, Fiona Mackie, on the final day. We looked out over the beautiful city of Liverpool as those attending the conference made their way home. We were totally knackered, but it was a special moment.

In contrast, as a SpAd, you dread conference. It is simply something which has to be endured. If it didn't exist, you definitely wouldn't invent it. For four days, everyone from the enthusiastic sixteen-year-old who wants a selfie with your minister to the captain of industry who 'just wants five minutes with the Secretary of State' will hinder your frequent and often fruitless attempts to get to the next appointment. And there are many. The diary is always full to bursting, and you generally don't have time to tie your shoelaces between business dinners, receptions, tidying up the latest draft of the speech or fielding yet another enquiry from a journalist about your conference announcement.

Nor do you have civil servants to help you, so the work of managing a Cabinet minister, usually done, in my experience, by twelve or fourteen people in a private office, is instead carried out by one or two SpAds. Some of my co-SpAds were more adept than others at turning up on time, organising meetings and keeping things on track; these time management skills are not always part of a SpAd's day back in Westminster, so they don't necessarily come naturally.

Then there are the demands from the department. Before leaving for conference each year, I always had a chat with the private office staff to ensure they understood how much pressure the political team would be under away from base. They could not expect either SpAds or ministers to check their email every half an hour. I also made sure

I had an out-of-office message on my email to make clear that replies would not be swift, with a request to ring me in an emergency.

Preparation is key. I put a lot of effort into getting the diary shipshape and Bristol fashion for my ministers well in advance of conference itself, employing a complex but ordered filing system for all the requests we received. Keeping your minister fed, hydrated, on schedule, briefed and with enough time to ring their spouses at least once a day is imperative, as you are on the go from early morning until late at night. A mobile phone charging pack is a must.

When you finally get to the conference venue after weeks of preparation, there's the matter of moving round the secure zone, which is a vast area encompassing both the conference hotel and the conference centre itself. I remember as a TV producer collecting Boris Johnson for his annual interview as Mayor of London with Jeremy Paxman at the Birmingham International Conference Centre in 2010. Boris's press officer asked me, 'How are you going to move him?' I naively replied, 'Well, we just walk across the conference centre to the studio and Jeremy will interview him.' She rolled her eyes – she had seen it all before. Boris was already thronged by well-wishers, and moving him about 300 yards to the makeshift studio where Jeremy was waiting patiently took about twenty minutes by the time all the selfies had been taken.

Boris was polite and warm as I dealt with him as a young producer. Unlike Theresa May, whom I got to know a bit during the 2017 election (see Chapter 8), I've never really spent much time with Boris. Our first encounter was when I was on work experience at *The Spectator* in 2005. On my first morning, he sent me out to buy him a latte, saying, 'And get one for yourself too.' The coins he gave me covered neither the full cost of his latte nor any of the price of my own cup of tea, so I'm afraid, Prime Minister, you have owed me £2.35 for the past fifteen years.

For two conferences when James was Northern Ireland Secretary, I somehow managed to conceal from him that my sense of direction – especially under pressure – ranges from appalling to non-existent. In 2016 in Birmingham and again the following year in Manchester, the protection officers knew exactly where we were going. During James's period at MHCLG in 2018, however, I was chief navigator at conference. Sadly, the International Conference Centre in Birmingham is labyrinthine, so we frequently got lost as we tried to find out where stage three was, eventually finding out that – of course – it was on level seven and beside room forty-nine.

Invitations for ministers to attend conference events can arrive anything from four months in advance to moments before the event begins. There is never enough time to do everything, but politicians don't like to tell anyone 'no' at conference, especially the party faithful or an important donor who puts the minister on the spot. It often falls to the SpAd to be the 'bad cop' in these situations, making clear that there is simply no time in the diary. Frequently, you are not popular. And once you actually agree to something, the organisers usually want to make it an annual event. Junior ministers can come in handy for providing a bum on a seat for the events the Secretary of State doesn't have the time, or inclination, to do.

Similarly, some ministers will agree on the hoof to interviews with journalists which have not been cleared with No. 10. Extracting your minister from these can be difficult, but it is an important part of any media SpAd's job. And it's vital to remember, in the heady atmosphere of conference, that every single word at every single event should be treated as on the record. Walls are thin and everyone's phone has a voice recorder. The last thing any politician wants to do is to become 'the story of conference' due to an unguarded remark. As we were reminded before each conference by the No. 10 high command, this was the case for SpAds too. You are always 'on'.

Dealing with the media from morning until night is fine when you are in the office in Westminster, but at conference you share the same lounges and event space, attend the same receptions and often even sleep in the same hotels. And, yes, occasionally the same beds. It is a cheek-by-jowl existence for an intense few days. Well in advance, I used to draw up a roster of half-hour coffee meetings my ministers would be having with national newspaper editors and political editors. We would often find ourselves sitting for three-hour stretches in one of the lounges, such as the London Lounge, run annually by InHouse Communications, which is the best organised and, crucially, has the best snacks. There, we would drink tea, eat numerous marshmallow buns and chew the cud with the media and others. We could have done the whole thing in London, but conference was the place many of the journalists wanted to meet, so that's what we did.

At conference, the media was mostly very well behaved, and it is actually a good opportunity to get to know them better. The temptation is to talk frankly about what might be coming up, and that's largely fine, though no exchange between politician and journalist is ever truly off the record. At one stage, however, ITV political editor Robert Peston managed to cause a minor diplomatic incident. In 2019, as Robert Buckland and I said goodbye to one set of journalists as their allotted half-hour ended and were about to welcome another to our reserved sofas, Peston barged in, sat down on the sofa and started talking to Robert. Sadly, this left Charlie Cooper from Politico and James Tapsfield, political editor of MailOnline, standing like lemons, wondering whether to sit down or not. Cooper and Tapsfield had asked for the appointment over a month previously and, as I had scheduled them in, it was left to me to point out gently to Peston that the two men hovering by the sofa had this time booked for a chat with the Justice Secretary and that he should come back later. In fairness, he did just that.

Mealtimes at conference usually involve journalists too, as they quickly book up lunches and dinners with Cabinet ministers. There are also party dinners that numerous ministers will attend. Robert was invited to a dinner with one organisation in 2019 and I was told by the organiser that there was absolutely no way I could also attend the event, at which journalists were present, as there just wasn't room. Fine, I said, then Robert isn't going – I am not going to allow a scenario where my Cabinet minister is at a dinner with national journalists and his media SpAd is not present. The organisers relented, and I was allowed in. I raised an eyebrow, however, when Robert's fellow Cabinet minister Andrea Leadsom turned up with *two* guests – her son *and* her mother.

Occasionally, a SpAd can slip away at mealtimes to see friends at receptions or for a bite when the minister is at, say, a party donor's dinner where SpAds are not required. I remember at one conference working out that I had been in the same Pizza Express just outside the secure zone four times in thirty-six hours, on three of those occasions dining with members of the media.

As a journalist, I used to gatecrash the odd party. News International, then the name for the publisher of *The Sun* and the *News of the World*, had a reception at Conservative Party conference in 2010 to which *Newsnight* producers were definitely *not* invited. I deployed the old 'two glasses of champagne' trick – you acquire two glasses of champagne from another reception in an adjacent suite and tell the security guards on the door you are 'just going back in', thereby gaining entry. There, possibly fuelled by the champagne, I marched up to Andy Coulson, who was then the Downing Street director of communications, and asked him why we weren't getting ministers for *Newsnight*, a long-running gripe (see Chapter 2). He was churlish and unpleasant, dismissing me in a sentence as if I were something on his shoe, turning to talk to someone else immediately as I attempted to reply.

I encountered Coulson on only one other occasion, when I was reporting on his phone-hacking trial at the Old Bailey, where his previously imperious attitude appeared to have left him.

The opportunities to give interviews are many and varied for any Cabinet minister at conference, with the associated organisation done by SpAds, alongside the party press officers. One of the very few times Jonathan Caine complimented me during the nineteen months we worked together was at the first party conference we attended with James as Northern Ireland Secretary. James was booked in for a morning round of media the following day, and Jonathan suddenly realised that he wouldn't have to get up at the usual early hour to support his minister. Instead, I had that privilege as media SpAd. Jonathan wasn't used to such an arrangement, having been the single SpAd for the previous six years. 'Oh, I suppose I can have a lie-in, then. There is a point in having you after all,' he remarked.

A few weeks before that conference, we received an email from Theresa May's political secretary – a very senior aide in No. 10 – Stephen Parkinson, now Lord Parkinson. Parky mentioned that ministers who had police protection, such as the Northern Ireland Secretary, would automatically have a room in the conference hotel within the secure zone. One SpAd would have a room in the same, luxury hotel, with additional SpAds staying in the less salubrious surroundings of the local three-star Holiday Inn fifteen minutes' walk away. Immediately, I deferred to Jonathan, pointing out that of course he should have the room in the nicer, five-star hotel as the more senior SpAd. Exactly a year later, in the summer of 2017, I remarked to Jonathan that we had received no similar email from Parky about the conference accommodation arrangements that year. Should I follow this up? 'Oh,' said Jonathan. 'I emailed him a few weeks ago to tell him *I* am taking the conference hotel room.'

In fairness, my Holiday Inn room wasn't terrible, and I shouldn't complain, mainly because the Conservative Party conference for the past few years has been held alternately in Manchester and Birmingham, which have excellent facilities for large conferences. Previously, most political parties in the UK tended to go to seaside resorts, some of them a bit grim. The standard of accommodation many SpAds experienced in days of yore are notorious. One SpAd, who worked in the press office for Conservative Party headquarters in the early 2000s, told me her memories of Blackpool are far from pleasant. She related her miserable experience as follows:

> We in the press office and some of the Research Department desk
> officers were billeted to a… well, 'B&B' is too strong a term – we

were billeted to a *place* that had nylon carpets. I'm not being precious about that; I'm just saying you didn't want to set yourself on fire.

All of the rooms very weirdly had up to five beds in them, with nylon sheets. So you're sensing the fire-related theme here. The bathroom was utterly disgusting, covered in black mould. I made sure my contact lenses were out as I went into the shower, because I didn't want to touch anything, or at least see what I was touching.

I was on early press duty one morning, which meant getting up at 4.45 a.m., and I had a shower and found I couldn't turn the shower off because the taps got stuck. All I could do was let the hot water continue to run.

I was leaving about a quarter past five for the office, so there was no one on the 'front desk' – again, that's too generous a phrase; it constituted an MFI bit of wood knocked together in someone's front room – of this alleged bed and breakfast. So I just ran up the hill to the main conference hotel.

In those days, you would have to watch the TV breakfast news programmes and listen to key interviews on the *Today* programme, transcribing them in real time. You would have the newspapers in hard copy – this was all before newspapers were properly online. You would photocopy relevant stories into a pack of cuttings. Hotel staff either hated you or you were their best friend, because you then needed to get that all photocopied about thirty times, and then run down corridors and get it hand-delivered to the Cabinet's hotel bedrooms by eight o'clock.

So I did my early morning duty and ran back down the road to the place we were staying in order to have breakfast. It was beans and sausages out of a tin. Literally, heated up and out of a can. It was disgusting.

Everyone else was quite upset that morning because they had had cold shaves or cold showers – they were all generally quite miserable. And the reason was me. I hadn't been able to turn off the hot water in my mould-ridden shower hours before everyone else got up. I used all the hot water – I'm the culprit. They were all in this grim, mould-ridden accommodation and they couldn't even have a hot shower.

It's not always plain sailing for journalists at conference either. Moments before one particular broadcast, Sky News' then political editor Adam Boulton had a minor wardrobe malfunction, resulting in what tailors call the 'seat' of his trousers loudly splitting.

Quick as a flash, his producer Clare Parry – the nicest person I worked with in a decade in broadcasting – constructed an intricate but effective solution, using black gaffer tape to seal the gap in the seat of Adam's trousers.

The problem was that while one side of the gaffer tape is black, the other side – in this instance, the side that was facing outwards – is white. Taking the correspondent–producer relationship to a new level of intimacy, Clare sourced a black marker and, with just moments to spare before going live, coloured in Adam's 'seat' to disguise the gaffer tape.

It's not strictly relevant to a chapter on party conferences, but perhaps this is also the point to inform you of not one but two other trouser-related incidents regarding my former colleague Adam Boulton; a master at political presenting, reporting and analysis but clearly not an expert when it comes to trousers.

One such incident came in July 2019 when Adam, now promoted to the intriguing title of Sky News editor-at-large, was standing in Downing Street wearing a white suit, about to broadcast. He promptly managed to sit on a Mars bar, which Sky News political editor Beth Rigby helped him peel off.

The other trouser-related story comes from my first day working at Sky News in Westminster in 2012. Starting that day as a political news editor, I had an introductory chat with my new boss, Esmé Wren, then Sky's head of politics. She was sitting, facing me, with her back to Adam's glass-walled office just yards behind her. As Esmé gently explained, 'Things are done in a slightly different way here at Sky News than other places you have worked, and you'll have to adapt to that quickly.'

As she spoke, Adam, in the glass office, dropped his trousers, took off his shirt and stood in his boxers and vest for all to see. He was changing into a suit before he went on the telly. My face must have betrayed my shock that someone would do this in a glass cubicle in an open-plan office. Esmé glanced back at Adam's state of undress, a frequent occurrence in the Sky Westminster office, as I was to learn. Without missing a beat, Esmé said, 'The benefits of a public school education, eh?'

Adam is a heavyweight of British political broadcasting in many ways. At the end of that first day, the then deputy political editor of Sky News, Joey Jones, very kindly took me for a drink to welcome me to the fold. 'What's it like being deputy to Adam Boulton?' I asked. Joey paused. 'Adam casts a long shadow,' he said, taking a sip of his gin and tonic, before adding, 'He casts quite a wide shadow too.'

Back to conference. I remember in 2017, just weeks after the disastrous election for the Conservative Party, numerous journalists were complaining that conference lacked atmosphere, sparkle and a 'story'. My answer was always the same: 'Just you wait until Mrs May's leader's speech on Wednesday – it's going to be amazing!'

I'd been in the hall as a journalist for leaders' speeches a number of times. The atmosphere is always one of great expectation and goodwill from the party faithful – who make up the vast majority of the audience. In 2014, Labour leader Ed Miliband forgot large sections of his speech, which he gave without notes, though few in the audience noticed. But what was remarkable regarding Miliband's first conference speech as Labour leader, in 2010, was what I was reliably informed had been cut out in the drafting stages.

Originally, I'm told, there were not one but two jokes at the expense of then Communities Secretary Eric Pickles (not to be confused with the cactus, Eric Prickles). Specifically, about Pickles being quite overweight. The first joke – 'The party never worries about losing Eric Pickles, because wherever he goes he always leaves a trail of crumbs' – you could probably just about get away with. But another proposed line: 'Eric Pickles: the only Cabinet minister who is visible from space', also apparently in one of the drafts, would have been a jibe too far.

At Conservative conference, Cabinet ministers are seated shortly before the leader's speech. Their arrival a few minutes before the leader has become an event in itself, designed to give the broadcasters some pictures. The speech is always the final engagement at Conservative conference, with most people rushing to catch trains immediately afterwards.

The hall is always very full, sometimes with people not getting seats – SpAds often end up standing around the sides. It's meant to be the highlight of conference – the reason thousands of delegates have paid substantial sums of money to attend. Having been to a number of these set-pieces, in 2017 I decided to wait in the hotel for half of it, watching it on telly, and then go backstage for the final half, as James and I had to leave immediately afterwards from there with the protection officers to catch a flight to Belfast. I didn't want to deprive one of the party faithful of a seat in the hall, especially as I had spent lots of time watching Theresa May give speeches during the election just months earlier.

One of the protection officers had kindly said I could wait in his hotel room, from which he had checked out, watch the speech, and pull the door after me. I sat in the empty bedroom watching May on the telly, which seemed to go well for about the first twenty minutes or so. That was until the moment a comedian called Simon Brodkin walked up to the podium and handed the Prime Minister a mocked-up P45 form. A friend who was in the hall at the time, working in the operations team as the whole nightmare played out, takes up the story. His job was to keep everything running smoothly, and as an ops person he was the first line of defence in the conference hall.

> It wasn't immediately clear to people in the room what was happening. We had a WhatsApp group to keep everyone working on the event in touch, both backstage and in front of the stage. A large 'box' is marked on the floor with white tape at the very front, to allow the photographers space to get their snaps. We had to make sure we kept an eye on the journalists and especially the snappers to ensure they had the best views of the Prime Minister.

But we were only keeping tabs on the media within that box, not anyone else who was coming into it – as Brodkin did.

Just before the speech, the final text is locked with just moments to spare. It's still being fine-tuned on the day, so there's always a press officer who receives the speech and has to very quickly format it on the computer and then photocopy about 200 copies. There's always that slightly comedy scene of a press officer sprinting down to the journalists near the stage so they can get their copy just as the Prime Minister starts to speak. If there is anything market-sensitive in the speech, obviously that is redacted.

The speech started and it was all fine. I saw the commotion, but it wasn't exactly clear what was happening, so I started walking closer. Obviously, Simon Brodkin had crept forward into the media box and handed over the P45. He then sat down and started talking to Boris, I think.

One of the other members of the operations team was the closest, and he was the first person to begin to escort the prankster out. In fairness, Brodkin didn't resist. At that point, the conference venue stewarding staff took over the handling and led him out of the room. There was an interesting scene with about four security staff trying to escort him through the exhibition hall. But by that stage he was surrounded by TV cameras and correspondents – a classic media scrum.

They walked slowly towards the front of the conference hall and it was a mess – they were slamming into charity stands, into walls. It was chaos, a ridiculous scene. Some police officers had joined in as well. They formally arrested him a bit later on, and just kept him in the conference security centre until things calmed down.

The media were waiting to interview him outside the security turnstiles, but the police kept him inside.

By the time I got back into the hall, about ten minutes later, the speech was still going. And then, the coughing started. She had a glass of water, but that started to run out. There was a lovely lady from the audio-visual team who was crouched down trying to find a good moment to give the Prime Minister another glass of water. Then Philip Hammond passed forward a cough sweet.

There's a big space just yards away from the main conference hall where the broadcasters sit on the other side of a curtain. Obviously, the political editors are seated in the hall, but the majority of the other broadcast people are in their makeshift office on the other side of that curtain. I remember hearing laughter from the broadcast area, and I thought that was very odd, as journalists usually never make a sound during the speech. Apart from the sketch-writers, obviously, who don't care.

I was thinking at this stage: we've had the protester, we've had the coughing, but now what? Then I walked round to the centre of the hall and it was clear some of the letters on the backdrop were falling off. I think we all had the collective thought at that point: how can this get any worse? Oh, wait, it just has.

Coincidentally, I happened to be in the main conference hall on the Tuesday night and saw the workmen attaching the letters to the backdrop. I did wonder at the time why they were doing that. The answer is that for the rest of the conference, when Cabinet ministers give their individual speeches, a lectern is used which can be moved up and down. High for the gigantic Chris Grayling, low for Alun

Cairns, the then Welsh Secretary, who is titchy. Incidentally, I was always very glad that Alun Cairns was in Cabinet for all of James's time – it meant that James was not the shortest man in the photos and TV footage.

But the Prime Minister has their own fixed-height lectern because they give the most important speech of conference, and that lectern can be used for other events, too. The point of having a slogan behind the Prime Minister is that the broadcasters sometimes don't put the words printed on the front of the lectern in vision – if it's directly behind the speaker, they can't fail to include it in the shot.

The main hall itself is set up in a different way to the rest of conference, with more seats added, as the Prime Minister's is the most popular event. The Cabinet is seated in a prominent position, and often the stage is made larger, with sometimes even an additional, smaller stage added to the main one, so that the Prime Minister and their lectern can be brought further out into the audience.

Factors including the number of people in the hall, the room temperature and associated moisture, as well as the vibrations of all the clapping throughout May's speech, combined to create the conditions for the letters – stuck on just a few hours earlier – to fall off.

'Things always happen and sometimes speeches are dominated by the one thing that goes wrong,' continues my friend, a veteran ops person.

> That day, three different things happened. One of those things on its own would have been really bad. But the thing I always remember is that the room was completely behind her. There were a lot of people I spoke to afterwards who said, 'Good on

her, she carried on, she was resilient.' It was embarrassing, but she stuck at it.

As well as the leader's oration, earlier in conference each Cabinet minister gets their moment in the sun. This causes another headache in its preparation, and the speeches are planned weeks in advance. A long process of drafting, redrafting, approvals, releasing extracts to the press and last-minute tweaks right up until the moment the final, 'locked' words go onto the prompter dominates the preparation for conference. Ideally, your announcements will be signed off by No. 10 in plenty of time, and in 2019, my final conference as a SpAd, this was done very efficiently. The gridders in No. 10 then carefully assemble a chart to keep the media beast fed over the course of conference, with everything timed so the announcements dominate the news cycle.

When I was at the Northern Ireland Office, Jonathan Caine wrote the speeches for James, and I had very little input beyond reading over them and adding some very minor changes. Similarly, at MHCLG, Liam Booth-Smith, the policy SpAd, was in charge, again with only minor amendments coming from me. Liam in particular is a talented and experienced speechwriter, and I think that speech was James's best as a Secretary of State.

I longed to write a conference speech myself but could never quite 'get' James's voice in articles and other speeches. It was only for the final of the four conferences I attended as SpAd, with Robert, that I held the pen. About 95 per cent of the final speech was my construction, and Robert delivered it well and he was pleased with the media reaction.

We had two, proper, well-thought out and costed measures in 2019: increasing the amount of time the most serious violent and sexual offenders spend behind bars to two-thirds of their sentence, rather than automatic release at the halfway point; and using sobriety tags on offenders on licence. The public was hugely in favour of both policies, with the two-thirds announcement garnering a 76 per cent approval rating in a poll taken afterwards. That was the highest approval rating of any Conservative Party conference announcement in 2019.

Liam was part of the conference speech approvals team at No. 10 by this stage, and his praise for the speech I drafted meant a lot. My rhetorical construction around the policy and its popularity as an announcement were not, however, the part of which I am most proud. Rather, what I will remember is a rather crude joke – which thankfully No. 10 didn't censor – about our investment in prison scanners which look inside people's bodies.

The context was that just days into his appointment, Robert and the new Prime Minister, Boris Johnson, had gone up to HMP Leeds to launch our £100 million policy to get these scanners into prisons. Duly, Boris and Robert looked at the scanners and saw that there was the plastic container you find inside a Kinder Surprise chocolate egg that had been used to conceal drugs. The container was placed in… well, a certain part of a prisoner's body which had come up on the scanner. In the footage, you can actually see the moment when Boris works out exactly where in the prisoner's body the Kinder egg container is and how it got there. At first, Boris had imagined Bowler had swallowed the container, but then worked out how it had got to where it was. In an article in *The Sun* headlined 'Bum deal', Boris is quoted as saying to prison guards, 'You're joking? He plugged it?'

Robert's conference speech duly went:

> In one of his first acts, the Prime Minister announced we will
> recruit 20,000 new police officers. More bobbies on the beat means
> more arrests, more victims getting justice. And an investment of
> £2.5 billion to deliver 10,000 new prison places. More and better
> prisons to support our brilliant prison officers, the unsung heroes
> who day in, day out face huge risks in their workplace.
>
> To help them, we have announced £100 million for new security
> measures, such as the scanners at Her Majesty's Prison Leeds,
> checking people as they go in and out of prisons. These scanners
> show us the ways drugs are smuggled in are often creative. When
> we visited HMP Leeds, the Prime Minister wondered what exactly
> the small plastic container coming up on the body scanner was –
> I think we all had something of a Kinder Surprise.
>
> The PM then wondered aloud how the small capsule had got
> to where it was. Now, there's always that moment with a new
> boss when you're not quite sure what you can and can't say. I did
> think about explaining, but I knew in *my* gut it was a bad idea.
> Much as the prisoner did.

Getting media coverage for our announcements at 2019 Conservative conference was a major part of my job. The planning for that
coverage, which I did in conjunction with a No. 10 SpAd, the efferves-
cent Meg Powell-Chandler, who runs the grid, couldn't have been
smoother.

Robert was to do a sit-down interview with the *Daily Mail* on
both announcements, with the smaller sobriety tags aspect held

back from other media as an exclusive for the *Mail*. The *Mail* is a key paper for the Conservative Party, especially on law and order. Everyone else would get speech extracts on the main policy – the sentence extension – but the sobriety tags plus interview was the *Mail*'s alone.

All went nicely in the sit-down, with Robert acquitting himself well in the interview with *Mail* associate editor for politics Jack Doyle and home affairs editor Ian Drury. I got on well with both men – Ian once told me he and I were 'the Lennon and McCartney of home affairs stories', and Jack had previously done the excellent 'from cancer to Cabinet' interview with James. (Saying that, I often josh with Jack that he was the first journalist ever to have been in the Brokenshires' kitchen and he missed the ovens story, which you can read about in Chapter 7.)

The sentence extension announcement was gaining traction as the embargoed press release hit the journalists preparing for the next day, and it would drop in the papers at around ten-thirty that night. And the sobriety tags policy was safely exclusively briefed to the *Mail*. I did a quick walk-round of the newspapers' different desks in the press centre at conference in the morning, and all was fine.

That is until one journalist from *The Sun* said, 'Yeah, tell me more about this sobriety tags thing.' I went white, stonewalling, and walked away as quickly as I could.

The Sun ran the tags story as an 'exclusive' the next day, under-standingly infuriating the *Mail* and, for that matter, me. Thankfully, the *Mail* ran the whole interview as their front-page splash, so all was not lost, but it made us look like idiots who couldn't keep a lid on the sobriety tags aspect of the story.

How on earth had our exclusive for the *Mail* leaked? I mentally went through all the people who knew about it, but it was in all of their interests to keep it under wraps, keep it exclusive to the *Mail* and stick to the grid. Nobody gained anything from giving it to *The Sun*, and none of the usual suspects for leaking knew a thing about it. The *Mail*'s editor, Geordie Greig, was also at conference, so it was doubly inconvenient. I was confused at what had happened, and incandescent. I had had an excellent relationship with the *Mail* – and not a bad one with *The Sun*.

A few days later, I found out that the *Sun* journalist had been at a drinks reception and one of the members of our Justice political team had had a few too many shandies and blabbed the story. Somewhat ironically, had that team member themselves had a sobriety tag attached, we could have monitored them and the story would have remained a *Mail* exclusive. As a colleague remarked to me after my, shall we say, full and frank exchange of views with the team member who drunkenly leaked it, 'He certainly had his card well marked by Cardwell.'

Nonetheless, my final conference as a SpAd was probably the one during which I was most relaxed. We didn't have to be in Manchester for the entire time, as Robert had to get his Lord Chancellor's ceremonial tights and wig on back in London for a ceremony to mark the start of the legal year. When we were in Manchester, I felt as if I finally knew what I was doing regarding conference, and perhaps as a SpAd too. There wasn't much that could have been thrown at me by October 2019 that I couldn't have dealt with. When I got home to London for a good sleep after conference, my housemate, Sam, told me I was treating the new job with Robert with the correct degree of professionalism and commitment.

'With Robert,' Sam said, 'it's clear it's a good colleague to good boss relationship, and you're dealing with that well.'

'Was that not the case when I was working with James?' I asked.

'No,' she replied. 'With James, it was more disciple–messiah.'

7

Breaking SpAd: When Things Go Wrong

The Secretary of State's press conference had gone well and, foolishly, we relaxed. It was time now to come inside; out of the blustery January wind off the East Belfast hills and into the comfortable, warm boardroom of Stormont House for a further conversation, this time with just print journalists. The scribblers often moan – usually with some justification – that broadcasters get more of a bite of the cherry at televised press conferences, so we thought we would give them a nice cup of tea while they had a chat with the newly appointed Northern Ireland Secretary, Karen Bradley.

She had acquitted herself well in Stage 1 outside. As her newly confirmed media special adviser, I sat behind the reporters, maintaining eye contact with Karen so I could send her subtle signals if things went off course. She was, let's remember, just ten days into her new job, one of the toughest in Cabinet. It was quite a contrast with her old department, the Department for Digital, Culture, Media and Sport.

For the UK government's man or woman in Belfast, every word matters in that part of the country, where, as I knew from previous experience, politicians are offended easily. A lunch was planned immediately afterwards with some of Northern Ireland's business leaders and an influential newspaper columnist. So no problems forecast. So far.

Enter Sam McBride, political editor of the Belfast *News Letter*, and perhaps the smartest journalist in Northern Ireland. Quiet, unassuming, hirsute Sam, small in stature but lethal in line of questioning, he made an excellent guess at asking a question on which Karen had not been briefed, with disastrous consequences. Karen kept on about how vital it was that devolution at Stormont – which had collapsed almost exactly a year previously – was restored, so that Northern Ireland could have the government it needed. Valiantly, she stuck to what she had been briefed by senior members of her team, including me. So far, so good. She was doing well in her first days – not bad for someone who had never even visited Northern Ireland prior to her appointment, as was so often the case with Secretaries of State.

In the days following the Conservatives' disastrous result in the 2017 election, Northern Ireland's largest political party, the Democratic Unionist Party (DUP), agreed what's called a confidence and supply deal with Theresa May. This meant the DUP's ten MPs would mostly vote with the May government to push agreed pieces of legislation over the line. Their side of the bargain was a £1 billion financial package for Northern Ireland, a part of the UK already generously subsidised by the British taxpayer.

McBride leaned forward slightly and in his soft voice asked whether the new Secretary of State was looking forward to new Northern

Ireland ministers being appointed soon, so the additional £1 billion could be spent? It was a skilfully constructed elephant trap by the talented hack.

Karen replied, 'Well, we need to do budgets, don't we, and budgets require ministers to administer those budgets. It's really clear to me – I'd a meeting with the Northern Ireland civil service first thing this morning… They need ministerial direction in order to do that.'

Sitting just yards behind McBride's fiercely scribbling pen, my face turned white.

A few minutes later, as the Press Association's David Young tweeted Karen's comments, the DUP went ballistic both in public and in private.

The party's Westminster leader, Nigel Dodds MP, tweeted, 'Oh dear … some [of the money] already released. Rest on way. This is not correct.'

Karen had inadvertently implied the cash would only continue to flow if the DUP went into coalition again at Stormont with their loathed rivals, Sinn Féin, and the DUP believed Karen's comments were tantamount to coercion. The billion, they argued correctly, was not contingent on devolution, and the new Secretary of State – a member of the party they were propping up – had erred badly.

Sometimes, over a drink at the end of a long week in one of Westminster's bars, SpAds will ask each other whether they had a *West Wing* week or a *Thick of It* week – have they been doing big, important things, writing speeches with soaring rhetoric and carrying out important work that makes a tangible difference to people's lives, or have they been flapping about trying to put the toothpaste back in the tube of whatever gaffe their minister has committed?

For me, this week fell emphatically into the latter camp.

The next forty-five minutes was a high-adrenalin, high-octane race to dig ourselves out of the omnishambles we found ourselves in as a result of some ill-chosen words. I rang two of the journalists reporting the story, Young and McBride, and asked them to stand by to speak to the Secretary of State, who, on speakerphone on my mobile, 'clarified' her remarks in further comments just minutes after her error. It was highly irregular for the Secretary of State to communicate with journalists directly in this way.

She told Young and McBride, in an effort to put the DUP's mind at rest, that her words had been 'a bit clumsy', reading out lines from a prepared script that Jonathan Caine and I had worked on. It was a desperate move, but the only one I could think of as the walls closed in around us.

Concurrently, political Twitter went crazy, Downing Street was menacingly on the line – reacting, of course, to the DUP's complaints, already made at the highest level – and the NIO press office's phones rang off the hook.

Oblivious to the chaos just yards away, the guests were arriving for lunch, soon exchanging pleasantries with Karen, the Permanent Secretary Sir Jonathan Stephens and me upstairs in the Stormont House dining room. A near-schizophrenic scene emerged, as I oscillated between making calm, polite small talk in the dining room and rushing into the adjacent office to try to calm down the DUP, Downing Street and the media as calls intermittently lit up my phone.

Nigel Dodds was extremely angry, and who could blame him? To use a wonderfully Northern Irish term, he ate the face off me. Would he hold for the Secretary of State so she could apologise in person?

'I certainly will not be holding, Peter,' he barked. 'Ring me back when she is free,' he added, concluding the call. I'd probably have done exactly the same thing in his position.

Correctly, the next day's *Daily Telegraph* reported that the episode had 'infuriated' Dodds. He didn't quite spell out that the hard-fought and always delicate confidence and supply deal could be at risk, but that was the clear undertone. It was not the first time a Cabinet minister had made inaccurate remarks around this issue, but it was a first for a Northern Ireland Secretary.

I called Karen out of the lunch, and it was clear she would not be eating the delicious fare the Stormont House chef Martin had served up but humble pie. My advice was simple – for the next five minutes on the phone with Nigel Dodds, just keep apologising until he calms down. It was sometimes the best strategy with the DUP, as I had learned over the previous eighteen months in politics, and indeed ten years as a journalist, having frequently interacted with Dodds and his colleagues. They were in the right, and we needed to take our medicine.

Karen did as she was advised and did well in the circumstances. It was all over as quickly as it had started, barring the media pick-up and disastrous headlines in the papers the next day, including the *Telegraph*.

Karen requested that I join her for dinner that evening in the beautiful village of Hillsborough, asking her private secretary to book us a table at a nice restaurant. Hillsborough is in County Down, about twenty miles from Stormont House. At the top of the picturesque and sleepy village, Hillsborough Castle is both the Queen's and the Secretary of State's official residence in Northern Ireland. This impressive historic building with magnificent gardens is well worth a visit, and I was privileged to stay there overnight on numerous occasions. The intricate wrought iron gates originally hung outside the castle in my home village, Richhill, thirty miles away, before they were 'acquired' (nicked) by Northern Ireland's Governor General in 1936. Do join my Facebook group demanding their return.

Anticipating further media attention the next day, I thought it would be a good opportunity to catch up with Karen, with whom I hadn't had much one-on-one time since she had been appointed the previous week, even though I had been at her side almost constantly. We could chat about the big issues she would be facing as Secretary of State: the legacy of Northern Ireland's Troubles; the equality agenda around same-sex marriage and abortion; the extremely thorny issue of the role of the Irish language in Northern Ireland, about which Sinn Féin had a major bee in their bonnet. Plus, the dinner would be an opportunity to guide Karen away from the kind of unfortunate remarks she had made earlier that day and lay the groundwork for a more successful interaction with the media. I could talk to her about what in politics are called the lines to take – effectively the script any Cabinet minister has to stick to about their department. And in Northern Ireland there are many.

In a busy restaurant, with her 24-hour police protection officers ever-watchful of their new, high-profile charge, we discussed another interview she was doing the following day for BBC Northern Ireland. The presenter was a Belfast journalist called Stephen Nolan, a particularly combative interviewer I had worked with previously. I had absolutely no intention of allowing him to interview Karen. I hadn't been entirely against the idea of Nolan interviewing Karen's predecessor,

James Brokenshire, but wiser heads rightly veered me from that particular precipice when it came down to the wire.

The compromise with the relevant producers was that two sixth formers would interview Karen the next day, on our turf, at Stormont House, for broadcast the following Wednesday evening. The idea of two bright students who represented the future of Northern Ireland getting face time with the new Secretary of State on the big issues of the day was a strong, positive signal to send.

We also suspected, at this early point, the kids might turn teacher and test Karen's general knowledge about Northern Ireland, so we went over some rudimentary questions I suspected they might ask. Karen remembers my telling her the FAT LAD acronym I had learned in primary school to remember the six counties of Northern Ireland – Fermanagh, Armagh, Tyrone, Londonderry, Antrim, Down. Thankfully, the good diners of Hillsborough were more interested in their red wine jus and balsamic reductions than my lesson for the new Secretary of State. Karen and I had certainly built a better dynamic over dinner, but I was still nervous about the next day, given how the previous one had gone.

Karen is a very nice person who worked hard at a relentless job which involves a huge amount of travel, time away from family, incredibly complex policy and dealing with some of the most intractable issues in UK politics. But just days into her new role, the Northern Ireland media was negatively comparing Karen to James. One seasoned hack in Belfast once described James as 'a civil servant's dream and a journalist's nightmare', given how slavishly he stuck to the script and never, ever slipped up. He was not loved by the media, but he didn't err. Was his successor, Karen Bradley, they asked, of the right temperament, with the right precision of language for Belfast's brutal political theatre? The BBC interview the next day would be yet another test of this.

Liz Sanderson, who as special adviser in No. 10 was one of Theresa May's closest confidantes, once said of Karen's predecessor, 'James Brokenshire has never unknowingly committed an act of news.' The aim for any senior politician, in any interview, is to get through it without 'committing' news you don't want to commit. This can be frustrating for interviewers and the public alike, but the majority of times a government minister speaks to the press, the aim is not to move the story on at all, but to hold the line and avoid these 'acts of news' being committed. Karen, without meaning to, had committed some serious news.

My co-SpAd, Jonathan Caine, had flown back to London that night and was reluctant to come into the NIO's Westminster office the next morning to brief Karen. Daily meetings took place between the London and Belfast offices 'down the line' via a secure video link.

'For God's sake, Jonathan, you saw what happened yesterday. You're coming into the office and that's that,' I barked down the phone, mildly hungover the next morning on my way into the office in a taxi. 'Get in the bloody car and we'll see you down the line at ten o'clock.' Lord Caine is a formidable person, many years my senior, and had thirty years' experience in politics. I hadn't spoken to any superior like that before, and nor have I since.

We briefed Karen for the guts of an hour, and while I have often heard people joke 'I was nearly sick over my boss', this almost became a most unfortunate reality. At one stage I was so nervous and green around the gills that Karen asked me if I wanted to leave the room and get some air or a glass of water. She was a picture of calm. I was not. And it was not just the mild excess of wine the night before that made me almost vomit over a Cabinet minister.

In the end, Karen's interview with the sixth formers went absolutely fine, with not a word out of place. They did end up asking her a few pop quiz questions too. It was broadcast to little reaction or fanfare, as is the case with most media interviews undertaken by politicians, and we lived to fight another day.

That interview, and many others Karen did, was at Stormont House, the NIO's headquarters on the Stormont Estate, not to be confused with Parliament Buildings up the hill, the seat of the Northern Ireland Assembly. Or Hillsborough Castle, which I banned the NIO using for anything media-related, except infrequent royal visits. Prince Harry came to James's garden party in September 2017 as the royal guest and brightened up a very wet and muddy afternoon. I even had a brief chat with him about his work with Heads Together, the prince's mental health initiative, which I strongly support. I wouldn't have been fit to appear at all if not for a lovely woman who worked at the castle, Dorothy Arbuthnot, who took one look at my muddy trousers and said, 'You can't meet the prince looking like that, Peter!' and took me down to the kitchens to clean me up with a damp tea towel.

But the castle's history as a country mansion – and status as a royal residence – feeds the critical narrative so beloved by some in Northern Ireland of a hoity-toity English MP flying in to visit the natives and patronising them while staying in a grand, palatial home. The fact that Karen was brought up living above a pub and went to state schools is neither here nor there – there are some sections of the Northern Ireland media who will happily perpetuate the Tory toff narrative, come what may.

Some years previously, Owen Paterson MP, who later re-emerged as a key player in the Brexit debate, was Northern Ireland Secretary in the Cameron administration. Paterson's plummy voice and privileged background fulfilled many more of the Tory stereotypes with which certain sections of the Northern Ireland media feel comfortable. About to undertake an interview at Hillsborough Castle with the BBC, Paterson's perhaps over-zealous press officer insisted that the camera angle be moved slightly, so a gilded gold mirror be taken out of shot. 'Yes, good idea,' said Paterson. 'I don't want to look like a toff in a castle.' Quick as a flash, BBC reporter Yvette Shapiro quipped, 'Secretary of State, with the greatest of respect, you *are* a toff and this *is* a castle.' Apparently, Paterson had the good grace to laugh.

~

As a media SpAd, the question always has to be: *why* are you granting an interview – and the answer cannot be simply to fill space in a newspaper or time on the airwaves; there's got to be a political purpose. When the *Sunday Times* Home supplement asked to interview James Brokenshire in May 2018, it wasn't an article I was expecting to be particularly significant in the scheme of things, but I did think it was worth doing. The new Housing Secretary, at home, with his wife, sitting in his living room and kitchen, talking about his political and personal life, housing policy and what his family home meant to him. It sounded pretty straightforward to me, so, in consultation with No. 10, James and his wife Cathy, I agreed to it. As was the case with every politician I worked with, the kids were totally off limits, and the condition that no images of them appeared in the paper was part of my negotiation with the *Sunday Times*, as it had been with other journalists who interviewed James at home.

James, Cathy and I ended up spending more than two hours with the *Sunday Times* journalists at the Brokenshire family home in Bexley, south-east London, in his constituency. James uttered not a word out of place, as usual, and assorted photos duly appeared alongside the interview in the paper that weekend.

By that stage – May 2019 – speculation was rife as to who would run for the leadership of the Conservative Party when Theresa May stood down. That made it understandable that, two days before the interview was published, I received a text from a *Sunday Times* reporter on the news section, asking, 'Did you do the interview because Brokenshire is running for leader?' I replied, honestly, 'No, we did the interview because your Home supplement asked us to.'

We were all very happy with the final article, a well-written and insightful piece in which James spoke honestly and movingly, about his family in particular. James told the interviewers about caring for his father, Peter Brokenshire, through his final days of pancreatic cancer. James also spoke about his own battle with lung cancer the previous year, as well as his mother's dementia. He told the paper, 'I remember doing a tough [Radio 4] *Today* interview and coming back to my mum, who was sobbing because she'd remembered, again, that my dad had died. That was tougher than cancer.'

But the interview will never be remembered for any of that. Instead, the only thing anyone will ever recall is the fact the Brokenshire kitchen has multiple ovens.

The eight-day media maelstrom that we soon began to call 'Oven-gate' had humble beginnings. A small *Sunday Times* news piece on page 2 in the main paper remarked on the fact that James and Cathy own two double ovens, referring to the profile in the separate Home section. This was followed up by the *Daily Mail* the next day with a huge picture of Cathy, James and the ovens headlined 'At home with the Tory housing supremo and his very middle class two double ovens'. Their consumer affairs editor, Sean Poulter, wrote:

> The extra double oven – there are also two dishwashers – was deemed necessary by his wife Cathy, who felt there was not enough room to cook for big family occasions. Mrs Brokenshire said she 'hates it when, come Christmas, there's not enough room in the oven'. It seems that while at one time a Porsche on the drive, a conservatory, wine fridge or garden studio were the evidence of middle-class success, now two ovens are the ultimate badge of honour.

Also covered in the *Mail* that day – in a tiny article on page 6 – was our 'gridded' item: a £92 million fund for local councils to provide secure accommodation for survivors of domestic abuse. There was at least some reaction to that story, though: to continue the completely surreal nature of Day 2 of Ovengate, the tweet from the domestic abuse organisation Women's Aid welcoming our announcement was retweeted by Mel B from the Spice Girls, who is herself a survivor of domestic abuse. It was the first time a pop star had welcomed a policy I had worked on, but it was totally overshadowed by the Brokenshires' multiple ovens. It's a lesson, as if it were needed, about how news items in the public interest are not always of interest to the public.

By the Tuesday, two days after the *Sunday Times* article, memes were flying thick and fast on Twitter, and James decided to lean into the ludicrous, and increasingly funny, reaction. He tweeted an old picture of him with a Victoria sponge cake with the line: 'Amazing what you can rustle up! Maybe some more hot potatoes next! #TwoOvens'.

With political Twitter going into meltdown, I received a text from a *Mirror* journalist asking a perfectly reasonable question that was nonetheless impossible to answer: could I clarify if the Brokenshires had two ovens or four ovens? I replied that they had 'two, normal double ovens' which was then of course quoted on Twitter as 'a source close to James Brokenshire' 'denying' he owned four ovens.

I think my favourite meme showed the notorious Iraqi 'Information Minister' Muhammad Saeed al-Sahhaf. During the 2003 invasion, he infamously denied that there were any American military in Baghdad, when in fact US tanks were just a few hundred metres away. In the meme, the Iraqi was wearing military fatigues at a press briefing, holding up his hands, with the following words displayed over his photograph: 'There are only two ovens here.'

The journalist Tom Peck wrote: 'There is a chance that James Brokenshire's ovens are being over-analysed, but what cannot be denied is that this is a photograph of a politician, standing in front of four ovens, saying he's got two ovens.' My comment to the *Mirror* was ridiculed by a comedian on Twitter, who wrote: 'A source close to Mr Brokenshire insisted he did not have four ovens, simply "one normal quadruple oven".'

Friends or contacts sometimes asked me to have a cup of tea with students to talk about political or journalistic careers. I brought one very talented young student, Catherine Kennedy, into Parliament, having been asked to speak to her by a mutual friend, the former Deputy Chief Constable of Northern Ireland, Judith Gillespie. Catherine asked a number of highly intelligent and pertinent questions about journalism and what it was like to work in the corridors of power as we sipped Earl Grey tea in Portcullis House, one of the buildings within Parliament. But our discussion was marred slightly by the fact that my phone was red-hot with phone calls from journalists from national newspapers interrupting our chat to ask, as one from *The Independent* did, 'Is it fair to say Mr Brokenshire denies having four ovens?'

Another favourite tweet included a comment on our media handling: 'Political messaging insight here: this is actually perfect for Brokenshire. We're all talking about him, no one actually cares about how many ovens he has (well, no Tory members do anyway) but this is all free publicity and makes him look human. Nine out of ten for technique.' I was very happy to accept that completely unwarranted praise.

And so it went on. YouGov did a poll asking how many ovens the UK public had. Seventy-five per cent of people had one oven, 20 per cent had two, 2 per cent had three, and 1 per cent four or more. One per cent said they didn't have an oven. I did also feel slightly sorry for the 1 per cent of respondents who claimed they didn't know how many ovens they had.

At events that week, journalists started asking other Cabinet ministers including Amber Rudd and Liz Truss how many ovens they owned. Amber, memorably, claimed to have only one, but, given the Brokenshires have one home and she, at that stage, owned at least three, I wasn't hugely amused.

But the most surreal element of all was the tin-hatted tweeter who suggested the ovens speculation might be an example of dog-whistle antisemitism. There was also a reference to a notable interview with Ed Miliband during the 2015 election when he appeared to attempt to hide the fact that his family home had two kitchens. Cathy is not Jewish, but the tweeter ignored this fact, writing: 'The hidden factor in this is that Brokenshire's wife is Jewish and presumably keeps a kosher kitchen – for family if not herself [this is factually incorrect]. "Two ovens" like Ed Miliband's "two kitchens" is a bit of nudge-nudge "by the way, did you know they're Jewish" I suspect.' James and Cathy Brokenshire are Anglicans, but let's not let that get in the way of this bizarre theory.

Then it got even more ridiculous. 'How do we know the cupboards above the four ovens aren't also hidden ovens?' joked one tweeter. At one stage, friends of James and Cathy's in America contacted them to say they had seen it on the news there.

A fun addendum to all of this is that, for my thirty-fifth birthday a few weeks later, James not only made me a delicious chocolate cake in one of the ovens (bottom left, since you ask) but also arranged for a personally signed birthday card from the Prime Minister, accompanied by a beautiful, classically designed edition of *Pride and Prejudice*, which is both Theresa May's and James's favourite book. The Prime Minister wrote: 'Peter, Happy Birthday and thank you for all your hard work. Theresa May.' I was absolutely thrilled. But there was more to come. Cathy also sent a photo featuring each of the oven doors emblazoned with a large poster, making up the four-word, four-door phrase 'Happy / 35th / Birthday / Peter!'

In November 2019, four months after James and I had left MHCLG, the press office held a baking competition. The winning cake had icing decorated with four differently coloured 'ovens'. It was attached to a piece of cardboard with the famous photo of James in front of his own ovens. In addition, the image of James had a speech bubble gently mocking his way of speaking in interviews: 'I am clear that my chocolate orange loaf cake has a real sense of deliciousness!'

I continue to enjoy an excellent friendship with James and Cathy. One SpAd who served in both the Cameron and the May administrations told me her relationship with her minister, while warm, felt more transactional in the end.

'I went around to her house all the time,' the former SpAd explained.

> I had smashed avocado on toast with her kids every morning no matter how many times I told her I don't like avocado. You learn about people's private lives, about their kids, their worries about their children's education. But you are not their friend, and the minute you forget that, to all intents and purposes, you're coming through the servants' quarters, as it were, is the minute you're in trouble because at any given point a SpAd has to take a bullet for their principal. The only exception I have ever seen to that is you and Brokey.

Any good working relationship, no matter how close, can still be tested, although I've never fallen out with James. I think he snapped, was in a bad mood or appeared ratty a maximum of two or three times during the almost three years that I worked with him. Usually, that was just due to extreme fatigue.

During one particularly intense period of our time at the Northern Ireland Office, we had no real alternative but to take a private plane from London City Airport to Belfast. Due to security concerns, for decades the Northern Ireland Secretary had travelled to and from Belfast in a private plane, but in 2010, the decision was made that they could fly commercially. With fewer than five exceptions I can remember, this is what James and Karen did. But on this particular occasion we had to take the private plane, necessitated by two things: the scheduling of tight government votes and the stage of the Northern Ireland talks process that started (and stopped, and started again) when Stormont collapsed in 2017. There we were, sitting in this ridiculous private lounge of London City Airport at about five o'clock in the morning when a familiar face passed us. 'That guy looks a bit like Kevin Spacey,' I quietly said to James. He replied, 'That *is* Kevin Spacey.'

On another occasion, we travelled to and from Belfast in an RAF plane, again due to a completely unavoidable logistical problem about votes and timings. Being served G&Ts by uniformed RAF stewards on planes used by royalty is only slightly less surreal than seeing Kevin Spacey in an exclusive lounge for people who use private planes.

Incidentally, the small plane used weekly by Secretaries of State for Northern Ireland before 2010 had to be for justifiable travel within civil service rules, as is any travel for governmental purposes. Gin and tonic in hand on the RAF royal flight, I'm not sure I could have looked the taxpayer in the eye, but I reflected on one story I was told about Shaun Woodward, one of the Labour Secretaries of State in the late 2000s. Woodward was married to a member of the Sainsbury family, and the joke was that he was so rich that his butler had a butler.

On being told by his civil servants that the use of the private plane was not justified for the journey he wanted to make to Belfast, Woodward simply asked how much the trip would cost – which would have run into five figures. He took out his chequebook and paid for it himself with the stroke of a pen.

Sir Patrick Mayhew, a Conservative Northern Ireland Secretary in the early 1990s, used to take his dog on the flight with him across to Belfast. A BBC journalist friend of mine once went to interview Mayhew at Hillsborough Castle and was standing waiting for the Secretary of State when she felt a cold, wet sensation on her calf – the hound was licking her leg.

A book on Peter Mandelson in 2000 by Donald Macintyre outlined how, when Mandelson was Northern Ireland Secretary, he was speaking to Sinn Féin leader Gerry Adams at Hillsborough when Mandelson's dog, Bobby, came up to the pair with a rubber bullet in his teeth. 'It's my contribution to decommissioning,' Mandelson is reported to have said.

The security around a Home Secretary is huge. Due to the very short period I was in the Home Office, I travelled with Amber Rudd only a few times, but I do recall going to a reception put on by the Foreign Office at the Commonwealth Heads of Government Meeting, which was being held in London. Sitting in the bulletproof, bombproof car, not dissimilar to the one used in the 2018 BBC series *Bodyguard*, with police protection officers in the front, I noticed that a road was being opened for us. A few moments later, we would be introduced to Prince Harry and his then fiancée Meghan Markle. I took a moment and just thought about what was happening to a wee lad from Richhill. The Windrush scandal (which I outline in more detail in Chapter 9) was in full flow at that point, so it wasn't the most relaxing time at work, but there was no doubt it was a tremendous privilege to work for the Home Secretary of the United Kingdom, even very briefly.

One other interesting experience with Amber was discussing women's rights with the former Prime Minister of Australia Julia Gillard in the Home Secretary's office. I found Gillard tremendously warm and friendly. Indeed, when I mentioned a friend, Sarah Wiley, who had worked as a political correspondent in Canberra during Gillard's time as Prime Minister, she sent Sarah her very best regards. Sarah was thrilled. I also told Gillard she was the answer to my favourite pub quiz question: 'Who is the only Prime Minister ever to have been born in Wales?' Most people guess Lloyd George, who was certainly Welsh but was actually born in Manchester. Gillard was born in Barry in Wales, leaving aged four for a new life in Australia.

～

I often put cuttings of the most significant press coverage we received on the wall beside my desk. Some I would rather forget – chief amongst them the outcome of an interview we didn't even do.

One morning in January 2018, my taxi pulled up to the Westminster bureau of the main UK broadcasters at 4 Millbank, as I turned up my collar against the cold. All the breakfast programmes were interviewing James, who was then Housing Secretary – with one notable exception.

James had told me the night before that he just didn't want to do an interview with *Good Morning Britain* if he didn't absolutely have to. And who could blame him? Piers Morgan frequently harangues his guests, asks them all sorts of random questions off the topic they have come to discuss, and rarely, if ever, keeps to the agreed time slot.

Despite having worked for *Good Morning Britain* as a reporter for two years, I had a very mixed experience of the programme as a media SpAd. The producers – my former colleagues – were unfailingly courteous. My chief reaction to them ringing me was generally sympathy – imagine your job is to try to persuade people to be interviewed by Piers Morgan. The programme's senior political producer, Anne Alexander, combines being one of the nicest people in Westminster with doing one of the toughest jobs in broadcasting.

Having worked as a producer with Jeremy Paxman – a very different type of interviewer, but equally feared by politicians – I have a lot of time for and sympathy with Anne. When I worked at *Newsnight*, SpAds would always ask, 'And who is presenting *Newsnight* this evening?' I would always note the slight exhalation of breath at the end of the line when I said, 'It's Gavin Esler tonight.' And so my day would immediately get a lot easier, with the SpAd much more inclined to grant the request with someone less aggressive than Paxman in the presenter's chair.

As the car pulled up outside Millbank, I received a message from Gareth Milner, then one of the tribe of scribes at the media monitoring unit at Conservative Party headquarters. It read simply: 'Piers has just been going for you on GMB, mate. Will send clip.'

I decided not to tell James for the meantime. He needed to concentrate on his media round with about a dozen other broadcast outlets. But I eagerly awaited Gareth sending the clip, wondering what on earth Piers had said.

Hours before, I'd had what I thought was only a minor contretemps with the editor of *Good Morning Britain*, Neil Thompson. He had been my boss when I had worked on the programme. Before emailing Neil, I checked with the No. 10 head of broadcasting, Dylan Sharpe, whether it was OK to exclude *Good Morning Britain* from the interviews. Dylan confirmed that was fine, drawing my attention to Piers's derogatory tweets about then Prime Minister Theresa May after an edition of BBC *Panorama* earlier in the week.

After the media round, back in the office at the Ministry of Housing, Communities and Local Government, I watched the clip of one of Britain's best-known presenters trashing James for four and a half minutes on national breakfast television in all its glory. And I personally was in Piers's sights too.

'Rather comically,' Piers told his viewers, 'Mr Brokenshire is doing every other programme apart from us today, and his SpAd – which are these weird little creatures, special assistants [*sic*] to the ministers, awful little people most of the time – the SpAd's told us the following...'

Piers then read out the email I had sent *Good Morning Britain*'s editor the night before. He adopted a nasal, mocking voice: 'I'm afraid we won't be doing *Good Morning Britain* tomorrow following James's treatment last time ... Piers's tweets following the *Panorama* special on Theresa May, making clear he does not think Theresa May is a leader and that Brexit is "a farce"...'

Susanna Reid chipped in: '...We live in North Korea now, apparently...'

Piers: '...make clear he cannot be relied upon by us to do a fair and balanced interview.'

Then came mocking laughter by both presenters.

Piers continued: 'As if the entire planet doesn't think Brexit is a farce or that your boss isn't a leader! So, Mr Brokenshire, we're all for this, honestly, we're all for you deciding, unilaterally, you're going to ban *Good Morning Britain* from your schedule today. The truth is, you're an unbelievably boring person...'

Susanna: 'Can we not make it so personal?'

Piers: 'I didn't even know we were going to be interviewing you. If I'd known, I'd have cancelled you, and you're now banned from ever appearing on *Good Morning Britain* as long as I'm sitting in this chair, Mr Brokenshire, you jumped up little prima donna. Who *do* you think you are? My message to anybody else in the government is, honestly, if you think we're North Korea and you can only come on if we're going to praise the great leader, Theresa, and say that Brexit's fantastic, if you only want to come on in those circumstances, you're all banned!

'Honestly, Brokenshire, mate, do yourself a favour – get a new SpAd. Sort it out, because this is the most pathetic thing I've ever heard in my entire life. You silly SpAd! Imagine being the parent of a SpAd! "Hello, dear, what's your new job?" [Nasal voice again]: "I'm a SpAd, Mum." "What?" "I'm a SpAd to James Brokenshire..."'

It went on for another full minute.

Towards the end, Piers said, 'We'll come back to Brokenshire throughout the programme. I wonder if his SpAd's watching? I've got the feeling somebody will be telling the SpAd about now. Can we find out who the SpAd is? Who is James Brokenshire's SpAd—'

'OK, that's enough,' Susanna interjected, knowing that Piers knew full well who I was.

Piers continued: '…who wants us to treat him like Kim Jong-un?'

As television, it was entertaining at least. As a way to treat a government minister and his SpAd, it wasn't brilliant.

I was pretty calm. I took it in my stride and sent the clip to a few friends – I remember one said I had 'arrived' as I had clearly enraged Piers so much. Downing Street, on the other hand, was furious.

Call me old-fashioned, but strongly criticising the Prime Minister on Twitter and telling everyone that her main policy is a farce doesn't strike me as the most impartial journalism as outlined in the Ofcom code, to which UK broadcasters must adhere. All any special adviser should ever want from broadcasters is a fair, balanced and impartial interview. Most of them did that for James, most of the time. I'm not entirely sure how that made us North Korea, but there you are.

Piers is Piers. If you watch *Good Morning Britain*, it seems most days he says something is the most outrageous thing he has ever seen or the most unbelievable thing he has ever heard – although I'm not sure he ever banned a Cabinet minister from the programme. I have bumped into him since that incident and there is absolutely no animosity from either side. He plays a role on telly, the programme gets the ratings and the clips on social media, and the ITV executives are happy.

But I'm afraid I don't feel the same way about Neil Thompson, the editor of the programme, who had decided my email should be read out on air. I had texted him some weeks previously about what I thought was a needlessly aggressive interview with James by another presenter, Ranvir Singh, and Neil sent a long text back disagreeing in strong terms. We agreed to disagree. I thought that was it, but he was clearly still annoyed, and it flared up again with my subsequent email about the interview with Piers and Susanna. Neil does an excellent job editing *Good Morning Britain* and I liked him when he was my boss, but I fear we are not now destined to go on a spa weekend together any time soon.

James Brokenshire was, as usual, cool as a cucumber. Back in his office, I reassured him that while Piers had called him a prima donna, 'to me, James, you've always been very much *post*-Madonna'.

Downing Street also backed me to the hilt. In fact, No. 10 director of communications Robbie Gibb had been one of my first line managers when I worked at *Newsnight* some years before, so we have known each other for a long time. He had been an excellent boss, and especially kind when I was seriously ill at one point, in hospital with salmonella. After the Piers incident, he rang me in solidarity.

Later, in Robbie's office in Downing Street, he decided to complain to ITV. I mumbled, 'Well, I suppose you could email Neil Thompson,' but Robbie wasn't really listening, shouting down the office, 'Get me the chairman of ITV on the phone.'

I have no idea where the complaint went, but rather amusingly we simply bit the bullet when James was asked onto *Good Morning Britain* just a few weeks later. Piers went ahead and interviewed the Cabinet minister he had 'banned from ever appearing on *Good Morning Britain* as long as I'm sitting in this chair'. The exchanges were fine, and fair – though it badly overran, of course.

A week afterwards, I was on the terrace of the House of Commons having a drink and encountered Dylan Sharpe, the Downing Street broadcasting honcho. He looked as if he hadn't slept for about six months, and perhaps he hadn't. 'We're still annoyed with *Good Morning Britain*, Peter, and you never have to do them again if you don't want to,' he told me. Now, it's impossible for any SpAd, even the No. 10 head of broadcasting, to be aware of every single interview every single minister does, so he was surprised when I said, 'Yeah, we just ignored the alleged "ban" and James did it last week.' Dylan looked totally shocked: 'Really? With Piers!?' 'Yeah,' I said, shrugging.

Suddenly, Dylan looked as if I'd just announced some life-changing news. 'But, Peter, you know what this means? We've won!' he exclaimed. 'We've won!'

I didn't quite see it in those terms, but if Dylan was happy, so was I. And James himself has never actually watched the clip of Piers's rant.

～

At Housing, James was totally on top of his brief, but this is not always the case with Cabinet ministers. The smooth running of the minister–SpAd relationship often depends on the raw material. At the time of writing, there have been six male Lord Chancellors since 2010, and I'll let you guess which one asked the following question of a crowded room of advisers and civil servants.

The meeting was an important one, dealing with a major issue for the tens of thousands of prisoners of whom the Cabinet minister was in charge: their sexual health while incarcerated.

The transmission of sexual infections, contraception and testing were on the agenda. The Lord Chancellor had done his reading, and his SpAds and civil servants were poised to discuss the issue affecting the predominantly male prison estate.

Yet he opened with an intriguing question: 'I've done all the reading and I think I understand the issue,' he told the room. 'But one thing I just don't get: how *are* these prisoners getting the women in?'

Later in the same meeting, he asked his special adviser to explain what a dental dam is and how it is used; a tricky enough discussion at the best of times, never mind with the Lord Chancellor of the United Kingdom, watched by over a dozen senior officials. I later related this story to my 62-year-old co-SpAd at MHCLG, Lee Scott, who blankly looked at me and asked, 'Peter, what *is* a dental dam?' I asked him to google it, rather than face the prospect myself of explaining the excruciating details.

The main things that went wrong during my time as a special adviser were, of course, the many problems we had with Brexit and the collapse of Stormont, which James and then Karen did so much to attempt to resurrect. Long, interminable meetings with Northern Ireland politicians ensued, some of which I was part of and some not, with Jonathan Caine being the lead SpAd in the vast majority of them. Jonathan has spent more time than any Conservative alive negotiating with Sinn Féin, so he knows them well.

It was slightly weird sitting opposite Gerry Adams and, until his death in March 2017, Martin McGuinness at a negotiating table. They were the terrorist bogeymen of my youth, so to shake hands with them at the start and end of meetings was an odd experience, though it swiftly became normal. McGuinness, in particular, had successfully cultivated a very charming and avuncular persona, while being underneath it a hard and canny negotiator who conceded nothing.

One of the few perks of these talks was the outstanding food. We were given excellent packed lunches with beautiful sandwiches, and there was soup, scones on tap and plenty of Diet Coke and Earl Grey tea to keep us sated. When you start in politics in Belfast, you are warned of the very real prospect of putting on what is called 'the Stormont stone', given how much food is in meetings due to the famous Ulster hospitality and determination that no cup of tea will be drunk without an accompanying stodgy, sugary accompaniment. I was certainly a victim of it, and my Stormont stone is perhaps the most enduring legacy of my time at the Northern Ireland Office.

These Stormont negotiations also took place over several weekends, although for religious reasons the DUP refused to negotiate on a Sunday. One Sunday, with no talks going on but James stuck in Hillsborough on his own, I invited him to have lunch with my parents at our family home thirty miles from Belfast. My mother was in quite a tizzy that the Secretary of State was coming, even though she had met James once before in London, but I assured her that he was very undemanding and to go to no trouble. She did, of course, bringing out the good china. At one point she said, 'It's very kind of you to come and have lunch with us.'

'To be honest, Sandra,' he replied, 'I'd just have been on my own rattling around in that big castle.'

Progress was definitely made during those talks, and, as Karen's successor Julian Smith confirmed, the foundations were laid for the eventual resurrection of devolved government in Northern Ireland in 2020. A cynic would say that the bad result of the 2019 general election for both the DUP and, to a lesser degree, Sinn Féin, was a deciding factor, forcing them back to Stormont. I was a tad frustrated that the eventual agreement they signed didn't look too different from what we were negotiating a year earlier, but Julian's team did brilliantly and I take nothing away from their achievement.

I generally got on with politicians and advisers from across the political spectrum, and remember one particularly jolly dinner sitting beside Mark Mullan, a Sinn Féin SpAd, at the British–Irish Council in Cardiff. I'm not the most tribal Tory and that probably comes from broadcast journalism, where your job is to interview people from all sorts of backgrounds, never allowing yourself to put any personal view into a report, while trying to understand everyone's perspective. One friend once accused me of never having an opinion on anything, which I don't think was true, but I certainly saw sides of arguments others didn't. I went from a job which necessitated having no opinion to a role where it was my job as special adviser to have an opinion on every conceivable issue. I had interviewed Sinn Féin and Labour politicians – the parties with which I personally disagree most – many times. Indeed, most of my job as *Newsnight* political producer was to schmooze MPs right across the House of Commons. I remember having an introductory coffee in 2010 with Tristram Hunt, an MP for Stoke. I asked him what he saw as his main role as a constituency MP. He answered, 'My main role as constituency MP for Stoke, Peter, is to try to convince people that Stoke isn't a shithole.' At least he was honest.

Some years later, I related this story to the then MP for Foyle in the north-west of Northern Ireland, Sinn Féin's Elisha McCallion. She was astonished, but confessed she loved the name Tristram, and had she had the chance she would have given the name to one of her three sons. 'Er... Tristram McCallion, in Derry, the son of a Sinn Féin MP?', I remember thinking at the time. I was unsure how such a posh English name would go down in the heavily Irish Republican area. 'So did you call your son Tristram, then?' I asked her. 'No,' she replied. 'They're called Dáithí, Malachi and Fiachra.'

Speaking of people from Derry, or Derry-Londonderry as it is often ludicrously called in Northern Ireland in a vain attempt not to offend anyone, it was one of the city's sons who once saved my bacon over an issue with nomenclature. One of James's opposite numbers in Labour, the shadow Northern Ireland Secretary for a time, was an MP called Dave Anderson. I got a text one evening from someone in the Northern Ireland Office telling me that Dave Anderson had died. That tragic event would have necessitated a statement from James as Secretary of State, paying tribute to Dave. Luckily, Dave Anderson's then political adviser – my own opposite number – was a Derryman called Ruaidhri O'Donnell with whom I would occasionally go for a pint. I rang Ruaidhri with my condolences, but he hadn't heard a thing. A thought crossed my mind: had I just rung Ruaidhri to inform him of the passing of his boss and, as a result, his own unemployment? And was I definitely acting on correct information? I asked him to check out what I had told him. A tense few minutes later he rang me back, telling me breezily, 'Dave's alive and well and playing with his dog.' It turned out that it was in fact a different Dave Anderson who had sadly died, a man who was the much-loved household manager of Hillsborough Castle for a quarter of a century and of whom colleagues in the Northern Ireland Office assumed I would have been aware.

~

Regarding Brexit, I've written in Chapter 9 about the gargantuan effort by James and Jonathan Caine to keep the DUP on board during a crisis in December 2017. It was in late March 2019 that the third meaningful vote was held in Parliament on the Withdrawal Bill.

We knew exactly which way it was going to go – yet another big loss for the government – and James was already lined up to do a pre-recorded interview with *Newsnight* shortly after the vote, at No. 10's request. Not only was he reliably on message and a strong media performer, but by that stage Theresa May was running out of allies who would put forward the government line.

The stage was set, with the *Newsnight* cameraman and producer waiting in Parliament's central lobby, just a few minutes' walk from James's parliamentary office. But we were half an hour late because, quite simply, we didn't know what James was going to say.

Before a minister does a broadcast interview, they get a briefing on what questions they might be asked. Media SpAds frequently get involved in this, but there is also a dedicated unit within No. 10 made up of SpAds whose job it is to give ministers across government the lines to take on issues which might arise. Sometimes, these briefings can go on for up to an hour, for example in preparation for a programme such as *Question Time*, while for other appearances they might last only a few minutes. We usually did a very short briefing at 6.45 a.m. before a morning round at Millbank to 'top up' the minister regarding what had occurred overnight. The call is set up through the No. 10 switchboard, with the weary briefer, still pyjama-clad, having spoken to us late the previous evening as well.

This briefing unit of bright young SpAds keeps on top of all the issues and the government's position on them, with ministers frequently asking the briefers on the phone or in person, 'What is the line to take on this?' Indeed, when Michael Gove admitted in June 2019 to having taken cocaine on several occasions, I had to have the slightly awkward discussion with James about whether he had ever used illegal drugs. Unsurprisingly, he has never done so. 'So the line to take', I suggested, 'is that you didn't take any lines.'

That March evening on which the third meaningful vote on Brexit was lost, James was up to be the government voice. For briefing, he turned directly to Robbie Gibb, the Downing Street director of communications. This was a sign of the importance of the moment and how much pressure the government was under to find a way out of the mess. On the government's message, the only person higher up the food chain than Robbie was Theresa May herself.

With the interview just minutes away, James asked Robbie a perfectly reasonable question. Given that the mantra had been 'no deal is better than a bad deal' and that the deal had been rejected by Parliament, was the policy of Her Majesty's government, at that moment, that a no-deal Brexit was the preferred outcome?

Robbie and James had an animated but friendly discussion, while the rest of us sat in the Secretary of State's office wondering what on earth he was going to say on *Newsnight*. I WhatsApped the *Newsnight* producer waiting patiently in Central Lobby, stonewalling. We knew we had now been keeping the presenter Kirsty Wark, the producers, camera crews and editors of *Newsnight* back in New Broadcasting House waiting for nearly half an hour. I emailed them later to apologise.

The phone call was nearly at an end, but we were none the wiser as to what James was going to say. Again, James, as the main May administration spokesperson on Brexit that evening, asked Robbie a simple question: 'If I am asked whether the Brexit policy of the government is now no deal, what is the line to take? What is my response?'

A tense pause ensued, before Robbie uttered the immortal line: 'James, I'll ring you back.'

8

Truly, SpAdly, Deeply:
Elections

W alking down Whitehall back to the Northern Ireland Office after an upbeat meeting in Downing Street with chief of staff Gavin Barwell, I felt pretty positive about what lay ahead. Granted, it did involve me resigning my post as special adviser, but that was OK, because we were riding high in the polls and were going to win a great majority in the 2017 election, returning to government in a blaze of glory. Right?

Theresa May had just told the British people they were going to the polls again. She had been Prime Minister for less than a year and felt the time had come to solidify and increase her mandate, having governed with just a small Conservative majority inherited from her predecessor, David Cameron.

I had covered many elections as a journalist and loved the drama of the contest, as well as the sheer fun of wolfing down your third Snickers while balancing your iPad on your knee in some random leisure centre so you can monitor Sky News while awaiting the results.

Being on the inside couldn't be that different, I thought. Surely this was one of the most exciting tasks for any SpAd? I was eager to get started to fight for the future of the May administration, headed by a Prime Minister in whom I strongly believed.

As I ambled along, I sidled up to long-serving SpAd Amy Fisher, then the most senior political adviser at the Home Office. 'Are you excited, Amy?' I asked the veteran of a number of election campaigns. 'Elections are fucking awful, Peter,' she replied. 'They're horrible. Long hours, no rest, crap food, crap hotels and you're never sure of the result until the last possible moment.'

'Surely it can't be that bad, Amy?' I asked, crestfallen. 'It's worse,' she said. 'I can't stand them.'

What I learned rapidly is that being a journalist covering an election is a bit like visiting Disney World. Being a SpAd volunteering on an election is a bit like *working* at Disney World.

There are odd employment rules when SpAds resign for elections, and the money side is a bit complicated. If you've been a SpAd for up to two years, you get a redundancy payment of three months' salary. Up to three years and it's four months'; four years and it's five months', up to a maximum of six months' salary. You then live on this money throughout the election campaign – the party doesn't pay you a bean as you're technically a volunteer. If you get rehired after the election into any SpAdding role, you pay back the Cabinet Office the extra money over and above your pro rata salary for the election period.

It's quite weird suddenly to get this large lump of cash into your bank account and the thing you want to do most is to win the election so you'll have to pay most of it back. History does not record the name of the SpAd who bet a substantial chunk of their payment on a large Conservative majority being achieved in the 2017 election. Presumably, he or she was condemned to eating beans out of a tin with a cocktail stick for some time afterwards.

I have an almost pathological hatred of owing anyone even small amounts of money, and within fifteen minutes of the bank details coming through to my NIO email following the 2017 election, I had transferred the full whack of what I owed back to the Cabinet Office. Jonathan Caine, my co-SpAd, took a rather more leisurely approach. He waited until several reminders had been sent out by the Cabinet Office, but eventually sent them a cheque for the full amount. The cheque was a wonderfully retro way of transferring money, and very Jonathan.

He and I stayed at the Northern Ireland Office for a few days following Theresa May's election announcement. He would soon go into Conservative Campaign Headquarters (CCHQ) on Matthew Parker Street in Westminster to write the party's Northern Ireland manifesto. There was a strange dynamic between the party in London and the party in Northern Ireland. The Northern Ireland Conservatives comprise just a few hundred activists, many of them extremely dedicated, good people, but they have sadly not enjoyed any electoral success recently.

There is currently not a single Conservative elected in Northern Ireland at the time of writing in early 2020, not even on a local council. Nonetheless, the party fielded candidates in a number of constituencies in 2017. Labour, in contrast, actually bans candidates from standing in Northern Ireland, something I have always thought is a disgrace. Jonathan, as the man with more experience of Conservative policy on Northern Ireland than any living person, wrote both the relevant part of the main UK manifesto and a separate document specifically for Northern Ireland voters. I did harbour doubts that many people actually read the latter manifesto. But there is no doubt it was a useful thing to have in our back pockets to show Northern Ireland Office officials, to make clear the terms on which we had been elected.

I hadn't been a paid-up member of the Conservative Party before becoming a SpAd and took impartiality – a rule of broadcast journalism under the Ofcom code – very seriously; more seriously, I would argue, than some of my colleagues over the years. Indeed, I hadn't been a member of any campaigning or political organisation before, unless you count Cats Protection and the MS Society. Part of that was having worked in Northern Ireland, where the political class – and public – are very quick to label journalists as being sympathetic to one 'side' or the other, and I was determined not to fall into that trap.

The Conservatives usually don't stand in my home constituency in Northern Ireland, where I have almost always voted. My friend Danny Kennedy of the Ulster Unionists was our local candidate and Northern Ireland Assembly member for many years, so my vote went to him the vast majority of the time. The exception was when things were very close for a while between the moderate nationalists, the SDLP, and Sinn Féin, so I voted for the SDLP, even though I am a unionist.

Just days before I became a SpAd, I had paid my £25 online and become a member of the Conservative Party. Since that moment I have always voted in my London constituency, and, of course, always Conservative.

SpAds, with very few exceptions, formally resign their role when elections are called, as I did twice, in 2017 and 2019. While in Belfast at Stormont House with James just a few days before Parliament was dissolved in 2017, Downing Street chief of staff Fiona Hill texted me with an instruction to join, as a volunteer, the press team at CCHQ, so I flew back to London and started there about a month before polling day.

My job was to write press releases, pen articles in the Prime Minister's name for a variety of publications, and work at events where the Prime Minister campaigned. I was also chosen to head up the party's engagement with black, Asian and minority ethnic (BAME) media – 'Who better than a middle-class white man to do that?' I asked rhetorically when given the role. I promptly set up a WhatsApp group for others involved with this task, entitled 'BAME: I'm gonna live forever'.

My initial entrance to CCHQ did not go brilliantly. When I asked about the possibility of getting a building pass when I was signing in, so I didn't have to be buzzed in and out every time I popped out for a sandwich, the slightly overzealous security guard clearly wasn't keen on the idea. 'There seem to be a lot of new people, all asking for building passes at the minute,' he grumbled, seemingly oblivious to the fact that the governing party might be increasing its headcount in its headquarters now an election was on. It took a few days and a lot of pushing to actually get the cherished pass.

Luckily, I had a full-sized desk to myself. Many others were not so lucky. With many of the SpAds coming in from different departments and all sorts of volunteers joining the main CCHQ operation, often one normal-sized desk would be shared by two people, as there were just so many bodies in Matthew Parker Street. Thankfully, we were on the ground floor, with many others exiled to the basement. I sat at an all-male bank of six desks opposite Robert Oxley, who was in charge of communications for the election. Robert would later go on to be Downing Street press secretary under Boris Johnson. It was a cramped, hot and uncomfortable place to work, and became a tad pongy after a week or two.

Another of my tasks was to be complainer-in-chief to the BBC about their news website, which frequently annoyed Fiona Hill and her co-chief of staff Nick Timothy, who by this stage had left Downing Street to work at CCHQ. They had good reason to monitor the website closely – it is the main source of news for hundreds of thousands of people every day, and so much more influential than the front page of any newspaper. The diplomatic difficulty was that the editor of the BBC website at that time was a guy called Nick Sutton, who is a friend and had been one of my superiors at *Newsnight*.

Throughout the election, Nick Sutton and I were to have numerous torturous, ultimately mostly pointless, conversations about a photo or a paragraph in the top article on the website that day. It was important to monitor and gently complain where necessary, but I have never felt entirely comfortable arguing with journalists who are essentially doing their job, rather than having an anti-Tory agenda. I have known Nick Sutton for nearly fifteen years and still have absolutely no idea how he votes, and nor have I ever heard him say anything even vaguely hostile to any political party that has not been clear, impartial analysis.

I did once manage to get a particularly unflattering photo of Theresa May changed, but most of the time the exchanges were circular. Nick is a quiet, softly spoken man, but he has a core of steel, and he and I both knew I was on a fool's errand. Very little the BBC did was not fair, balanced and impartial in the website content I saw. More often than not, I was chatting to him on the phone as Fiona or, more often, Nick Timothy was standing silently behind me. Fiona would look on disapprovingly and Nick Timothy would peer over his huge beard, monitoring the call.

During that time, Fiona once rang *Good Morning Britain* while they were on air to bollock them about a line of questioning, expecting the poor producer on the end of the line to somehow have some magical power to stop Piers Morgan saying whatever he was spouting. Alas, I had to calm the producer down after the conversation, and I'm afraid she didn't know who Fiona was or the clout she wielded, so the exercise was a tad pointless. From the producer's initial perspective, it was just some random woman barking down the phone at her.

Ghost-writing articles for friendly editors to use was another function of our unit, but I had my doubts as to the effectiveness of the media strategy. I took great delight in writing one particularly excoriating article about how Jeremy Corbyn was going to turn the UK into a socialist wasteland like Venezuela, but I had no conviction that it would make the slightest difference to the election result.

At one stage I stupidly managed to put out a press release spelling the surname of the then chairman of the Conservative Party, Sir Patrick McLoughlin, as 'McLaughlin'. Journalists' responses were swift and withering. 'How do you expect to win an election when you can't spell the name of the chairman of your own party?' one asked. I apologised immediately to Sir Patrick, who was very gracious and said it happens all the time. Quietly, as others fussed over my mistake, the Dean of SpAds Sheridan Westlake showed the class for which he is so admired throughout Westminster. An email arrived in which he outlined the top ten screw-ups he had seen in his fifteen years plus in politics. The political adviser who, in 2007, had sent the entire list of confidential conference announcements to what he thought was Matt Hancock's email address but which turned out to be that of the Lib Dem MP Mike Hancock. The Conservative Party press officer who sent his expenses claim to all the political journalists based in Westminster. The person who, during the Crewe and Nantwich by-election in 2008, managed to send the electoral roll for the entire constituency to a radio station on the Isle of Man. The highly amusing list was a thoughtful and very funny gesture from Sheridan to a much less experienced SpAd.

One of the least pleasant duties in the office was to brief the top brass at a 6 a.m. meeting about what had 'cut through' overnight in the press. They would have seen the newspaper front pages and watched the BBC *News at Ten* and received the many digests pumped out at all hours of the day and night by the media monitoring unit (MMU), a group of four people in CCHQ, to hundreds of people on the payroll. These digests keep everyone from the Prime Minister downwards informed as to what is being broadcast, and MMU also attach a judgement on the coverage as to whether they believe it to be fair. The MMU has a key role in transcribing interviews, too, and I was told that this tiny unit took down and emailed out nearly 1 million words over the course of the 2017 election. They are a truly under-appreciated resource in CCHQ.

But the question for the leaders of the campaign at the start of the day was what was gaining traction in the media, and the press SpAd on rota – occasionally me – had to work out what was cutting through. Either in the Thatcher Boardroom at CCHQ or on a conference call were Fiona Hill, Nick Timothy, campaign guru Sir Lynton Crosby,

Lynton's right-hand man Isaac Levido (who later ran the 2019 campaign) and a few others.

The on-duty press SpAd joined only the start of the meeting and spoke briefly. It was intimidating at first, and I am absolutely not a morning person so was generally still half-asleep, but I soon got the hang of it. In addition, we often sent out a short email summary, and it was quite weird to think the Prime Minister was reading what I had written, her personal email address being one of those on the long list of recipients of those morning emails.

The Australian election guru nicknamed the Wizard of Oz, Sir Lynton Crosby, was one of the main leaders of the campaign. As a foot soldier, I only interacted very occasionally with him, although he did ask my view on the campaign press material on Jeremy Corbyn's historical links to Irish Republicanism. The typical way these stories were given to the media was that research was done on an attack story, providing plenty of information and what are called source quotes, to make the task of writing it up as easy as possible for the journalist. It was usually given to a friendly publication which would endorse the Conservative Party nearer the election.

Typically, a senior member of the team would put together an excoriating quote about how awful Corbyn was. This was signed off before being given to the reporter, who would quote 'a senior Conservative source', relevant spokesperson or sometimes even a Cabinet minister, depending on the story.

As well as a coherent strategy to win the 2017 election, CCHQ also lacked sufficient toilets. Almost every time I went to the CCHQ loos there was a wait, and sometimes a queue, so occasionally I nipped into the single-stall ladies' and used that. I got away with it almost all the time, but on one occasion I met Lynton coming out of the gents' at exactly the moment I exited the ladies'. 'You're not a girl!' he exclaimed in his Australian drawl, and he was right. 'Maybe I identify as a woman, Lynton,' I countered. 'And anyway, my bladder was at DefCon 3.' He was unimpressed.

Being in such close quarters to your colleagues did not just mean queues for the gents' (or, occasionally, the ladies') but when food was brought in for those working in the evening, the strong smell of lasagne, curry or other glutinous fare could be smelt throughout the ground floor. Speaking of aromas, one worker on that election also had a particularly strong reaction around Fiona Hill – her perfume brought this staffer out in hives, so she had to retreat from the chief of staff every time Fiona came near. The volunteer never felt as if she could explain to Fiona the reason she kept stepping away.

The timing of the food was a matter of contention too. Having been up since 5 a.m. to do the morning briefing, I always looked forward to the 7.30 a.m. breakfast. However, there was one extremely pedantic worker at CCHQ who was insistent that it was not OK to pour yourself a bowl of cornflakes or push some bread down in the toaster at 7.27 a.m. – no, it had to be 7.30 a.m. So you had the ludicrous spectacle of weary SpAds and other election volunteers – some who had just come from very important jobs in government in departments with multi-billion-pound budgets – standing in an early morning queue in the basement of CCHQ being told they had to wait another three minutes until the milk could be produced.

There was huge ambiguity as to who was actually in charge of the 2017 campaign, and when it all eventually went horribly wrong there was a lot of finger-pointing. Fiona and Nick certainly had some responsibility to take, especially for the disastrous policy on social care, which quickly became known as the dementia tax. Both fell on their swords immediately following the result – but they were not the only people to blame for the catastrophe that was both the campaign and the outcome. The key role of Ben Gummer as co-author of the 2017 manifesto alongside Nick is rarely mentioned, unfairly I think. In the fallout that followed, I was sad to see such deeply personal and critical things written about Fiona in particular. Aside from the fact that I will always be grateful to her for bringing me into SpAdding and changing my life, the level of personal vitriol did seem excessive at times.

In 2019, it was entirely clear that bearded Antipodean Svengali Isaac Levido was in charge, but in 2017 I don't think anyone knew who was actually running the show. Being so far removed from the top of the campaign, I didn't feel it was my place to ask. Lynton, Nick and Fiona were certainly the three people I *felt* were in charge, but the lack of a clear hierarchy was just one problem. Another was the much-mocked campaign slogan. Two years later, the brilliant, simple phrase 'Get Brexit Done' was something almost anyone could have said – and indeed did say – in the normal flow of conversation down the boozer. But show me the person who has ever, in the history of humanity, said to their mates in the pub, 'Do you know what, I really think we need strong and stable leadership in the national interest.' I am not an expert, but I do know that any campaign slogan has to be memorable and resemble something people might actually say. The 2017 campaign slogan was far from that.

A major part of my job at that time – perhaps even half of it – was assisting the party and the media at campaign activities around the UK. There is an excellent team of operations people, whose job it is to ensure every event attended by senior politicians goes smoothly. Red flags include signs reading 'EXIT' above politicians' heads as they address the assembled masses, or any potential problem with protesters. Every step the Prime Minister takes is planned, camera angles checked, checked and checked again, with even a little piece of black tape stuck to the floor a few feet from the camera to tell Theresa May where to stand while she is being interviewed by a reporter for the evening news. The logistics of parking spaces for satellite trucks, how long cables from those trucks are and whether they can reach the place where the Prime Minister is speaking, and how many journalists are going to be allowed into the building all have to be planned. The ops team and press team basically take over whatever venue the Prime Minister may be visiting for at least a few hours and often longer. Days of preparation can go into a twenty-minute prime ministerial visit.

I remember one particular firm in the west of England which had agreed to Theresa May visiting its factory. They were very kind and accommodating but seemed overwhelmed by the large number of people who arrived about three hours before the Prime Minister herself. As usual, we breezed in making all sorts of requests to move equipment, pre-interview people who would be speaking to the Prime Minister to make sure we knew what they were going to talk about with her, walk through exactly where May would go and even check there was a supply of the correct tea bags in case she wanted a cup of tea (Earl Grey, small amount of milk, no sugar, since you ask).

This was to say nothing of the process of bringing in the small army of cameramen and women, sound personnel, journalists and engineers who were descending on their factory, sometimes with a number of names on the list changed or added at the last minute. I did feel slightly sorry for those businesses. But they did eventually get the resulting photographs and good publicity that came with a visit from the Prime Minister, which I hope made up for the disruption.

Escorting May to interviews was occasionally part of my job. For the first time I was actually having quite a lot of face time with the Prime Minister of the United Kingdom. I found her very polite, warm and appreciative of everyone's efforts, and she made time for party volunteers especially.

The election date in 2017 was Thursday 8 June, and almost exactly a week beforehand it was my thirty-third birthday. Walking the Prime Minister to a BBC interview, we were chatting, as usual, about who the reporter was and what she was likely to be asked. Despite everything else going on and the thousands of things on her plate that day, she said, 'Oh, Peter, someone told me it was your birthday. Happy birthday!' 'Thank you, Prime Minister,' I replied, 'that means a lot.' 'I'm sure you didn't expect to be spending it in a conference centre in Derby with me!' she continued. 'No, Prime Minister,' I replied. 'I was meant to be in the south of France having a nice glass of wine with some friends at this exact moment and then YOU ruined it.' Thankfully, she burst out laughing.

It was a fun moment with a lovely woman, a true public servant and someone who I believe was an excellent Prime Minister despite very trying circumstances. And I strongly suspect my friend Liz Sanderson, also at the event that day, tipped her off before this special birthday moment.

I also got to know many of my fellow SpAds much better during this time. Seeing how they operated both in the office and in the field was a great education about how to be a good SpAd (or not, as was sometimes the case). I lost count of the number of trains, planes and taxis during that short space of time, as well as the number of insalubrious hotels. One particularly fun visit was to Edinburgh; I have fond memories of a lovely evening tucking into haggis, neeps and tatties at a hilltop restaurant as the sun went down the night before the launch of the Conservatives' manifesto for Scotland.

Another campaign visit took us to Northern Ireland's main agricultural event, the Balmoral Show, at a venue outside Belfast on the old site of the infamous Maze Prison. As the SpAd who knew the Northern Ireland media best, I was heavily involved. James Brokenshire as Northern Ireland Secretary was there too, and he and Theresa May were mobbed as they walked through the tented stands on a gloriously sunny day, sampling the fine fare Northern Ireland had to offer. James even proved adept at cooking, donning an apron at one of the stands and preparing some tasty Ulster fish as people crowded to watch him in action.

At one stage, May met and had her photograph taken with all the Conservative candidates in Northern Ireland, none of whom had any chance of winning a Westminster seat, sadly. Farming is a significant industry in Northern Ireland, and many local politicians go to the Balmoral Show, so Arlene Foster, the leader of the DUP, heard the PM was also attending that day and came up to say hello. Later, we were accused of stage managing the meeting, but that was not so. Indeed, a member of the Northern Ireland Conservatives even alleged to a Belfast newspaper that party candidates who were there were instructed to take off their rosettes so as not to offend the DUP. The problem for that member was that he was not actually there. The party later suspended him for six months as a result.

At one stage, just in advance of some planned media interviews, someone realised no private briefing space had been set aside for the Prime Minister to go over what might be asked, something that is done before every interview. Quick as a flash, Home Office SpAd Mo Hussein convinced a stallholder in one of the gazebos to allow us to brief the PM in a tiny area where stock was stored. It was a tad surreal going through the lines on Northern Ireland and Brexit with the Prime Minister of the United Kingdom as she sat on a plastic chair surrounded by boxes containing hundreds of bags of cheese and onion crisps. But in the interviews with the Northern Ireland media she was word-perfect and we breathed a sigh of relief afterwards.

I was used to travelling with James and his protection officers, but with the Prime Minister it is a more elaborate affair. There is a long convoy of numerous vehicles, what the Americans call a motorcade. The Northern Ireland visit was the first time I had travelled with police motorcycle outriders and their flashing blue lights, and it really was quite cool as they sped alongside us. The Prime Minister was only in Northern Ireland for a few hours, but I will remember that bright, brilliant day for a lifetime.

~

Former Prime Minister Tony Blair wrote in his autobiography, 'The single hardest thing for a practising politician to understand is that most people, most of the time, don't give politics a first thought all day long,' and this excellent analysis is most strongly felt by SpAds within an election campaign. The fight does seem to drag on interminably – the 2017 campaign was fifty-one days long, compared to twenty-one days in February 1974 – although I've found that a sort of switch is flicked in the public consciousness in the final week. People not usually very interested in politics seem finally to focus just before polling day. A number of more left-wing friends, many of whom had never voted Conservative, would ask me in 2017 whether Jeremy Corbyn would really be that bad as Prime Minister. My answer at that stage was always the same, especially as there had been a number of recent terrorist attacks in London: 'OK, so imagine there's another terror attack. Who do you want in Cobra as Home Secretary making decisions? Amber Rudd or Diane Abbott?' That soon shut them up.

My hero of that election was Gareth Milner, one of the scribes at the media monitoring unit. More often than not, I would WhatsApp Gareth with something like: 'James did an interview with *Channel 4 News* and I was wondering if I could get a five-minute section transcribed? No rush at all.' Gareth was frequently on the early morning shift, meaning he'd been up since 5 a.m. But even if I sent Gareth the message late at night not expecting a reply for hours, the transcription would be in my inbox within thirty minutes, without fail. Gareth had been a soldier working in Army intelligence before he joined CCHQ, and he did his work with military precision and huge commitment.

He had quite a memorable week just before the election. On Tuesday 30 May, someone from Diane Abbott's office managed to email a document to the wrong person in Parliament, and that document eventually made its way to Gareth, a man with great political nous who knows an opportunity for an attack story when he sees one. Those instincts would later see him promoted to SpAd to Secretary of State Steve Barclay at the Department for Exiting the EU. Indeed, I joked with Gareth when he was a SpAd that his chat-up line should be:

'Hi, I'm Gareth from DExEU. Care to leave the single market before Britain does?'

Abbott's document was on Labour's secret plans to bring back a discontinued visa, allowing many more unskilled immigrants to the UK. This damaging story for Labour was of course given to the press by CCHQ without delay, resulting in three front-page stories the following morning in the *Daily Mail*, *Daily Express* and the *Daily Telegraph*, all key newspapers for the Conservatives in an election. It was a nice birthday present for Gareth, who turned thirty-two on the Wednesday of that remarkable week. A further splash generated from the Abbott document followed the next day.

But it is Friday 2 June 2017 that will be remembered in the Milner household for many years. Because it was not only the day Gareth's younger brother Richard got married but the occasion on which Gareth's place in CCHQ's firmament was secured. And it happened without Gareth even being on duty in party headquarters, as he was in the north of England at the wedding.

A tad worse for wear after the festivities, Gareth boarded a train at Newcastle, bound for London King's Cross. By a complete coincidence, when the train stopped at York a very important man boarded the train and sat a few seats away from Gareth, settling himself and drinking a glass of white wine. It was Corbyn's right-hand man, Seumas Milne.

At the time, Labour was under pressure over Corbyn's opposition to nuclear weapons. In his drunken daze following the wedding, Gareth became vaguely aware of Milne, who was sitting in front of him speaking on his phone. Milne was speaking to someone called 'Ed' and then another person called 'Jeremy'. These turned out to be

Ed Miliband, who was preparing for an interview on the Radio 4 *Today* programme the next morning, and Jeremy Corbyn.

Fumbling with his phone, Gareth messaged another Conservative stalwart, the man they call N – Richard N. Jackson, head of CCHQ operations. The use of his middle initial is not because he is another intelligence operative; rather, those in Westminster use it to distinguish Richard N. Jackson from another Richard Jackson, nicknamed 'Tricky', who was head of No. 10 operations. For a time, N and Tricky worked together, so both the head of No. 10 operations and his deputy were called Richard Jackson. There was, for a time, a third Richard Jackson working on operations for the Conservative Party, so it was even more confusing.

Back to the train. Utilising some of his military skills gained during two tours of Afghanistan, Gareth surreptitiously took a picture of Milne, sending it to N for a second opinion. N concurred – it was Milne. So Gareth started secretly recording the conversation; the former Army spy hadn't lost his touch. Back in London, N got his team together, poised over their keyboards to receive the audio files Gareth would send through periodically, transcribe them and use what was in them to scupper the Labour election effort as much as possible.

Milne's series of calls on the train that night was almost continuous, and Gareth was sleepy. So Gareth actually fell into an ale-fuelled doze in the middle of the conversations, his mobile phone still recording Milne. To this day, there are parts of the train journey that are a drunken blur for Gareth.

But that didn't matter. Because what Gareth had recorded of Milne was incendiary. 'Without looking defensive,' Milne told Corbyn on the phone that night, 'we need to seal down the Trident thing so it doesn't keep intruding in the next few days. We just need a form of words ... to shut down the nuclear question.'

The *Mail on Sunday* was the lucky recipient of the transcript of the recording, with Gareth's reward the front-page headline 'May Goes Nuclear'. The copy, by political hacks Simon Walters and Glen Owen, read:

> The Prime Minister received a boost last night from a sensational leaked conversation between the Labour leader and his Left-wing spin doctor Seumas Milne.
>
> In a phone call two hours after Mr Corbyn was heckled by the audience in the BBC's *Question Time* Leaders' Debate on Friday for refusing to say if he would use nuclear weapons, the two men agree that launching such a strike would be 'bonkers'.
>
> They discuss finding a 'form of words' to 'shut down' the embarrassing row over his anti-nuclear views and stop it wrecking the final stages of his election campaign.
>
> And they mock those who support using Britain's Trident deterrent, including Mrs May, in a series of jokey exchanges.

Ironically, for some days afterwards, the man at the centre of this subterfuge remained blissfully unaware of exactly what had happened during the train journey and concurrently in CCHQ. When Gareth eventually woke up with a hangover the next day, he got some semblance of it, but the full story wasn't explained to him until after the election about a week later, when he finally had the chance to catch up properly with N and relive the evening. But coming into the office for his regular shift on the day the *Mail on Sunday* front-page article appeared on newsstands and dropped through letterboxes across the UK, just days before the election, Gareth was given a much-deserved hero's welcome by Sir Lynton Crosby – indeed, all of us – at CCHQ.

My own contribution was much less impressive than Gareth's, but I did win one of a series of awards for excellent work that Lynton gave out during the campaign. Mine came after taking a late train back from the prime ministerial campaign event in Derby the night of my birthday and arriving at King's Cross after midnight. Bleary-eyed, I was back in the building at 5.30 the next morning to brief the top brass on the media overnight, and somehow struggled through both that briefing and the day itself until about 7.30 p.m., before collapsing into my bed at home in west London. A few days later, my name was called out during Lynton's awards, my stamina rewarded by the cherished prize of a Nicola Sturgeon face mask, which I have to this day. There was no way I was going to say 'no thanks' to that.

~

I had been in touch regularly with James during the election, mainly working on the logistics of the numerous visits he was doing through-out England, as well as the Northern Ireland trip with Theresa May. I also played another important role for James, however: keeping him updated on the election gossip, such as decisions from the top of the campaign to sideline certain people from the media rounds – including Philip Hammond, the then Chancellor, which struck me as crazy. On election day itself in 2017, I went down to his constitu-ency of Old Bexley and Sidcup in south-east London and helped his volunteer team there. On polling day, it's all about getting out the vote – 'knocking up' doors to ask people whether they have voted, encouraging people to get to the polls and vote Conservative.

It was all going very much as expected by the late afternoon – many people had voted; others were on their way to the polling station or just weren't back from work yet. I only encountered one person who told me she couldn't be bothered and it wasn't worth voting because they were all the same anyway. Plus she had to make the dinner and, well, it was a busy evening, so she wasn't going to make it to the polls. 'I can assure you they are not all the same, madam, and James Brokenshire is a very good man who has been an excellent MP for this area. Is there anything I can do to persuade you to go to the polls this evening?' I asked. When she said there wasn't, the correct thing for any canvasser to do is to move on to the next house, rather than waste precious campaigning time speaking to someone who cannot be convinced. But I stood my ground. Was there anything she wanted to know about the Conservatives' policies? 'No,' she replied. I got desperate. 'Have you heard of the suffragettes, madam? They were a group of women who 100 years ago made all sorts of sacrifices so women could have the vote. One of them even threw herself in front of the King's horse at the Derby.' No, she hadn't heard of the suffragettes. Time to move on.

Matthew Parris, the *Times* columnist, once said to me, 'The problem with you, Peter, is that you are incurably folksy.' I'm afraid he may have had a point, because I took a note of that woman's address, and a week later I posted her a DVD of the excellent film *Suffragette* starring Carey Mulligan. I know I shouldn't have, but I don't regret it.

Election night itself was as tense as expected. Just before the crucially important 10 p.m. exit poll was announced, James, Cathy and I went to College Green opposite Parliament and climbed the steps to Sky News' temporary outdoor studio, where he was to give an instant reaction to the predicted result on behalf of the Conservatives. The exit poll is the moment when all broadcasters simultaneously report a survey of tens of thousands of people done on election day. It is almost always closely reflective of the final result and sets the tone for the whole evening.

The three of us crowded around my phone to watch the Sky News output of presenter Adam Boulton announcing the result, broadcasting from the platform just yards away. James was due on in a few minutes and had already had his studio makeup done. The three of us greeted the catastrophic exit poll with silence and a sinking heart. Far from the increased majority we'd hoped for, a hung parliament was predicted – the campaign had been a huge failure. Apparently, just a few hundred yards away in CCHQ, someone vomited at that moment, and everyone heard the retching because the offices were so silent. I felt a bit sick too, but James had to go on.

The shadow minister Emily Thornberry was on as Labour's guest, standing just a few yards away from us as she, too, prepared to join the panel. The key thing, in victory and defeat, is to be graceful and magnanimous with your opponents. Thornberry was neither. Smug, churlishly guffawing and sneering at us, she strutted onto the set with a big grin. Cathy Brokenshire can't stand Thornberry to this day and, believe me, when you've lost Cathy Brokenshire you're doing really badly.

The welcome contrast to this was two and a half years later, when I met my former opposite number as Northern Ireland Office SpAd,

Ruaidhri O'Donnell, who advised a number of Labour's shadow Secretaries of State for Northern Ireland. I bumped into Ruaidhri, a loyal fan of Jeremy Corbyn, at an event at the Irish Embassy in London, only for him to instantly shake me by the hand and congratulate me on the 2019 campaign. I simply do not adhere to the notion that you cannot have friendships across the political divide, and I've always found it quite weird when people feel they cannot debate, discuss and drink with those who disagree with them. Perhaps I should invite Emily Thornberry for a pint.

After the Sky News appearance, James travelled the half an hour or so down to Bexley for his own constituency count; the result there was never in doubt, as it's about as safe a Conservative seat as there can be. I went back to CCHQ, where the atmosphere was as abysmal as you can imagine. Theresa May and her husband Philip came out from the VIP area to address the troops and were extremely thankful and gracious for all our hard work. As she walked past with the Prime Minister, I quietly mentioned to JoJo Penn, now Baroness Penn, May's deputy chief of staff, that should she need any help with the DUP, who it was clear even then would hold the balance of power, I was happy to assist. I went home at about 6 a.m. or so, chatting to a few journalists standing outside CCHQ on my way to the Tube station. We were still going to be the government, but it was a disaster. We had lost our majority. When I got home, I slept the moment my head hit the pillow. The inevitable reshuffle would come next.

Thankfully, it came quickly and was very simple. May reappointed James as Northern Ireland Secretary, and within minutes he rang to tell me he was reappointing Jonathan Caine and me as his SpAds. So I was back at my desk in Whitehall the next day. But it was over two weeks later before the confidence and supply deal with the DUP was signed. There were big decisions for May ahead, and for me too. I decided, when we got back in, that due to the fact I had made Jonathan Caine dozens, if not hundreds, of cups of coffee during the previous nine months – and he had made me the sum total of zero – that I wasn't making him any more. It was a watershed moment in our relationship, but it was the right thing to do. He reacted by getting one of the private secretaries to make him coffee instead.

My favourite story of the 2017 election, though, came not from Westminster, but from my home village of Richhill in Northern Ireland. When taking a short break after the election, I was speaking to a friend, Suzanne, who is my age. Her little sister Jasmine was then just six years old. Jasmine had enquired as to why her school, which was being used as a polling station, had to be closed for the day. Suzanne gently explained to her infant sister: 'Every few years we have this thing called an election, because people need to pick someone to run the schools. And we need to pick someone to run the hospitals and the roads and so on.' 'Oh,' replied Jasmine, deep in thought. 'I hope they don't pick me.'

~

In 2019, the task of convincing people to vote Conservative was a lot easier, and my experience of the campaign was completely different. My boss by that stage was Robert Buckland, the Justice Secretary. His seat of South Swindon was uncomfortably marginal, with a majority in 2017 of just 2,464. This made it a key target for Corbyn's Labour, and their candidate, Sarah Church, is a former Army officer and on the reasonable wing of the Labour Party.

It was very clear that the best use of my time as Robert's media SpAd would be to go to Swindon and work as a volunteer on his constituency campaign rather than on the national effort in London. To be brutally honest, I didn't relish the prospect of squeezing into CCHQ for any repeat of 2017. As the 2019 election was called, a friend rang and said, 'Ah, you must be looking forward to the election?' To which I replied, 'I'm still recovering from the last one.'

Having resigned from the Ministry of Justice on the dissolution of Parliament a few days previously, I worked from home in London for the first days of the campaign before things got properly busy. Robert picked me up on his way back to Swindon from the Cenotaph service on Sunday 10 November. The journey was memorable because the gossip was that Sian, his wife, was convinced that Carrie Symonds, Boris Johnson's then girlfriend, was pregnant. Carrie had apparently disappeared from the Foreign Office reception a number of times heading for the toilets, something Sian felt was evidence of morning sickness. I WhatsApped a fellow SpAd, someone who is very close to Carrie, who flat-out denied it. That message didn't age too well, as, a few months later, Sian secured her position as successor to the greatest predictor of them all, Paul the Octopus, who correctly called the result of matches in the 2010 World Cup. Throughout the election, Sian gestured gleefully to pictures online of Carrie holding her dog, Dilyn, in front of her stomach as yet further evidence of a bump being covered.

That car journey was one of many between Swindon and London, as Robert was frequently interviewed on broadcast media from Millbank throughout the election. We were happily at CCHQ's beck and call for that, and the exposure is something any Cabinet minister in any constituency during an election will not turn down, especially those in marginal seats. Plus, Robert is a good media performer. We also made sure to include his local radio station, BBC Radio Wiltshire, in every media round we could, and not just because the excellent journalists there were always fair, balanced and impartial. SpAds should never forget BBC local radio in their minister's constituency. It is still hugely popular, especially amongst the over-55s, who reliably turn out at the polls, so it should always be included in a round of political interviews.

A few nights before polling day, Robert was called upon to calm things down on the media the morning after a particularly bad story of a child in A&E in the north of England having to sleep on a pile of coats. Off we went to London again for another morning media round. To help him rest and prepare for the interviews, I was unofficial chauffeur, with Sian very kindly insuring me on their Audi, with she and I sharing the vehicle during the course of the election.

Both Cathy Brokenshire and Sian Buckland are extremely supportive wives to their husbands, and it would be very difficult for either James or Robert to do such demanding jobs without their considerable support. I had less interaction with Karen Bradley's husband Neil, but it's clear he also fulfils this role. Sian is a formidable person, and my greatest nervousness at the election wasn't the prospect of Robert losing to his Labour opponent; rather, it was incurring the wrath of Sian if I managed to prang her car. I discussed my concerns with James, who knows the Bucklands well. 'I wouldn't worry about it too much, Peter,' chuckled James. 'If you prang that car, you'll just be dead. Sian will have you killed and you will be dead. It'll be quick. So don't worry!' he said breezily, as my heart sank.

Before I was let out on my own on the unsuspecting people of Swindon, Sian supervised a short driving lesson to let me get used to the Audi, with her in the passenger seat as instructor. No pressure there, then. She looked on disapprovingly as I struggled with the clutch, frequently pointing out just how slowly I was progressing when we eventually made it on to Swindon's roads. 'You are allowed to go over fifty miles an hour, you know,' she said more than once.

During our impromptu driving lesson, Sian also kindly took me across one of Swindon's greatest cultural highlights, the so-called Magic Roundabout, which I'm fairly sure was designed by someone who was, at the time, on glue. Five mini-roundabouts surround one circle, and somehow drivers are meant to negotiate this bizarre and confusing system, which I eventually mastered a few days before leaving Swindon. Swindon generally appears to be obsessed with roundabouts: on one twenty-minute journey from the centre of the town to north Swindon, I counted nineteen of them.

Having learned how to drive Sian's car properly, my role was to be the number two to the campaign manager, Alex Williams. Alex is an old head on young shoulders, and calmly and with military precision he mapped out all the different canvasses across Swindon's streets and housing estates. Any campaign needs dedicated volunteer campaigners, and every political party is mostly made up of these people, who are too often overlooked when kudos is being handed round for an election victory. Alex kept Robert's volunteer canvassers informed at every point through WhatsApp groups, which were strictly policed so no non-relevant content was posted to the sixty or so people who helped. Some volunteers came only once during the campaign to canvass; others were out every day, or nearly every day – the latter group a small but dedicated band including a lovely retired gent called Lawrence Elliott, with whom I struck up a friendship.

While I went on quite a few canvasses, my role was more about coordinating visits and media, attempting to make life easier for Alex in the process. I would focus on the air war, Alex on the ground war. By day, Alex would be out in all weathers with the canvassers. By night, he typed all the information he had gathered into the central database, every keystroke beamed back to CCHQ to help paint a nationwide picture of how things were going. Alex and I stayed in his parents' house at the start of the campaign, as they were in New Zealand, our frequent takeaway pizzas keeping us fed, with episodes of *The West Wing* played on the telly to keep us inspired. Sian even christened Alex 'Bruno' after Bruno Gianelli, the election guru in the series, and me 'CJ' after the White House press secretary, although it was made very clear by Sian that this was in reference to CJ's period as press secretary only, and not at the latter point in the drama series when she becomes chief of staff to the President. I was not to get any ideas above my station.

Several Cabinet ministers and other senior politicians came to campaign for Robert, with the regional media covering most of them extensively. Chancellor Sajid Javid, Health Secretary Matt Hancock, Work and Pensions Secretary Thérèse Coffey and former Chief Whip Mark Harper all made the journey to Swindon. The Bucklands' friend Nicky Morgan, then Culture Secretary, also helped, arriving about ten minutes after Robert did to our rendezvous point in a car park beside a housing estate. Getting out of his car, Robert asked, 'Has Nicky arrived yet?' I replied, 'She's running a little late, but knows where we are. So we'll have no problem finding NiMo.'

And the most welcome visit of all was from my former boss, James, who kindly came along for two sessions, punctuated by a lovely pub lunch with Robert. I even gave James a lift from Swindon railway station in the Audi, with him miraculously remaining uninjured by my appalling driving and even worse sense of direction.

For the final two weeks of the campaign, I stayed with Sian and Robert in their home, a generous gesture on their part. The weather wasn't great for campaigning in early December, but knowing Sian had prepared a hearty, hot meal for the end of the evening canvass was a great incentive to keep posting those leaflets and banging those doors during the rain and wind.

Despite the brilliant hospitality, laundry, food and the loan of Sian's car, it is nonetheless a slightly odd experience to be quite literally within twenty yards of your boss almost continuously for two weeks. It is testament to the kindness and generosity of the Buckland family that they put up with me for such a long period, especially as for much of the time I was on my laptop in the kitchen, munching biscuits, drinking Diet Coke and working away. A great deal of coordination of the campaign press, visits and logistics was done at that table, and no one in the house even complained about my very loud voice, unlike everyone else I have ever lived with.

Sian has an opinion on most things, however, and my purchase of the breakfast cereal Just Right was a particular bugbear. She christened it 'the world's most expensive breakfast cereal™' and reminded me of that line every morning as I scoffed a bowl. She also had frequent thoughts on my volume of biscuit consumption.

For much of the campaign, we had secured a prime spot on a main route into Swindon for a huge roadside poster of Robert. A few days before the election, some clown painted over part of the B of Buckland, making it into an F. As they say, all publicity is good publicity; secretly, I wasn't entirely disappointed that it had happened and therefore had Robert's poster all over the local media a few days before polling day. I don't know who the vandal was, but his or her law-breaking only served to help our campaign.

Election day itself was such an odd atmosphere – calm without being in the slightest relaxing. In the evening, after having done some canvassing and visiting polling stations, one of Robert's supporters had many of us over for food. After that, we went back to Robert's, and I had about an hour to kill before the polls closed. A nap was out of the question, so I watched an episode of *The Office* to take my mind off things, before coming down to the living room just before 10 p.m. to watch the exit poll with Robert and Sian.

I genuinely couldn't, and didn't, believe what the 2019 exit poll suggested. Robert was ecstatic at the margin of victory, with the initial prediction showing a majority of eighty-six for the Conservatives. I was honestly expecting a majority of twenty-four or twenty-six maximum. My first question was: 'What is the margin of error?' But even within that margin we were home, even if the poll was badly out. It felt totally surreal finally to see our strategy vindicated.

Election counts are usually held in leisure centres or other council venues. For both the North Swindon and South Swindon constituencies, the counting was done instead at a venue called Steam, the museum of the Great Western Railway, historically one of the largest employers in the town. For some reason, there were absolutely massive posters of various Bond films adorning the walls of the count centre. I quickly made many friends due to my stash of biscuits and crisps, offering them round throughout the evening. Underneath the poster of the most recent Bond film, there was something of a feast at the Spectre.

Hours of waiting were punctuated by several media interviews for Robert, including a chat down the line with the main BBC election night programme presenter Huw Edwards, which had always been one of Robert's ambitions. The North Swindon result was very positive, and Alex and his team were extremely confident by that stage about the South Swindon constituency, but the result had still to be declared. At 2.20 a.m., it finally came through: a majority for Robert of 6,625, almost triple his 2017 margin. We had done it, and done it well. I felt relieved that Robert was an MP again, and knackered too. There were then yet more interviews to do, and I was pretty sure Robert, Alex or I was going to fall over at one point with tiredness as I called time on the media round about 3.30 a.m. and we finally got into the car.

We returned to Robert's house, where I presented him with a victory gift of a signed copy of the third volume of Charles Moore's biography of Margaret Thatcher, which is right up his street. Generally, I don't drink any more, but I did have a very small glass of champagne to celebrate with him, Alex and some of Robert's closest political friends in Swindon.

Just hours later, Robert and I were back in the Ministry of Justice in London, having meetings with officials. In the mini-reshuffle immediately after the election, Robert's position was confirmed, and he told me he was reconfirming me as his SpAd. We were back, with all the promise and privilege of a full term with a huge Conservative majority.

After thirty-seven hours straight, I retired to my bed in London and slept as soon as my head hit the pillow. That weekend, I reflected on an election well fought, the friends I had made, and the lessons about politics I had learned. But the true victory in December 2019 was that Sian's Audi was returned to her in mint condition: washed, valeted, full of petrol and – crucially – prang free.

9

Far From the SpAdding Crowd: Getting Sacked

SpAds are political mayflies, lasting on average less than two years in government. I was lucky. When I was sacked, I had been a SpAd for almost exactly three and a half years, in four departments, under four Secretaries of State. Apparently, at the time of my defenestration in February 2020 there were just ten of us, out of some 105 SpAds, who had more than two years' experience. This was partly due to the fact that in the summer of 2019, when Boris Johnson became Prime Minister, so many SpAds had left, taking with them much experience and expertise. In Downing Street, I think only about three of forty May-era SpAds survived – including, of course, Super SpAd Sheridan Westlake, a man it would make sense to stand next to in the event of a nuclear bomb.

But the end may not always be the end, as I found out not once, not twice, but thrice. I went through a range of emotions on each occasion. The first time I lost my job as a SpAd was actually the hardest. That's because it wasn't to do with me but rather because James

Brokenshire was very seriously ill. In December 2017, about a year and a half into my time at the Northern Ireland Office, I suspected something was not right with James's health.

In the days leading up to Thursday 7 December, and continuing into that night, James and Jonathan Caine had been in long, extremely intense negotiations with the DUP over Brexit. At the conclusion of the talks, in the early hours of Friday 8th, Theresa May flew out to Brussels for an early morning press conference with the then President of the European Commission, Jean-Claude Juncker. Previously, a joint report on Phase 1 of the Brexit negotiations concerning citizens' rights, EU budget contributions and, crucially, Northern Ireland, stated that a hard border between Northern Ireland and the Republic would be avoided, if necessary, by Northern Ireland maintaining 'full alignment' with the rules of the customs union and single market. This was controversial for the DUP, as it raised the spectre of a customs border between Northern Ireland and the rest of the UK. The Conservatives' confidence and supply partners had objected to the report, delaying its announcement from 4 December. Over the next few days, concessions were made, including the addition of a clause, paragraph 50 of the report, which stated that there would be 'no new regulatory barriers' between Northern Ireland and the rest of the UK.

The negotiating team at No. 10, which included James and Jonathan Caine, had played a blinder to get things over the line, keeping the DUP on board. Jonathan had actually been on the phone to one of the DUP negotiators, then MP Emma Little-Pengelly, a former barrister with a precise mind, until 3 a.m. The late-night call was to reassure Emma on the legal heft of the additional paragraph they had negotiated. At the time of their conversation, Theresa May was actually travelling to the airfield where the RAF plane that would take her to Brussels was powering up.

I was not in the No. 10 negotiations but monitored events as closely as I could from the office and home, a bit like the BBC's South Korea correspondent. Denzil Davidson, a veteran SpAd who was one of the key No. 10 Europe and Brexit negotiators, later said he had been in some tough negotiations in his career but the DUP drove the hardest bargain of the lot.

James was scheduled to make a number of phone calls about the outcome of the deal to the Northern Ireland party leaders on the Friday afternoon. That morning, though, there was a doctor's appointment, about which he was keeping tight-lipped.

It was obviously not my role – or anyone else's – to ask James personal questions about his health. There is always a line you do not cross between SpAd and minister, no matter how friendly you are. James had had a number of such appointments in the previous weeks and, despite my curiosity – which usually manifests itself simply as nosiness – I somehow managed to keep my mouth shut and let him get on with it. But I was certainly concerned about him.

After just a few hours of sleep, and a short time after the Prime Minister touched down in Brussels, James rang me late in the morning to say he was too tired to do the afternoon calls. This was not the James Brokenshire I knew, by any stretch. The man has a Stakhanovite work ethic. He often left me, seventeen years his junior, knackered, stumbling into my bedroom late at night at Hillsborough Castle as he happily sprinted up the stairs to the Secretary of State's flat for another two hours of red box work before bed. He had also rung *me* specifically – not Holly Clark, his principal private secretary – on a diary matter. That alerted me that something wasn't quite right, but I said nothing and simply communicated the message to the private office staff that he would not be making the calls.

It was when Jonathan Caine and I were saying our Christmas farewells to James in his office in Parliament just a few days later that James told us he was unwell. There were to be some more tests, and he would keep us informed. During that meeting, he said casually that he might have to have a bit of his lung cut out. For the first time, I hugged him. I worried about him all over Christmas but kept my mouth shut.

It wasn't until the very first days of 2018, following a Brokenshire family holiday to visit family in Australia, that he rang me to tell me about the devastating confirmation from his doctors he had received just hours before: he had lung cancer. I was standing in a friend's kitchen in Belfast, getting ready to go to a pub quiz, and I was stunned.

My initial reaction was to be energetically reassuring – it would all be fine, we would support him in the office completely and he'd be right as rain after the operation. We would get back to the crucial Northern Ireland talks into which he had put so much time and effort. We could weather him being out of action for a few weeks and would support him in any way he needed.

No, he said, firmly, he had to have a very serious operation and a potentially long recovery period. He had to resign as Secretary of State. He was sorry, but that was it – he had to put his health and his family first. He apologised, knowing I would lose my job. I was pretty overwhelmed and hadn't had the chance to consider the implications for myself in that moment – I was so upset, and worried, for him. As I started to go through the implications, I thought: what if he wasn't going to be OK? What if he was going to die? What about his lovely family, who had shown me such kindness over the past year and a half? I told no one. It felt a lot more than a simple employee–boss relationship at that moment.

Later that evening I went to the pub quiz outside Belfast with some friends, but I was miles away. I broke off from my friends, who were concerned about me but bewildered as to what was wrong, and rang James again. We had a long chat.

After a few days, the media in Belfast had started to ask questions about James's whereabouts, especially as a new round of talks was planned. Where was the Secretary of State, and why had these new talks aimed at restoring devolution not started? As his media SpAd, I stonewalled, never lying but never telling the full truth about James's private medical information.

Back in London, we were eventually told that James's resignation was going to be the start of a planned reshuffle, and that Monday 8 January was the date. I got the media plan in place – with James's sign-off, of course – and at the last possible moment I rang a friend and former colleague at Sky News and told them to send a camera to the Northern Ireland Office in Whitehall because they needed to record a clip, which would be sent to all broadcast outlets. James was resigning on health grounds, I told them, embargoing the information until 2 p.m.

By a cruel twist of fate, it was James's fiftieth birthday that day. Everything he had worked for since he had given out his first Conservative leaflet thirty-five years ago as a fifteen-year-old boy was potentially coming to an end. But his political career – previously one of the biggest things in his life – was now a secondary consideration to his health.

Miraculously, we kept a lid on the story until an hour before we had planned to release the clip, when a *Sun* reporter broke the news online. My phone exploded: Laura Kuenssberg, Robert Peston, my mother, my housemate, school friends, dozens of people getting in touch via Facebook. One contact wrote: 'I see Brokenshire has cancer – are you sacked?' I defriended that idiot immediately.

In contrast to that crass and insensitive message, James's letter to the Prime Minister was beautiful and entirely of his composition. Her reply was even warmer, all but guaranteeing that when James was better – although it was a big if, at that stage – he would return to Cabinet. The Prime Minister was as good as her word: four months later when she appointed James Housing Secretary.

When the media maelstrom and associated phone calls died down, and with the clip running across the news, we packed up James's office. I asked if I could keep a little memento, a lovely notepad with an engraved message from the Gaelic Athletic Association in Northern Ireland. James had been the first Northern Ireland Secretary ever to attend a Gaelic football match – a heavily nationalist sport – and it remains a reminder of a very special evening.

As I packed into James's boxes an unopened bottle of champagne I had given him for being reappointed in the post-2017 election reshuffle, I wondered whether there would ever be cause to serve it.

I then invited James to come down the corridor to another ministerial office, where we were joined by the private office and senior officials with whom we had both worked so closely for the previous year and a half. I had arranged for a projector and screen to be set up for his fiftieth birthday surprise: *Brokey: The Movie.*

For the previous three months, Cathy and I had been secretly assembling video messages from many of James's friends and family, including a very short 'Happy Birthday' from his elderly mother, Joan, who was suffering from dementia and died just two years later.

The actress Joanna Lumley, with whom James and Cathy shared a selfie at an event one evening, sent a video message and was featured. We had also arranged clips from one of James's favourite contestants from *The Great British Bake Off*, Northern Ireland's Andrew Smyth. Theresa May, Cathy and the Brokenshire kids, Jonathan Caine and I also recorded messages, and we did a sweeping shot of the department's London and Belfast open-plan offices, with the staff waving and wishing him well. A friend who is a Sky News tape editor had done a terrific edit as a favour to me, adding music and graphics. James was visibly touched. I had also managed to wangle a West Ham shirt out of the club with 'Brokenshire 50' printed on the back, and an invitation signed by the club captain for James and his family to go to a match as West Ham's guests. My final gift was the Emergency Snickers, squirreled away in my office in case James had a meltdown some day and needed some chocolatey goodness to get him back on track. But of course we never needed the chocolate bar, because James didn't have meltdowns.

James and Cathy left the building soon after, and, bereft of the best boss I had ever had, as well as a great friend, his future uncertain, I wept.

The Northern Ireland Office Permanent Secretary, Sir Jonathan Stephens, was considerate that day. Often SpAds are immediately marched from the building with a box of their possessions. Instead, Sir Jonathan said to wait and see who the next Secretary of State was. There wasn't very much to do for a few hours except watch Sky News and monitor Twitter at my desk to see how the reshuffle was going. After such a fraught time, there was an eerie quiet, simply waiting for news of who the incoming Secretary of State would be and what that would mean for Jonathan Caine and me.

An excellent source told us at around 3.30 p.m. it was to be Karen Bradley, the Culture Secretary, with whom I had exchanged only a quick hello on the campaign trail the previous year. About an hour later, Twitter had it. I knew little about Karen, but after some basic research I asked a journalist friend who has an extensive political database for her phone number. I didn't really know what I wanted at that stage, but Jonathan Caine had been in this situation many times before and was going into overdrive about what lay ahead.

At 6 p.m. or so, Karen was appointed. We briefly said hello when she came into our offices in the Treasury building a few hundred yards from Downing Street. The new Secretary of State received initial briefings from senior civil servants with SpAds not present, before leaving. I went out with friends and got well and truly plastered.

My sad week then became a deeply weird one. Sir Jonathan allowed Jonathan Caine and me to go to Belfast with Karen, but we were to keep a low profile, as our reappointments as SpAds had not yet been confirmed.

Jonathan Caine was having kittens, worried he wouldn't be kept on after the reshuffle. Having been reappointed by no fewer than four Northern Ireland Secretaries previously, he had nothing to worry about, but he was in a panic anyway.

While Arlene Foster, the DUP leader, got on personally with the Permanent Secretary of the Northern Ireland Office, I think it is fair to say she did not consider Sir Jonathan Stephens to be the strongest unionist. True or not, that was her perception.

Arlene, Jonathan Caine and I had always got on, and he had known her for many years. Now, he felt, he needed her. From her perspective, having two strong unionists in the SpAd team at the NIO was useful. So he rang Arlene directly and got her to speak to Downing Street chief of staff Gavin Barwell to ensure our future as SpAds – a deft move and a kind one, as he spoke of the need, as he saw it, to save 'the SpAd team' rather than simply attempting to look after himself. I had once been warned that when this moment came Jonathan would throw me under a bus, but he absolutely did not.

Winding up Arlene on the phone, Jonathan said, 'I mean, Arlene, if the SpAd team isn't retained here, you may as well hand the whole thing over to Sir Jonathan...' Arlene snarled down the phone in her Fermanagh brogue: 'We're *nat* havin' *that!*'

I'm ashamed to admit that for the next few weeks, when anyone proposed anything we didn't want the Secretary of State to do, Jonathan Caine and I just looked at one another, grinned and impersonated Arlene, repeating the line: 'We're *nat* havin' *that!*'

One of the private secretaries in the department knew that I love inappropriate humour, even at my own expense. At one point she said, 'I think Karen should just do it *X Factor*-style. "Peter, Jonathan... I'm afraid you need to pack a bag... [Dramatic pause.] BECAUSE YOU'RE COMING WITH ME TO BELFAST!"'

Soon afterwards, Jonathan was told he had survived, but there was never really any doubt as he had done the job for such a long time.

Karen was completely inexperienced in Northern Ireland matters, whereas Jonathan Caine is the doyen of policy in the area.

On the Wednesday morning after her appointment, less than forty-eight hours after being made Northern Ireland Secretary, Karen asked me to stay on as her media SpAd. I agreed, but I really wasn't sure what I wanted at that point. I asked my great friend Amy Fisher, then a Home Office SpAd, for advice. There was some talk of making Jonathan, who had been made a peer by David Cameron, let's remember, a minister in the Lords, which didn't come to anything. Despite my reappointment, the situation seemed fluid. On the Wednesday, Amy informed me that Amber Rudd was to be given an additional SpAd, as she had been given extra responsibilities in the reshuffle. Would I be interested in having a chat?

Amy and I spoke on the phone for some time about the role and what it would involve. At one stage, Amy told me, 'The Prime Minister and Home Secretary have discussed you,' which was surreal. I privately asked the advice of Eamon Deeny, our brilliant head of comms in Belfast and a trusted friend and colleague. 'Go for it,' he urged.

As I prepared to fly back to London, Amy rang to ask whether I would be free to have breakfast with Amber the next day. 'Well, Amy, I have Pilates at 9.30,' I joked, 'but I suppose I could probably miss it just this once to have breakfast with the Home Secretary.'

I felt emotionally drained by a week in which my beloved boss had resigned because of a cancer diagnosis. It was also a week in which a new, inexperienced boss had come in and needed guidance as she undertook the many 'firsts' a new Secretary of State must complete. And now there was a prospect of a big promotion to the Home Office.

I needed to prepare for breakfast with Amber the next day, and to my enduring regret I'm afraid I ducked out of James's fiftieth birthday celebrations that Thursday night to concentrate on prepping for my job interview. Half the Cabinet, including Theresa May, attended, a token of their huge esteem for James. At least *Brokey: The Movie* got a second showing.

On the Friday morning, in a very ordinary café near Amber Rudd's home in west London, I sat with Amy and the Home Secretary over a cup of Earl Grey. Amber gently grilled me on Brexit, my experience at the Northern Ireland Office and James's health, before appointing me on the spot. Amy told me later that Amber's exact words to her about her decision to appoint me were: 'He had me at Fulbright Scholar,' referring to an academic award I had received some years previously. I knew the then head of the Fulbright Commission in the UK, Penny Egan, would be happy to hear this. She and her colleagues had given me the opportunity to study abroad for a year at Columbia University in New York in 2007.

Beaming as we left the café, Amber already en route to her Hastings constituency, I took the Tube with Amy back to the office. I immediately told Karen, who kindly gave me her full blessing. James, of course, had been talking to me about what I should do throughout, a curious reversal of roles – the adviser becoming the advised.

The next step was squaring it all off with No. 10, who were not mightily amused I was moving departments. At one stage, a senior SpAd there suggested I do both the NIO and Home Office jobs simultaneously, a bizarre and completely impractical request as I had been in Belfast around half the week for the previous eighteen months. Cabinet Office mandarin Sue Gray (see Chapter 2), a woman once dubbed 'the most powerful woman you have never heard of' and formerly known as 'deputy GOD' (GOD being the former Cabinet Secretary, Gus O'Donnell, her boss for many years), asked me to agree to Karen's request to stay on at the NIO. I found her mildly terrifying, so it was a difficult thing for me to say no, I wanted to go to the Home Office. But the fact was that moving from the tiny Northern Ireland Office to one of the Great Offices of State represented a significant promotion, and I was determined to go. Eventually, after much faffing, a compromise was reached: I would stay with Karen for about ten weeks to help her get her feet under the table. I eventually started at the Home Office on 2 April 2018.

And on leaving the NIO, there was a nice surprise in store from Karen. The Northern Ireland Secretary gets a number of tickets for Buckingham Palace garden parties, and Karen gave me two of them. It was a typically generous and thoughtful gesture from her. I brought my mother to the garden party and we had a brilliant day. At one point, having met the heir to the throne, whom Mum found very charming, she said, 'I can't believe I have just met Prince Charles!' I added, 'And here comes the Prime Minister and Mr May. Would you like to meet them?' After a pleasant chat with the Mays, I asked whether it would be all right to get a photo. Philip May, who is as down-to-earth as his wife, suggested he take the picture. 'I want you in it too!' I exclaimed. It is a very special photo to my mother and me.

Losing my new job exactly four weeks after starting at the Home Office, on the night of Sunday 29 April, was an altogether stranger and more brutal affair than moving from there from the Northern Ireland Office.

The initial warning came in my first week as I was still finding the loos in the cavernous and confusing Home Office building at 2 Marsham Street in Westminster. A WhatsApp group of Amber and her four SpAds pinged with a message from the Home Secretary. She was concerned about reporting around 'this Windrush thing. I think it could be a difficult one,' Amber wrote. And so it proved.

People who are members of the Windrush generation came to the UK from Caribbean countries which were part of the British Empire. Many had been born British subjects. In some part due to the pressure on the Home Office to reduce immigration figures, some had been wrongly detained, been denied their legal rights and in some cases been threatened with deportation or actually deported. Some lost their jobs or homes as a result, or were denied benefits to which they were entitled, or even medical care. It was a mess, and hugely unfair on those many people affected who have given so much to this country.

And inside the bunker, in the Home Office SpAds' office, the leaks and tsunami of negative media coverage presented a daily, sometimes hourly, trial for Amber's longer-serving SpAds Amy, media SpAd Mo Hussein and especially Simon Glasson, who dealt with immigration as part of his policy areas. I remember on one occasion Simon went out to get his hair cut for half an hour, earning him the wrath of a member of private office that he dare leave the office. Such were the tensions and heightened emotions for some.

Four weeks later, after the drip, drip, drip of leaks to *The Guardian* in particular, the Windrush affair forced Amber out. As she resigned, so our jobs ended too. Amy and Simon had served Amber loyally for almost two years at the Home Office, and Mo for even longer, having worked with Amber at her previous department, Energy and Climate Change. The three SpAds had been heavily involved with the developments over that final critical weekend and they had helped draft the eventual resignation letter from Amber. The final word came on the Sunday evening, with a breaking news alert from the BBC at 10 p.m. It was confirmation that, as expected, I had lost my job. Again. Amy, in particular, was extremely apologetic that I had to leave through no fault of my own. But I will always be grateful to Amy and Amber for the opportunity, however short, to serve at the Home Office.

SpAd defenestration can be brutal, but just before our email accounts were shut down, about ten o'clock the next morning, we received an email from the No. 10 chief of staff Gavin Barwell's office, asking the four of us to go and see him in Downing Street.

Earlier that morning, Sajid Javid had been promoted to Home Secretary and his three SpAds had moved with him from the Ministry of Housing, Communities and Local Government. Concurrently, and having quickly and fully recovered from his illness, James was then brought back into the Cabinet in Javid's old job. I messaged James immediately to congratulate him.

Again, Dean of SpAds Sheridan Westlake was scrambled. I asked Sheridan's advice on how to best communicate what I was thinking. His response was very simple: 'You need to tell them – they are not mind readers.' I fired off messages to Gavin Barwell and his deputy, JoJo Penn, telling them the logical thing was to send me to Housing, Communities and Local Government to become James's SpAd again.

We four now jobless SpAds went into the Home Office, picked up our personal items in the half-hour window we were allocated and left, agreeing to meet up later for the No. 10 meeting. A particular low point was carrying my mini-fridge past a TV crew on the way out of the Home Office building. A former Sky News colleague, Shona Somerville, asked me, not unkindly, what I was going to do now. 'I'm going home to have a cup of tea,' I said, quietly.

Having dropped off my possessions at home, I came back into Westminster and headed to No. 10. Gavin took the meeting, flanked by director of policy James Marshall, who was the SpAd personnel supremo, and a private secretary. I felt a tiny bit of a fraud as I had only been at the Home Office five minutes and was pretty sure James would take me with him to Housing. It was a difficult dance, as I wanted to be as supportive to them as possible, especially Amy. Simon, who as immigration policy SpAd had been even more at the centre of the Windrush fallout than the other two (if that was possible), looked particularly exhausted. He had worked for George Osborne at the Treasury and was pretty adamant his SpAdding career was over. He told me he wanted to go into the private sector, which he eventually did. Mo wasn't quite sure what he wanted initially, but, like Simon, ended up in public affairs, occasionally giving expert analysis on the telly as a pundit.

Gavin was gentle and kind, saying he and James Marshall had a good record of redeploying people, and it was fine to take some time to think about what we wanted to do. We outlined our plans in short individual meetings immediately afterwards. I was direct: I wanted to go and work for James at Housing. They were fine with it if he was. At around seven o'clock that night, James rang me, saying, 'Peter, would Fridgey and you be free to come and work with me at MHCLG?' Laughing, I confirmed both my mini-fridge, Fridgey, and I would be honoured. I started the next afternoon, carrying the fridge back into the same building at 2 Marsham Street, the government building which houses the offices of both the Home Office and MHCLG.

Many other SpAds have not been so lucky in the past. One SpAd at the Department for Work and Pensions was relieved of her mobile phone, computer and pass and was walked out of the building even before her Secretary of State had left 10 Downing Street, where he was still in the process of resigning his ministerial office. The senior official who did that has, I understand, since said sorry. But it is at this critical point that SpAds are reminded, yet again, that the civil service is permanent and SpAds are utterly dispensable. In recent years, one Secretary of State who resigned late in the evening had her SpAds come to the department the next morning to be presented with a cardboard box of their personal possessions. Their passes had been revoked and officials did not even allow them to get past security.

And the most brutal sacking of all in my experience was Sonia Khan, who was summarily dismissed from her job as special adviser to the then Chancellor, Sajid Javid, by No. 10 de facto chief of staff Dominic Cummings in the summer of 2019. Sonia's phone and pass were taken from her and she was escorted from Downing Street by an armed police officer. The news of her sacking spread quickly across the SpAds WhatsApp group, with the lurid details – some true, some not – appearing in the next day's papers. A photograph of Sonia was plastered on the front of *The Times*, a fate I would not wish on my worst enemy. Her dismissal is, at time of writing, subject to a legal case, so it's best I don't offer any further thoughts on it, except perhaps to note that every other dismissal of SpAds since has been done – it would appear – rather differently.

The convulsions that saw the demise of Theresa May's government and the ascent of Boris Johnson ushered in my next sacking, in the summer of 2019. James, after a lot of thinking and having consulted his three SpAds, had backed Boris for Conservative leader early in the campaign and wrote an excellent op-ed for the *Mail on Sunday*, although they published only extracts of it, which annoyed me greatly. To me, it needed to feel like a 'moment' when such a May loyalist backed Boris Johnson, and James's drafted words, which he had sent me to review, were characteristically sincere.

Instead, James's endorsement of Boris fell a bit flat. Around the same time, it became clear that Liam Booth-Smith was to have a senior role at No. 10 in the event of a Boris win, perhaps even deputy chief of staff to Sir Eddie Lister. Eddie had been Boris's chief of staff at City Hall in London, and the expectation was that he would fill the same role in Downing Street. I had also had a beer with Eddie Lister a few weeks previously, asking him about a possible move to the No. 10 press SpAds' office, but it didn't come to anything.

Boris's leadership campaign was deftly fought, and many of the key names went on to jobs in No. 10, including Lee Cain, Ben Gascoigne and Eddie himself, who was heavily involved at every stage. One name attached to the Boris team – indeed, the alleged chairman of the entire operation – was Iain Duncan Smith, who was clearly chosen to throw some red meat to the Conservative Party's right-wing Brexiteers to keep them on board. Some of these people believed Boris's commitment to their cause beyond Brexit may have been suspect, so this was a good strategic move.

But relations between chairman and candidate were not good. Indeed, on one occasion, just days before Boris was announced as the new leader of the Conservative Party, IDS attempted to ring him several times to suggest they have a strategy discussion at the campaign's headquarters at the home of Andrew Griffith, a Sky executive who later worked in Downing Street and became an MP in December 2019.

Boris ignored both calls and texts until finally IDS texted to say he was on his way round. With IDS en route, Boris quickly ordered his entire team to race up the stairs to the first floor of the house and, well, hide from their alleged campaign chairman as he rapped on the door of the building, demanding to be let in.

It was a farcical scene, orchestrated by the man who would be Prime Minister of the United Kingdom just hours later. Eventually, IDS gave up knocking on the door and ringing the bell, and the Johnson team gingerly made their way downstairs again to their makeshift offices to resume their work.

James Brokenshire's sacking the day Boris became Prime Minister was brutal. He was one of seventeen Cabinet ministers who were dismissed, after meetings lasting not much longer than five minutes in Boris's office at the House of Commons.

There had been all sorts of speculation that James would be kept on, and of course I had a key role in creating that impression. As one of the main May loyalists, James could be crucial, I argued, in helping Boris unite a party deeply divided over Brexit – yet somewhere in the back of my mind I was pretty sure James was going to get the chop. I had been talking him up for weeks to anyone who would listen, but I wasn't sure anything I said made the slightest difference. In the end, it didn't feel like much of a shock. And I think James might have felt the same way. His *Mail on Sunday* endorsement article had earned him no reward. Several other Conservative figures who might reasonably have been expected to back other leadership candidates also backed Boris, but they went similarly unrewarded, with several of them being sacked.

It was Lee Scott, my co-SpAd, who rang me about 5.15 p.m. that day to tell me James had been called to Boris's office in the House of Commons. That was to be the location of the sackings, meaning the ministers relieved of their posts didn't have to walk down Downing Street having just been given their marching orders. As soon as Lee said the words 'Boris's Commons office', my heart sank.

Less than five minutes later, James rang me to tell me he had been dismissed. He was very angry and sad to lose his job, especially given how much time and effort Boris had put into courting his endorsement just weeks beforehand. He told me Boris had assured him that people did sometimes come back to government, and in the reshuffle of early 2020 James did indeed return, this time to his old job as Security Minister at the Home Office. It is not a Cabinet post, but it's a hugely important position and James is well equipped for it.

No reshuffle is entirely on merit, but what annoyed me most about this one was any suggestion that James had been Housing Secretary simply because he was a May loyalist. James had numerous tangible wins under his belt, such as the decline in rough sleeping, a massive spending commitment on social housing for years to come, more secure tenancies for renters and a £600 million fund to remove and replace dangerous flammable cladding on privately owned buildings similar to Grenfell Tower. He had battled for months to make the latter case despite strong resistance, so it was a big win.

James would have served Boris in Cabinet as loyally as he had Theresa May, but our long-running campaign to keep him in the

Cabinet failed miserably, and I felt very bad for him as he contemplated life on the back benches. And of course, I didn't know what was next for me, either. Yet again, I had packed up my belongings and gone home. All I could do was wait to see if the door was entirely closed. I was fairly convinced it was.

It quickly became clear that the question for most SpAds who wanted to stay on – many did not – was whether you were on Dominic Cummings's blacklist or not. Some SpAds, such as some of those who had worked for the former Business Secretary Greg Clark, were told there was no way back. Clark remains a hate figure for Dominic. Indeed, Dominic told us in an all-SpAds meeting that Clark was, to him, someone who had acted proactively in government to 'frustrate the will of the people' over Brexit, which to be honest is probably true.

Rather handily, Liam, whom I now nicknamed 'Jimmy Big Bollocks' due to his exalted role in Downing Street as senior adviser to the Prime Minister, was put in charge of SpAd hiring and reallocating. I wanted to stay on, but I had to convince Dominic, a man I did not know at all and who did not know me, via Liam, that I was a sound person. I couldn't just be presented as a May loyalist or one of Liam's mates. You could say my battle was a sort of pound shop version of the unsuccessful one we had fought to convince Boris about James. It took some time to get me sorted, but Liam was helpful, loyal and good humoured throughout. He absolutely saved my SpAd career at that crazy time, in between sleeping on his office couch on numerous nights as Boris's Downing Street took shape.

Reshuffles are a time of crazy emotions – in the summer of 2019 it took nine nail biting days for my future to be worked out. Initially, I was told that No. 10 wanted to send me to Transport, something I said a flat 'no' to, much to Liam's surprise and, I think, annoyance. Quite simply, I didn't believe in HS2, and I have basically no interest in transport policy. I had seen the zeal and level of expertise that my friend Simon Jones, the previous policy SpAd in Transport under Chris Grayling, had for the role he loved, and I could never match that. The next few days involved much wrangling, missed phone calls, calls not returned or promised calls not made by certain Secretaries of State, including Julian Smith at Northern Ireland, not that a sequel at the NIO was what I necessarily wanted.

For about a week, I got nowhere. At one stage, I was in a state of depression, the not knowing being the toughest bit. Also, the brutal reality for people in this position is that you have to spend your days trying to pin down extremely busy people whose priority is understandably not some random, jobless SpAd from a mid-ranking department seeking to be employed in another one.

I was sitting in an Italian restaurant near my home in west London having their discount lunch of spaghetti bolognaise and a Diet Coke, pondering my fate, when a face from the past popped up on my WhatsApp. It was former No. 10 director of communications Katie Perrior, wondering whether I had considered contacting Robert Buckland, the newly appointed Justice Secretary and Lord Chancellor, about being his media SpAd. I knew next to nothing about Robert, but Katie assured me that he and I would get along. I asked James for advice and he said Robert and I had a similar political outlook, though Robert's personality and way of operating were probably very different to James's.

Robert was actually on holiday in Florida with his family, and when we spoke the next day he took the call in the Mickey Mouse

Theatre at Disney World. I had an odd vision of Robert in my head, wearing the Lord Chancellor's long wig with the cartoon mouse ears on top of it, perhaps swinging around the teacups as he spoke to me from the theme park. It was quite a distracting thought as I tried to convince him I was the man to guard his media profile and image.

We spoke for about half an hour before he told me he wanted twenty-four hours to think about my answers to his questions. I had another interview scheduled the next day with another Secretary of State, and I had spoken to a further Cabinet attendee earlier that day who said he was keen to appoint me.

Things were moving at last. I told Robert I didn't want to back him into a corner, but Justice was my first choice. If he offered me the job, I would take it. He said to do the other interview the next day and then he would speak to me again. All I could do, again, was wait.

But it wasn't to be for very long at all this time, because my phone rang precisely three minutes later. It was Robert. I presumed he had hit my number again by mistake. No, he said, he had actually made his mind up in those few minutes that he wanted to appoint me. That was that. I was back.

I rang Liam, whom Robert had texted to confirm his choice. Liam told me to come to the No. 10 SpAds' meeting the next day, square it off with director of communications Lee Cain and start at the Ministry of Justice the following Monday.

For obvious reasons, I was extremely keen to tie down Lee for that final sign-off meeting. I did not anticipate a problem. We had worked together on the 2017 election and were perhaps not friends but certainly good working acquaintances.

Poor Lee was less than two weeks into his job, one of the most relentless in No. 10, and being pulled in a number of directions. So even last thing on a Friday afternoon it was something of a battle to tie him down for a one-on-one meeting, even for just a few minutes. I was aware I was not top of his priority list. We exchanged pleasantries as I nervously waited for the questions I would have to answer before I could be approved. An awkward silence. 'Here we go,' I thought. 'What on earth is he going to ask me? Will this be scuppered at the final hurdle?' Erm, no. The awkward silence was Lee not knowing what the meeting was meant to be about.

I simply said, 'Liam tells me you want to approve all media SpAds. The plan is to send me to Justice, I think.' 'Oh yeah, yeah, whatever, yeah, all good mate,' Lee replied, waving his arms in a very general, dismissive way. 'So, what did you want to see me about?' It was a comic moment, for me at least, when the previous nine days of uncertainty and unemployment had been anything but fun.

The fourth time I lost my job, in February 2020, was the most memorable, as I actually stopped being a SpAd at the end of it. No nine lives for me; just the four.

In retrospect, it was something of a miracle that I had survived the previous six months, which had been down to Liam saving my bacon. So many other SpAds had not survived, or had chosen the end of the May administration as their moment to go off into the sun – also known as the much better remunerated, less stressful world of the private sector.

In January and February 2020, as the eighty-strong majority was clear and Brexit got done, we all knew a reshuffle was coming; it was merely a question of when. Speculation abounded about who was up, down, in, out of the Cabinet and whether Dominic would have a 'bonfire of the SpAds'. Having worked with us for just over six months, by now he would presumably have formed an opinion on the performance of SpAds he did not initially know well personally. Eventually, about twenty of us lost our jobs, around a fifth of the SpAd contingent.

A substantial amount of the Cabinet reshuffle speculation involved whether our Prisons Minister, Lucy Frazer QC, would be appointed Attorney General, a role Robert had coveted before he was promoted to Justice Secretary. I was fairly convinced Lucy was a shoo-in. There was almost no doubt that Robert would remain in his position as Lord Chancellor and Justice Secretary.

Sadly, promotion didn't come for Lucy, and she remained in her position as Prisons Minister. It was positive for the prison service at least to have some continuity – had Lucy moved, there would have been four Prisons Ministers in less than a year. But I was sad for Lucy, who is a great minister and would have been an excellent Cabinet minister. She would also have avoided the initial gaffes of Suella Braverman, who eventually got the job as Attorney General, and whose interview on *Channel 4 News* on her day of appointment was a disaster, with the new Cabinet minister tongue-tied and unable to answer basic questions convincingly.

Dominic Cummings had confirmed the previous Friday at the SpAds' meeting that there would be a reshuffle. Contrary to inaccurate reporting, he did not say, 'I'll see half of you next week'; rather, he said, 'I'll see you next week.' I know this for certain, because when he said it, I turned to Liam, who was standing beside me, and said, 'Or not!' and we both laughed a dark, hollow laugh. What we did not know at that stage was that Liam was safe but I, and many others, were not.

Robert's slot with the Prime Minister at No. 10 was scheduled for 11.10 a.m. on the day of the reshuffle, but the whole thing was badly delayed because of the machinations around Sajid Javid resigning as Chancellor after being told his SpAds all had to be sacked if he wanted to stay on. American President Harry Truman said, 'You want a friend in Washington? Buy a dog,' and sometimes it can feel the same in Westminster. Saying that, this was a reshuffle which resulted in the former Chancellor's cavapoo, Bailey, losing his position as No. 11's canine-in-chief.

The points of contention over Saj's leaving government, I am reliably informed, were little to do with policy and much more about personal politics. I can certainly see it from Saj's perspective. Just a few months previously, he probably thought he was in with a real chance of being Prime Minister. Now he was being told that his SpAds were going, come what may. You can't be much clearer than that as a Prime Minister to a Chancellor. Eddie Lister was, I'm told, in with Saj for nearly an hour trying to convince him not to resign, but Dom stayed out of it. I don't know him particularly well, but Saj was always very friendly and all his SpAds were fiercely loyal to him, and many of my friends worked tirelessly on his leadership campaign. Indeed, one still runs the Twitter account of Bailey Javid, @ExNumber11Dog. The pooch's ghost-writer, I can exclusively reveal, is Gareth Milner, who was a SpAd to Secretary of State Steve Barclay at the Department for Exiting the EU.

As news emerged throughout the morning of various other SpAds being sacked, my co-SpAd at Justice, Rajiv Shah, asked a curious question, although in fairness it was the first reshuffle he had been through. 'What's the protocol for contacting people whose ministers have been sacked?' he asked. Perhaps a little too sharply, I replied, 'The protocol is that you're a human being. Here's a Post-It note with their names, here is the list of their phone numbers – text everyone and say you're sorry what has happened and you're sorry they have lost their jobs,' I said, slamming the papers down on his desk. I had been doing the same throughout the morning, commiserating with those who had lost their jobs. I had been there before and knew all too well the range of emotions SpAds go through during this very public process.

Eventually, Robert had his appointment with Boris and we got word from the Justice Secretary's driver, Vic Lima, that he and Robert were on their way back to the department. I had been stressing for days, weeks probably, that I would be given the Spanish Archer ('el bow') and I quickly knew that was exactly what had happened. On his reappointment, I strongly expected Robert to have rung, in order: Sian, his wife; Jack Cole, his principal private secretary; and then me, which I would have probably put on speakerphone for Rajiv too. Robert had rung the first two, but not me – nor Rajiv, for that matter. Something was up.

Robert returned to the Ministry to a round of applause from his private office, and from Rajiv and me. Rajiv and I went into Robert's office adjacent to ours, where I gave Robert a big hug and said well done, and he spent a few minutes telling us about the conversation he had had with Boris. Robert was clearly extremely happy, but his face fell a few minutes later when I asked, 'And did they say anything about SpAds?' Robert asked Rajiv to leave for a few minutes, and before the door had clicked shut I said, 'I'm out, aren't I?'

Robert confirmed that was so. Dominic and his team were choosing which SpAds to sack, replace, move to other departments or change their responsibilities, and it was decided that I was for the high jump. I was to be succeeded by a man called Alex Wild from the Home Office, whom I knew a little and with whom I had happily worked on cross-cutting policies. Robert said he made sure I would get references from him and from Lee Cain if I asked for them, and offered help, if I wanted it, in the search for a new job.

SpAds need two approvals to remain in post – a ministerial say-so and agreement from No. 10. What had happened to me, Robert explained, was that the latter had been revoked. I returned to the SpAds' office a few yards from Robert's and called in Rajiv and my private secretaries. I needed help, I told them, in packing up the office, because I'd been dismissed. At least this was something I was quite good at by now.

It was odd to be getting congratulations messages regarding Robert's reappointment from people who very understandably pre-sumed I had also survived. They were all very well meaning, but it was obviously difficult to see my phone pinging with congratulations, knowing I would be out of the building within a very short space of time. A phone call came quickly from James Brokenshire, who was genuinely shocked.

I told the principal private secretary, Jack Cole, and Ministry of Justice acting head of news Simon Barrett of my news. I just wanted to get out of the building quickly, so I arranged to address the press office and private office for a few moments to say goodbye.

Rajiv was a bit strange in his behaviour, oscillating between saying nice things, ignoring what was happening, and just tapping away at his phone. 'Anne-Marie Trevelyan's gone to DfID!' he exclaimed at one point. I didn't really care. He offered to buy Fridgey McFridgeface off me, and that was a nice gesture, but a slightly emotional moment for me when I considered the many thousands of Diet Coke cans it had housed in the past few years. Much as T. S. Eliot's Prufrock measured out his life with coffee spoons, my SpAd career was probably measured out in Diet Coke cans. Perhaps Greggs sausage rolls and Snickers bars, too.

I sent a quick tweet: 'I am delighted @RobertBuckland has been re-confirmed as Justice Secretary. Sadly, in reshuffles special advisers sometimes do not survive, and after three and a half wonderful years I am leaving government. I wish the Johnson administration and everyone in it all the very best.' Replies were swift and generally complimentary, which gave me great comfort. I even got a nice tweet from Labour's Andrew Gwynne MP, who had been James's shadow at MHCLG.

With my coat on and rucksack packed, the rest of my possessions to be sent on, I stood outside the SpAd Pad one final time and told the Lord Chancellor's private office they were fantastic people who had supported me very well in the previous six months. I had had a wonderful time working with such talented and dedicated civil servants, I told them, and I wished them all well. I said Robert was an excellent Lord Chancellor and he would continue to do a brilliant job. I asked them to support the new political team as well as they had helped me, and I wished everyone all the luck in the world as they dealt with the many challenges that lay ahead.

With that, I went down in the lifts, handed my pass back to my private secretary, hugged Rajiv, and left the building. My next stop was the pub for a pint of Diet Coke with Amy Fisher, who kindly slipped out of work to commiserate with me and plan next steps.

Next came a return to Downing Street, to be formally sacked by Lee Cain. In the same office where we had met for our meeting to confirm me six months previously, in the same seats, he used the rather chilling words: 'The Prime Minister no longer has confidence in your ability to do your job.'

Not a brilliant line to hear, you'll agree, although I suppose it does imply that at some stage the Prime Minister *did* have confidence in me, something I had not previously considered. In reality, I expect Boris Johnson is only vaguely aware of my existence, although I have met him a number of times and sat in meetings with him around the Cabinet table.

As Lee spoke, I raised a wry smile as I reflected on the short shelf life of SpAds and on how sometimes the end is the end, but sometimes it is not. Because it was just a few months earlier that Robbie Gibb, then director of communications in 10 Downing Street under Theresa May, was playing the good cop when bollocking a friend of mine about not sticking to the government grid of stories that were agreed to be announced that week.

'Let me give you two examples', said Robbie to my friend, 'of two people – one who played the game and one who did not. Example one: Dylan Sharpe. He did the right thing. He stuck to the grid. He kept us informed. When [Chancellor of the Duchy of Lancaster] Damian Green had to resign and Dylan lost his job as SpAd at the Cabinet Office, we looked after him. We made him head of broadcasting at No. 10. He'll always have that on his CV. Now, let me tell you another example. Someone who didn't play the game. Someone who didn't stick to the grid. Someone who didn't keep us informed. Someone who will never set foot in this building again: Lee Cain.'

As Lee Cain sat in Robbie's former office, in Robbie's former chair, sacking me, a little part of me wondered whether I would ever be in this office, or this building, again. One day you are cock of the walk, the next a feather duster. Both Lee and I had realised that at various points.

I walked away from the famous black door of 10 Downing Street as the evening moved from twilight to darkness, thinking of all the new SpAds who would soon be unpacking their things, just starting out on a similar adventure to the one I had embarked on three and a half years previously. As I slowly approached the black steel gates of Downing Street that had been opened for me hundreds of times but would now be closed to me, perhaps for ever, I reflected on the words of David Cameron at his first Prime Minister's Questions in December 2005. Cameron, the newly elected Leader of the Opposition, leaned across the dispatch box, stared directly at Tony Blair, pointed at the Prime Minister and reminded the House of Commons: 'He was the future once.'

AFTERWORD

Turning left out of the Downing Street gates on Whitehall, it was a ten-minute walk to Leicester Square and the LBC radio studios, where the presenter Iain Dale had asked me to do an interview about my sacking and the reshuffle. Less than ninety minutes after being formally dismissed, I was back broadcasting. Since leaving politics, I have continued to be interviewed regularly for many TV and radio stations in London, Belfast and Dublin. The early interviews were generally about the politics of the day, although I was once asked about my favourite comfort food by an interviewer on BBC 5 Live (boiled eggs and soldiers prepared by my father, since you ask). One interviewer even asked me, 'Why doesn't Dominic Cummings like you?'

I got asked a lot about Dominic, of course, and interviewers sometimes found it strange that I remained so loyal to the man who sacked me, but I believed in government and still believe now that he is a strategic genius and probably the best living campaign strategist in world politics. And I'm afraid it was absolutely his prerogative to hire and fire whomever he wanted, whenever he wanted. That's the game. Accept it, move on, you had a good run and don't be bitter, because nobody cares – that's my mantra. And who knows what the future holds?

In those early months I also spent time writing a few articles for national newspapers, as well as giving some university seminars on politics and journalism, and consulting for a strategy firm, charities and others. But mostly I just had a rest. After the life I led for three and a half years, you do need a little bit of a sit-down.

And between endless cups of tea, catching up with friends, Netflix marathons, walks in the beautiful County Armagh countryside and reading some wonderfully trashy novels, I concluded the following: SpAds are something we need in UK politics. They help government function as it should. They're not perfect, and more can be done to train, support and scrutinise them, but the role they play is absolutely vital, especially in this media age. There will always be tensions between SpAds and the civil service, but that's fine, because there is no one correct way of running the country. And the power balance between SpAds, the civil service and elected politicians will always shift in varying directions.

I never thought I would find myself agreeing with any words uttered by Andrew Adonis, but he is right that SpAdding is a good apprenticeship for a life in elected politics, too – some of the best MPs and ministers have been SpAds. My former SpAd colleague Claire Coutinho, who became an MP in 2019, is one example of a name to watch. I have absolutely no intention of standing for election myself, though. I have seen the toll elected politics can take.

I will always be grateful for the period of my life covered in this book, the experiences I had, the friendships I made and the daily laughter and fellowship of working in politics with some fantastic people.

True, being a SpAd is not for the faint-hearted, but it is nonetheless the best job in the world. If you ever get the chance to do it, grab it with both hands. It will be many things, but it will not be boring.

ACKNOWLEDGEMENTS

It was my friend and former *Newsnight* colleague Michael Crick who suggested I write this book, and it was he who put me in touch with many of the interviewees from previous administrations via his unrivalled network. He also introduced me to Olivia Beattie, my brilliant, fun and extremely patient editor at Biteback. Michael, Iain Dale, Ruth Dudley Edwards and Christopher Wilson – who also writes under the name T. P. Fielden – gave me excellent tips on the process of book writing. Lucia Henwood provided outstanding research and fact-checking with a diligence and maturity that belie her teenage years; her help with the historical chapter was especially invaluable. Professor Stephen Hanney of Brunel University very kindly allowed me to draw on his 1993 PhD thesis on special advisers in a large part of the historical section, which he also read and on which he provided comments. One of the interviewees, David Cowling, did this too, and was also very helpful with other points of detail. Michael Selby and Frank Kennedy took my raw copy and improved it tremendously. My father, Ken Cardwell, also improved very early drafts (and sorry again for the bad language in the book, Dad!). Other friends including Daniel El-Gamry, Patrick Foster, Simon Henry, Patrick Maguire,

Rosa Malley, Natasha Proietto and Ryan Wilson joined Michael Crick and Ruth Dudley Edwards in reviewing slightly later drafts, making a number of helpful suggestions and providing essential guidance, particularly on tone. Ruth even calmed me down on the phone one evening when I was having a bit of a moment. Many people within the Westminster world – most of whom wish to remain anonymous – were extremely helpful with anecdotes. None was more brilliant than the unrivalled storyteller I will codename 'Judy', without whom this book would be much poorer. My lovely parents kept tea and snacks coming as I wrote in their front room during the coronavirus lockdown, never deviating from their insistence that I should stop drinking so much Diet Coke. More broadly, their influence, life lessons and the opportunities I have had as a result of their sacrifices are reflected on every page. Kathryn McCready lent me her laptop to write much of the book during the lockdown, later selling it to me at a knockdown rate. Charlie Beckwith and Pat Brickhill transcribed some interviews. Namkwan Cho created a great cover. Ben Turner took the very flattering author photo – and they say the camera never lies – with Laura Makin-Isherwood assisting with makeup, ironing and delicious steak sandwiches. I have made every effort to check the facts in this book and accurately recount what I have written. Any errors are, of course, mine alone.

GLOSSARY

4 Millbank: a building in Westminster where most UK broadcasters have studios. Interviews take place there during the media round.

Attorney General: a Cabinet minister who acts as the chief legal adviser to the government and oversees law officers, who ensure government actions are within the law.

Cabinet Office: the government department responsible for supporting both the Cabinet and the Prime Minister.

Cabinet Secretary: the most senior civil servant. The Cabinet Secretary acts as a senior policy adviser to the Prime Minister and the Cabinet, as secretary to the Cabinet, and as head of the home civil service.

CCHQ: Conservative Campaign Headquarters.

Confidence and supply: an agreement where a political party

251

supports a minority government on votes involving the Budget and on motions of confidence in Parliament.

CRD: Conservative Research Department. A department of CCHQ responsible for policy research where many SpAds and MPs begin their political careers.

DCMS: Department for Digital, Culture, Media and Sport. A government department which is responsible for public spending on and regulation of areas such as the arts, creative industries, broadcasting, the internet, tourism and leisure.

DefCon levels: a system used by the US Armed Forces to monitor danger levels. They range from DefCon 1, which denotes the most dangerous situations, for example nuclear war, to DefCon 5, used in ordinary peacetime.

Deputy director: a role in the senior civil service below that of director.

Diary secretary: a civil servant in a minister's private office responsible for organising their diary, meetings and movements.

Director: a role in the senior civil service below that of director general and above deputy director.

Director general: a senior civil servant who reports directly to the Permanent Secretary and oversees a group of directors.

DUP: Democratic Unionist Party. The largest unionist political party in Northern Ireland. Between 2017 and 2019, the DUP supported the Conservative government in a confidence and supply agreement.

Fulbright scholarships: an American programme of scholarships, named after Senator J. William Fulbright of Arkansas, the longest-serving chairman in the history of the Senate Foreign Relations Committee. The scholarships were created in 1946 for US students to study abroad and foreign students to study in the US and were designed to promote cultural exchange and understanding.

Junior minister: a minister below the Secretary of State in a government department. They include parliamentary under-secretaries and ministers of state.

Lines to take: the policy position on an issue that special advisers and politicians are expected to express when speaking to the press.

Media round: a series of interviews on TV and radio programmes at 4 Millbank undertaken by a minister, usually in the morning.

MHCLG: Ministry of Housing, Communities and Local Government. The government department responsible for housing, building and planning regulations, local government, urban regeneration, regional growth and a number of minority community issues.

Minister of State: a junior minister in a government department. There are several in most government departments and they are usually given responsibility for specific policy areas as well as helping to represent the department in Parliament.

MMU: media monitoring unit. The group at CCHQ responsible for monitoring political press coverage.

MoD: Ministry of Defence. The government department responsible for the armed forces and other military matters.

MoJ: Ministry of Justice. The government department responsible for the judiciary, courts, prisons and the probation system, as well as aspects of constitutional policy and human rights law.

Nationalist (Northern Ireland): opposed to Northern Ireland's membership of the United Kingdom and in favour of unification with the Republic of Ireland.

NIO: Northern Ireland Office. The government department responsible for supporting the Northern Ireland devolution settlement and for aspects of the governance of Northern Ireland not devolved to the Northern Ireland Assembly's Executive, for example electoral services and national security.

No. 10 Policy Unit: an office of civil servants and special advisers who provide policy advice to the Prime Minister.

Permanent Secretary: the most senior civil servant in a government department. They are responsible for supporting the minister who heads the department, acting as the chief accounting officer for the department and overseeing its day-to-day running.

PPS: principal private secretary. A civil servant responsible for running a Cabinet minister's private office and acting as the main link between the minister and the civil servants in their department.

Private office: a group of civil servants who work closely with and are responsible to the Secretary of State, running their daily schedule. They are the key point of contact between the Secretary of State and their department.

Private secretary: a civil servant working in the private office.

Prot: short for 'protection officers'; the police officers responsible for protected ministers' safety are part of the Metropolitan Police's Royalty and Specialist Protection branch. The Northern Ireland Secretary is one Cabinet minister who receives 24-hour protection from this unit and their Police Service of Northern Ireland colleagues.

Secretary of State: the most senior minister in a government department. They also serve in the Cabinet.

Short Money: financial assistance given to opposition parties in the House of Commons to fund their parliamentary business, expenses such as travel, and the office of the Leader of the Opposition. The amount is determined by a combination of the votes and seats won by the party. Named after Ted Short, the leader of the House of Commons who pioneered the system in the mid-1970s under Harold Wilson.

Sinn Féin: a left-of-centre republican political party in Northern Ireland and the Republic of Ireland, long widely regarded as the political wing of the IRA.

SpAd: special adviser. A political adviser to a Cabinet minister or the Prime Minister; officially, a temporary civil servant with political impartiality requirements waived. Most Cabinet ministers have two SpAds, one to offer advice on policy and one to help them deal with the media.

Stormont: a term for the devolved government of Northern Ireland, after the seat of the Northern Ireland Executive at Parliament Buildings on the Stormont Estate in East Belfast.

Unionist (Northern Ireland): in favour of Northern Ireland remaining part of the UK.

Whip: an MP within a political party responsible for ensuring that MPs vote with that party in Parliament.

Whitehall: a term for British government ministries and the civil service, named after the street in Westminster which is home to the offices of many government departments.

DRAMATIS PERSONAE

Diane Abbott: Labour MP, ally of Jeremy Corbyn's and shadow Home Secretary from 2016 to 2020.

Gerry Adams: Sinn Féin politician who served as president of the party between 1983 and 2018, playing an important role in the Northern Ireland peace process. He has always denied being a leading member of the IRA.

Ed Balls: former Labour MP; shadow Chancellor from 2011 to 2015. He was one of Gordon Brown's SpAds during his time as Chancellor.

Gavin Barwell: former departmental SpAd, Conservative MP and later Downing Street chief of staff under Theresa May from 2017 to 2019. Now a peer.

Tony Benn: Labour politician and a prominent figure on the party's left wing. He held a number of ministerial positions under Harold Wilson and James Callaghan, including Industry Secretary and Energy Secretary.

Edward Bickham: Conservative special adviser who worked for Jim Prior and then Douglas Hurd at the Northern Ireland Office from 1983 to 1985. Bickham subsequently worked for Hurd at the Home Office from 1985 to 1988 and at the Foreign Office from 1991 to 1993.

Tony Blair: Labour politician; Prime Minister from 1997 to 2007.

Liam Booth-Smith: former special adviser at MHCLG and head of the 10 Downing Street and Treasury joint economic unit at the time of writing.

Karen Bradley: Conservative MP; Secretary of State for Northern Ireland from 2018 to 2019.

James Brokenshire: Conservative MP, serving as Northern Ireland Secretary from 2016 to 2018 and Housing Secretary from 2018 to 2019. He is the Security Minister at the Home Office at the time of writing.

Gordon Brown: Labour politician, Prime Minister from 2007 to 2010 and Chancellor from 1997 to 2007 under Tony Blair.

Robert Buckland: Conservative MP; Justice Secretary and Lord Chancellor since 2019.

Tom Burke: environmental campaigner and special adviser to Michael Heseltine, Michael Howard and John Gummer at the Department of the Environment between 1991 and 1997.

Lee Cain: former journalist, head of broadcast for the Vote Leave Brexit campaign. Downing Street director of communications at the time of writing.

Jonathan Caine: special adviser at the Northern Ireland Office from 1991 to 1995 and from 2010 to 2019 and a peer since 2016.

David Cameron: Conservative politician and Prime Minister from 2010 to 2016, leading a coalition government with the Liberal Democrats and then a Conservative majority government from 2015.

Alastair Campbell: media adviser to Tony Blair and the Labour Party, Downing Street director of communications and strategy from 2000 to 2003, writer and campaigner. Widely believed to be the inspiration for the character of Malcolm Tucker in *The Thick of It*.

Barbara Castle: former Labour MP and later MEP who held several ministerial roles under Harold Wilson, including First Secretary of State from 1968 to 1970.

Nick Clegg: former Liberal Democrat MP, leader of the party from 2007 to 2015 and Deputy Prime Minister of the coalition government from 2010 to 2015.

Jeremy Corbyn: Labour MP on the party's left wing; Leader of the Opposition from 2015 to 2020.

Andy Coulson: former editor of *News of the World*, later imprisoned for his role in the phone-hacking scandal. Downing Street director of communications under David Cameron from 2010 to 2011.

David Cowling: special adviser to Peter Shore at the Department of the Environment from 1977 to 1979 and later a senior BBC analyst and polling expert.

Lynton Crosby: political strategist who worked on Conservative Party campaigns in the general elections of 2005, 2015 and 2017 and the London mayoral elections of 2008, 2012 and 2016.

Tony Crosland: former Labour MP and Foreign Secretary from 1976 until his death in 1977. He was the author of an influential book, *The Future of Socialism*.

Richard Crossman: former Labour MP who served as Social Services Secretary from 1968 to 1970.

Dominic Cummings: highly influential chief adviser to Boris Johnson and former special adviser to Michael Gove from 2007 to 2014; director of the Vote Leave campaign.

Melanie Dawes: civil servant who was Permanent Secretary at MHCLG from 2015 to 2020 and is chief executive of Ofcom at the time of writing.

Nigel Dodds: former DUP MP and leader of the party in the House of Commons from 2010 to 2019. Now a peer.

Bernard Donoughue: academic, politician and first head of the No. 10 policy research unit from 1974 to 1979 under Harold Wilson and James Callaghan. Now a peer.

Iain Duncan Smith: former Conservative MP; leader of the Conservative Party from 2001 to 2003. He was Work and Pensions Secretary from 2010 to 2016 and later a prominent Leave campaigner and titular chairman of Boris Johnson's 2019 leadership campaign.

Amy Fisher: special adviser for most of the period since 2010, having worked in Conservative politics for most of the past two decades. SpAd to Caroline Spelman at the Department for the Environment, Food and Rural Affairs; to Chris Grayling at the Ministry of Justice; to Amber Rudd at the Home Office; and to Brandon Lewis at the Northern Ireland Office. She was also a director of the Conservative Party at CCHQ on two occasions.

Arlene Foster: DUP Member of the Northern Ireland Assembly, serving as leader of the party since 2015. First Minister of Northern Ireland from 2016 to 2017 and from January 2020 to the time of writing.

Jo Foster: special adviser and deputy chief of staff to Nick Clegg as Deputy Prime Minister from 2011 to 2013.

Ben Gascoigne: private secretary to Boris Johnson as Mayor of London from 2009 to 2015, special adviser to Johnson at the Foreign Office from 2016 to 2018 and political secretary to the Prime Minister at the time of writing.

Simon Glasson: special adviser from 2015 to 2018, first to George Osborne at the Treasury and later to Amber Rudd at the Home Office.

Michael Gove: Conservative MP, serving as Education Secretary from 2010 to 2014, Chief Whip from 2014 to 2015, Justice Secretary from 2015 to 2016, Environment Secretary from 2017 to 2019 and Chancellor of the Duchy of Lancaster to the time of writing. He was also a prominent Vote Leave campaigner and briefly acted as Boris Johnson's campaign manager in his 2016 leadership bid before withdrawing his support and running himself.

Sue Gray: civil servant, director general at the Cabinet Office for around twenty years until 2018 and Permanent Secretary at the Northern Ireland Department of Finance at the time of writing.

Chris Grayling: Conservative MP, serving as Justice Secretary from 2012 to 2015, Leader of the House of Commons from 2015 to 2016 and Transport Secretary from 2016 to 2019.

Justine Greening: former Conservative and later independent MP, Transport Secretary from 2011 to 2012, International Development Secretary from 2012 to 2016 and Education Secretary from 2016 to 2018.

William Hague: former Conservative MP and leader of the party from 1997 to 2001. He held a number of Cabinet positions under both Cameron and Major including Foreign Secretary from 2010 to 2014 and First Secretary of State from 2010 to 2015. Now a peer.

Philip Hammond: former Conservative and later independent MP. He was Foreign Secretary from 2014 to 2016 and Chancellor from 2016 to 2019, amongst other Cabinet roles.

Richard Heaton: civil servant who was Permanent Secretary at the Ministry of Justice from 2015 to 2020.

Michael Heseltine: former Conservative MP and Cabinet minister under Thatcher and Major, including as Environment Secretary from 1979 to 1983 and from 1990 to 1992 and as Deputy Prime Minister and First Secretary of State from 1995 to 1997. His leadership campaign against Thatcher in 1990 led to her resignation. Now a peer.

Jeremy Heywood: civil servant who was Cabinet Secretary from 2012 to 2018.

Fiona Hill: special adviser to Theresa May at the Home Office from 2010 to 2014, when she was sacked after a dispute with Michael Gove. Chief of staff to Prime Minister Theresa May at 10 Downing Street alongside Nick Timothy from 2016 to 2017.

Jeremy Hunt: Conservative MP, serving as Culture Secretary from 2010 to 2012, Health Secretary from 2012 to 2018 and Foreign Secretary from 2018 to 2019. He campaigned against Boris Johnson to be leader of the Conservative Party in 2019.

Mo Hussein: special adviser to Amber Rudd from 2015 to 2018, first at the Energy and Climate Change Department and then at the Home Office.

Sajid Javid: Conservative MP who has held several Cabinet roles including Home Secretary from 2018 to 2019 and Chancellor from 2019 to 2020. He resigned as Chancellor following Boris Johnson's demands that his advisers be replaced by a joint No. 10–Treasury economic unit.

Roy Jenkins: Labour MP who served as Home Secretary from 1965 to 1967 and from 1974 to 1976 and as Chancellor from 1967 to 1970. One of the four founding members and first leader of the SDP. He was also President of the European Parliament, Chancellor of Oxford University and a historian and writer.

Boris Johnson: Conservative politician who has served as Prime Minister since 2019. Foreign Secretary from 2016 to 2018 and Mayor of London from 2008 to 2016, he was a prominent Vote Leave campaigner.

Laura Kuenssberg: journalist who has been political editor of BBC News since 2015.

Andrea Leadsom: Conservative MP, serving as Environment Secretary from 2016 to 2017, Leader of the House of Commons from 2017 to 2019 and Business, Energy and Industrial Strategy Secretary from 2019 to 2020. She campaigned against Theresa May to be leader of the Conservative Party (and therefore Prime Minister) in 2016.

Quentin Letts: journalist and sketch-writer for the *Daily Telegraph*, *Daily Mail* and, latterly, *The Times*.

Isaac Levido: political strategist who worked for the Conservative Party on the 2016 London mayoral election campaign and the 2017 general election campaign and ran the 2019 general election campaign.

Eddie Lister: political strategist and former civil servant who was chief of staff and deputy mayor at the Greater London Authority from 2011 to 2016 while Boris Johnson was mayor. Chief strategic adviser to the Prime Minister at the time of writing. Now a peer.

Peter Lilley: former Conservative MP; Trade and Industry Secretary from 1990 to 1992 and Social Security Secretary from 1992 to 1997. Now a peer.

David Lipsey: journalist and special adviser to Tony Crosland as Foreign Secretary from 1976 to 1977 and to James Callaghan as Prime Minister from 1977 to 1979. Now a peer.

Ed Llewellyn: special adviser and Downing Street chief of staff to David Cameron from 2010 to 2016. Peer and Ambassador to France at time of writing.

Damian McBride: special adviser to Gordon Brown from 2005 to 2009 and Downing Street press secretary from 2007 to 2009.

Martin McGuinness: Sinn Féin politician, formerly a leading member of the IRA and Deputy First Minister of Northern Ireland from 2007 until shortly before his death in 2017.

Francis Maude: former Conservative MP and Minister for the Cabinet Office from 2010 to 2015. Now a peer.

Theresa May: Conservative politician who served as Home Secretary from 2010 to 2016 and Prime Minister from 2016 to 2019, leading a majority government from 2016 to 2017 and a minority government with the support of the DUP from 2017 to 2019.

Ed Miliband: Labour MP who served as Leader of the Opposition from 2010 to 2015. He was a special adviser to Harriet Harman and Gordon Brown and was later Energy and Climate Change Secretary from 2008 to 2010. He is shadow Business, Energy and Industrial Strategy Secretary at the time of writing.

Nicky Morgan: former Conservative MP, serving as Education Secretary from 2014 to 2016 and Culture Secretary from 2019 to 2020. She was made a peer in 2020.

Mo Mowlam: former Labour MP and Northern Ireland Secretary from 1997 to 1999, during which time the Belfast Agreement ending the Troubles was signed.

Gus O'Donnell: civil servant and economist who was Cabinet Secretary from 2005 to 2011. Now a peer.

Priti Patel: Conservative MP, International Development Secretary from 2016 to 2017 and Home Secretary since 2019. She was a prominent figure in the Vote Leave campaign.

Jeremy Paxman: broadcaster and journalist who was presenter of the BBC Two news and current affairs programme *Newsnight* from 1989 to 2014.

Robert Peston: journalist who was BBC News business editor from 2006 to 2014 and economics editor from 2014 to 2015. He has been political editor of ITV News since 2015.

Eric Pickles: former Conservative MP who was chairman of the Conservative Party from 2009 to 2010 and Communities and Local Government Secretary from 2010 to 2015. Now a peer.

Dominic Raab: Conservative MP, Brexit Secretary in 2018 and Foreign Secretary and First Secretary of State since 2019. He previously served as Minister of State for Housing and Planning.

Amber Rudd: former Conservative MP, Energy and Climate Change

Secretary from 2015 to 2016, Home Secretary from 2016 to 2018, when she resigned due to the Windrush affair, and Work and Pensions Secretary from 2018 to 2019.

Philip Rutnam: civil servant who was Permanent Secretary at the Home Office from 2017 to 2020. He resigned following clashes with Priti Patel, the Home Secretary, and announced he was suing for constructive dismissal.

Lee Scott: Conservative MP from 2005 to 2015 and special adviser to James Brokenshire at MHCLG from 2018 to 2019.

Rajiv Shah: special adviser to Robert Buckland at the Ministry of Justice and to the Prime Minister on constitutional affairs.

Dylan Sharpe: special adviser to Damian Green as Cabinet minister in 2017 and to Theresa May as Prime Minister from 2018 to 2019, working as 10 Downing Street head of broadcast.

Peter Shore: former Labour MP, Trade Secretary from 1974 to 1976 and Environment Secretary from 1976 to 1979.

Julian Smith: Conservative MP, Chief Whip from 2017 to 2019 and Northern Ireland Secretary from 2019 to 2020.

Jonathan Stephens: civil servant who was Permanent Secretary at the Northern Ireland Office between 2014 and 2020 and at DCMS from 2006 to 2013.

Jack Straw: former Labour MP, Home Secretary from 1997 to 2001 and Foreign Secretary from 2001 to 2006. He worked as a special adviser to Barbara Castle at the Department for Social Security and Peter Shore at the Department for the Environment.

Rishi Sunak: Conservative MP and Chancellor since February 2020. He served as Chief Secretary to the Treasury from 2019 to 2020 and as Parliamentary Under-Secretary for Local Government from 2018 to 2019.

Carrie Symonds: former Conservative special adviser and CCHQ director of communications. Boris Johnson's partner since 2018.

Emily Thornberry: Labour MP, shadow Foreign Secretary from 2016 to 2020 and shadow International Trade Secretary at the time of writing.

Nick Timothy: special adviser to Theresa May as Home Secretary from 2010 to 2015 and as Prime Minister from 2016 to 2017 when he was joint chief of staff with Fiona Hill.

Theresa Villiers: Conservative MP, serving as Northern Ireland Secretary from 2012 to 2016 and Environment Secretary from 2019 to 2020.

Sheridan Westlake: the only special adviser to have served since the Conservative Party won power in 2010, first as SpAd to Eric Pickles at the Department for Communities and Local Government from 2010 and, since 2015, at 10 Downing Street.

Harold Wilson: Labour politician and Prime Minister from 1964 to 1970 and from 1974 to 1976, during which time the role of special adviser was formalised.

Gavin Williamson: Conservative MP, serving as Chief Whip from 2016 to 2017, as Defence Secretary from 2017 to 2019, when he was sacked following the Huawei leak, and as Education Secretary since 2019.

Stewart Wood: academic and special adviser to Gordon Brown at the Treasury from 2001 to 2007 and at 10 Downing Street from 2007 to 2010. Now a peer.

INDEX